QUÉBEC 5.0

An Act of 'Tough Love' for the Love of My People

Jean Ovide Bourdeau

© Copyright 2020   Jean Ovide Bourdeau.

QUÉBEC 5.0
An Act of 'Though' Love for the Love of My People

Edition 1 (revised 2025)

ISBN: 9798694976794

jobourdeau@gmail.com

January 2025 *

Works by Jean Ovide Bourdeau

REVISED AND NEW ESSAYS: *(Generation 2)*
Generation 1 thematically reassembled, revised, and updated

Series 1. **POLITICS OF DESPAIR**
FORBIDDEN THOUGHTS
On the Intellectual Disease of Self- Righteousness.
DYSTOPIAN THOUGHTS
On the Planetary Centralization of Power and Authorities.

Series 2. **POLITICS OF INTEGRITY**
AUDACIOUS THOUGHTS
On Sanity, Ethics, and self- actualization.
UNBOUNDED THOUGHTS
On Our Compulsive Urge to Fuse with The Infinite and Eternal.

POST- SERIES 1 and 2 PROJECTS
SACRILEGIOUS THOUGHTS
Our Murdering Species.
BLASPHEMOUS THOUGHTS
Beyond Orthodoxy and Political Correctitude (eBook only).

Series 3. **SPECIAL PROJECTS**
SECRET DAUGHTER
A Pathology of Intended Circumstances.
WORKMAN STREET
Wretched Lives in a Land of Plenty.
RUE WORKMAN
Des vies misérables dans un pays d'abondance.
QUÉBEC 5.0
An Act of 'Tough' Love for the Love of My People.
QUÉBEC 5,0
Un acte d'amour survolté, déchaînée, et acharné envers mon peuple.
ISABELLE and ANTOINE
Unexpected Love in The Winter of a Life.

Series 4. **VANITY PROJECTS**
JUST A FEW
A Few Remembered Artworks.

ORIGINAL ESSAYS: (*Generation 1*)
Discontinued and withdrawn early in 2019.

Series 1 **POLITICS OF DESPAIR**
Book 1. IMMACULATE PERCEPTIONS:
The Marketing and Selling of Dogmas
Book 2. ETHICS OF ONE:
Debunking Dogmatic Moralities
Book 3. GENOCIDAL LEGACY:
The Incomprehensible Obliteration of Reason
Book 4. BROTHERHOODS:
Patriarchal Missions of Despair and Death
Book 5. DOCTRINAL CANONS:
The Social Sacrament of Self- Righteousness
Book 6. SECULAR IMPERIALISM:
Ongoing Rational Totalitarianism
Book 7. THEOLOGICAL IMPERIALISM:
Ongoing Religious Totalitarianism
Book 8. GLOBAL TOTALITARIANISM:
Apogee of the 'Most Special Group on Earth'
Book 9. APES OF WRATH:
Imperialism of The Most Special Group on Earth
Book 10. TABOOS and TOTEMS:
Social Biases to Be Challenged
Book 11. POSTSCRIPT:
Appendices and Added Notes to Politics of Despair Series

Series 2. **POLITICS OF INTEGRITY**
Book 1. TOTAL MYSTERY:
On the Ambiguity of Conscious Existence
Book 2. TOTAL POSSIBILITY:
Open- ended Imagination and Infinite Potential
Book 3. ANGUISHED FREEDOM:
Choice of Dystopian or Ethical Civilizations
Book 4. PRIMAL IMPULSE:
On the Yearning for Eternal Life and Other Social Concordats
Book 5. ETHICAL SELF:
On This Nascent Ethical Age Now Beginning
Book 6. ASTONISHMENT:
A Few Moments of Wonder
Book 7. UNLIMITED ETHICS:
As the Supreme Principle of Conscious Existence
Book 8. EXISTENTIAL MISSION:
Communities of Interests and Benefits as Crucial Competitors of Human Eusocialism Now in Progress

Dedication

To all vulnerable people unable to fend for themselves
and at the mercy of others.

Dédicace particulière et un remerciement spécial

Chaque jour mes pensées se dirige vers ces '**Anges de Rigaud**', qui se dévouent constamment, et particulièrement celles que je cite ici par ordre alphabétique:

Carole, Corrine, Diane, Emilie, <u>Guylaine P.</u>, Guylaine, Isabelle, Jacquie, Joanne, Lyne, Lucie, Marie-Eve, Marilou, Martine, Solanges, Veronique, Yvette, et toutes les autres dont je ne connais pas les noms ou simplement celles dont je ne me souviens des noms.

J'exprime ici ma profonde gratitude envers elles pour les bons soins et l'amour qu'elles ont apportées à mon épouse, **Dolores Maureen Pierson**, décédée le 8 octobre 2019, qui pendant cinq ans était lourdement handicapée et résidente du CHSLD de Rigaud, Québec, Canada.

Je vous en suis éternellement reconnaissant.

Jean Ovide Bourdeau
8 octobre 2020

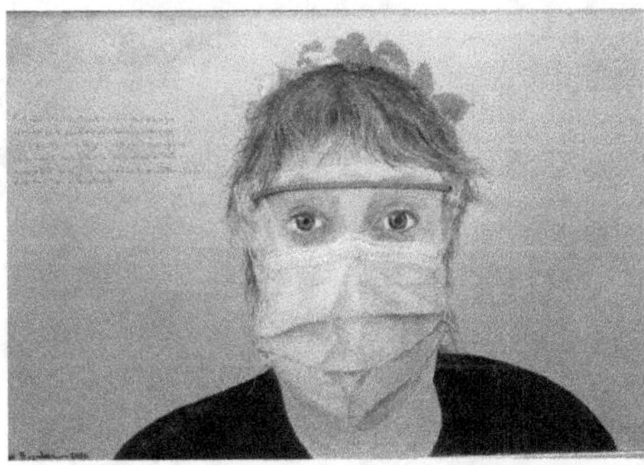

Thirdly, this is further dedicated to the secular values, meanings and standards that should be assigned to a free and ethical society … and rightly promoted by **Bernard Drainville**, … although I do not agree with his separatist leaning.

Acknowledgment

Cover designed by Monica Atwater.

Artwork "Coureurs de bois"; 1989, par Jean Bourdeau.

With kind permission of Denis Leroux,

Sainte-Justine-de-Newton, Québec, Canada

9

Table of Contents

Warning

This is a brutal attack on the "modèle Québecois" in particular and several aspects of the Québec culture in general, which will with many of my compatriots **rightly be considered as blasphemous and sacrilegious** about a number of Québec's values, meanings, and standards.

This approach, however, is not done out of malevolence or meanness.

On the contrary, it is expressed throughout and despite its harshness as a frantic **act of love for the love of my people**, on the part of this departing very old man, … in order to wake us out of our inculcated and preprogrammed social and political somnambulism generally and ethical apathy with the future of our children's inadequate education in the 21st century, the treatment afforded our oldest generation, and the mismanagement of our economy in the context of a privileged North America.

Preamble

This is a double exercise.

The first is one of tough love addressed to my very own people, French-speaking French-Canadians from the province of Québec in Canada. A community that did not take care of, nor provided for me and those like me, at that most vulnerable time of life: such as the poor people of southwest Montréal.

The second satisfies in great part many of the frustrations I experienced from time to time about my people during my lifetime. My way to vent once and for all what I consider still as ethnically self-inflicted harm on the part of the ethnic group from which I emerged.

Tough indeed it is, I admit, but a love of my people, nonetheless, sadly expressed in English, since my community of the Forties and Fifties did not see to it that I receive a proper French education – except for a very limited one in primary school. I was after all too poor and not Roman Catholic enough (if I ever considered myself religious at all) in that small world of Ste-Cunégonde within the broad St. Henri area of my origin, so well described by Gabrielle Roy. It is also and further an expression of hope for the future, as I peer into what I believe we, as a community, can contribute to the generations following us as well as for the rest of the world.

***

This begins with a short overview of the French-speaking reality in the 21st century, followed with many unorthodox political discussions between two serendipitously and propitiously partnered older but newly found soul mates each in the winter of their life.

Interconnected and intermingled themes here are discussed by means of unorthodox political discussions by adopting two general themes, that only two older soul mates with keen interests and steeped in Canadian politics over the years – our thespians in this case – are capable of.

These imagined heated discussions are divided into two themes.

Theme 1.

How the Québec French-speaking French-Canadian community through their good nature, joie de vivre, imbedded religious fear (still effectively active from their original ultra-religious lineages transferred from France), carelessness, social retrenchment, and lack of political wisdom, were abandoned by their mother country as a useless collateral cost due to France's traditional geopolitical mismanagement, more or less in exchange for sugar after France lost a war with England. This then allowed their own small elite and entrenched Medievally constituted Roman Catholic Church to trick them into inaction and a fear of the future (or Québec 1.0, 2.0 and 3.0). And incomprehensibly also, how my ethnic group metamorphosed and reconstituted this inherited religious model of logic into a secular political control system in many fields shaping their escape from the death grip of that Church from the beginning of the 'révolution tranquille' in the 1960s to this day (or Québec 4.0).

Theme 2.

How the Québec French-speaking French-Canadian community through their good nature, joie de vivre, intelligence, creativity, ability to change and learn as well as join the globalization movement, including an inevitable adoption of English as second language by default, … can become a world leader in any field it chooses (or this sought after Québec 5.0).

Forward

Modèle Québecois 1.

We discovered in the course of the Covid-19 pandemic in 2020 that our French-speaking French-Canadian society here in the province of Québec had sadly joined the rest of the world.

While believing the myth we had created for ourselves as a special people allegedly tightly knitted as a society ("tricotée serré" in Québec parlance) and as a marginalized people, in order to survive in the dominant society of English speaking Canada and our most powerful neighbor to the south of us; allegedly learning from the lessons provided by our ancestors and still propagated by our aging generation; we were simply kidding ourselves, when proclaiming that we cared deeply for those who preceded us including today's oldest, frail, and defenseless generation.

We in fact, like most of the world elsewhere, don't give a shit about those who preceded us and still couldn't care less what happens to the latest one. Although never admitting this out loud but satisfied nevertheless to park the oldest members of our society into terminal death cells, which we camouflage under series of pseudonyms expressed as nursing homes or in bureaucratic Québec vernacular, as CHSLD.

We, like the rest of our uncaring world at large similarly and continually ignore our old people and at best warehouse them in centers – wherein many share the same death cell – and this with a minimum of support, and then forget about them, presuming through our wishful thinking and ongoing prevalent mythology that the bureaucracies we instituted to take care of what we perceive as an inconvenience, will do the minimum at the lowest costs possible, since their effectiveness as a member of our Québec society is nil because of age or illness or at least insufficient enough to bother with anymore, and that therefore their date of usefulness is past due in our evaluation.

Indeed, we are not the purportedly caring 'nation' we pretend to be, and the solidarity we assumed to possess as an ethnic group about vulnerable people of our society is a myth. The so-called "modèle Québécois" in this case is something we should rightly be ashamed of as ethical human beings.

That is the reason, so many older people died alone and often a miserable death in the diapers full of stinking excrements in the course of the Covid-19 pandemic. We should indeed be ashamed, embarrassed, mortified, humiliated, offended, and horrified, … **but regrettably we are not**.

Indeed, our attitude toward an aging population reflects the fact that we are unwilling to face up to our own end of life, which must inevitably come regardless of who we are or whom we pretend to be.

Regrettably, we, Quebecers, follow the Western tradition's social model of an allegedly effective and efficient society wherein youth is glorified, mystified, sanctified, and sacralized—and wherein as well old age is ignored as if it would not or could not take place for the younger generations.

We like the rest of people in the Western world, while in good health fantasize a strength we do not possess as vulnerable human beings, which is why, we send our aging population à la dérive, so we do not have to assume the responsibility and accountability of our very own, inevitable, and most certain end of life.

Modèle Québecois 2.

We additionally ignore the harm caused to our vulnerable children by uncaring parents and other psychopathic individuals pretending that by instituting another "modèle Québécois", we merely created a bureaucratic machinery, wherein again no one is ever held accountable for the future of the next generation.

We again should indeed be ashamed, embarrassed, mortified, humiliated, offended, and horrified, … **but again we are not**.

We are then, beginning a sort of dystopian world of our own – a new, more pervasive, more all-encompassing, and again uncaring second "modèle Québécois".

Modèle Québecois 3.

A third "modèle Québécois" shows itself as a Left-leaning often groundless political protests from Quebec's spoiled, whining, ill-mannered, and insolents French-speaking, French-Canadian '**enfants-roi**', including those now adults, causing mayhem.

People who do, or did so, either just for entertainment at the expense of their fragile provincial economy, or simply to annoy the population at large generally and hard-working stiffs in particular.

And all this for dubious, out of context, and manipulative tactics meant to paralyze their democracy through hyperbolic and circular abuse of their parliamentary environment, while practicing the sport of abusing practices taught to them for so long by Québec's silo-oriented labor unions now enriching themselves at the expense of the workers, they supposedly protect as well as taxpayers.

All this again to shore up their inadequacies and pretend that such behavior is normal and valid.

I further suggest in this that these '**enfants-rois**' already know they're not only ethnically trapped but educationally ensnared, while also caught within an unforgiving self-inflicted preprogrammed ignorance of financial and economic realities along with a linguistic snare taught to them by the religious class for about four centuries.

We once more should indeed be ashamed, embarrassed, mortified, humiliated, offended, and horrified, … **but once more we are not**.

And this ironically while their instincts no doubt surreptitiously tell them to join the English-speaking winning team in the rest of Canada and the USA along with all those others across the world.

Prologue

The maxim that *"Nul n'est prophète dans son pays ou dans sa culture"* is a truism I encountered time and again during my life.

I strongly suspect it to be the main reason for this book, as I once more find myself going against the current to cleanse psychological, political, and sociological arguments and assessments through the censoring filters of *'Political Correctitude'*.

Nevertheless, the approach here is through invented conversations of two fictitious older Canadian soul mates with keen interests in sociological matters and steeped in detailed Canadian politics over the years.

Our thespians in this essay are Isabelle Sundström and Antoine Chevalier who three years ago in the middle of a gorgeous summer, as the story goes, accidentally met in Vermont in the USA at an outdoor musical venue called the "Mostly Mozart Festival".

A friendship that developed into an intense love only possible between two soulmates, and this at a speed and depth that can only take place between two older people, while quickly reaching a mutually rational consensus and an early patina of familiarity.

A process that took place through discussions, arguments and at times hyperbolic observations on subjects otherwise forbidden to less intellectually mature, less compassionate, and less open-minded individuals.

In-depth conversations without the filters of the 'bien pensants' that could and had to eventually and by necessity take place between only true soul mates late in life if their relationship was to continue.

A couple that planned and did spend the first year of their life together in Québec and the second one in British Columbia, on the south Pacific side of Vancouver Island, where they permanently settled eventually.

Several months of courting were followed by a couple of years spent discovering and rediscovering together a few of the most interesting areas of Canada, these two down-to-earth Canadians of good will from both sides of the traditional Canadian cultural divide became interested during that time – and among many other subjects of course – in exploring among other things the highly emotional subject of French-Canadians across Canada generally and those in Québec: that very part in particular presented in this essay.

Throughout this process they unwittingly overcame their ethnic biases and parochial prejudices by facing them squarely, as they examined and commented on the past, present as well as the potential future of that community.

A most delicate subject indeed – especially for two people on the move at the end of a long life; at a time when allegedly one's opinions and belief system have solidified.

We speak here of political reflections pertinent to Canada particularly by two Canadian-born individuals – now life partners – especially about that Québec French-Canadian conundrum as a probable and negligible North-American minority in the face of an accelerating 21st century globalization of just about everything, if it kept unchanged its present attitude and active modus operandi in the management of its affairs.

This includes its programmed exclusion of English as the preeminent and preferred language of worldwide and especially North American business corporations, the scientific world, along with that of the elite and political classes around the planet, which took place particularly during the 20th century and will most likely continue throughout the course of the 21st.

The general aim being, although intermingled throughout:

1. A struggled elucidation of the conundrum in which the Québec French-Canadian community and particularly its unilingual French-speaking segment now finds itself, and will eventually end up, if no change in attitude takes place.

2. A notion of an evolving Québec 1.0, Québec 2.0, Québec 3.0, and Québec 4.0 intermingled with ad hoc considerations of an open-minded, educated, entrepreneurial, and financially sound future secular Québec – the notion of a Québec 5.0.

3. An exposé beginning with a serious concern about **education** and ending with a continued alarm Quebec's **education system.**

This refers to the situation as of September 2024 … and my 88th turn around our sun soon now in progress.

Introduction

Bawling and Underperforming.

In Québec, we are generally bawling and underperforming, which means that we are constantly asking for help from the state in almost all areas, when we should be acting as entrepreneurs.

Insularity Crippling A Social Evolution.

Quebecers overconcentration on local when not simply parochial issues and problems ensures they generally ignore geopolitical ones.

Their self-imposed insularity cripples their social evolution in a pathetic pandering to local labor unions, a continued awarding of a special and unearned status to medical doctors and lawyers in the same manner as their previously favored ecclesiastical masters, … ensuring an insularity, which they refuse to admit and correct as their financial debt level increases and the level of education of their French-speaking vielles souches population diminishes significantly, … rather than retrain, reskill, and reinvent themselves.

And for this revelation I will no doubt be accused to be a traitor to the cause of my people, I suppose, … although this is expressed as an act of tough love for the love of my people as I near the end of my life.

Part 1.

POLITICALLY INCORRECT DISCUSSIONS

Temporarily Hovering Over a Fragment of Discussion 1.

The Québec Education System

Knowing that everyone she ever talked to had strong opinions if not plain biases on this subject, while expecting that several other subjects directly or indirectly tied to it would inevitably emerge as well, Isabelle Sundström wanted her say on the educational system – a subject dear and near to her.

And so, wanting to clarify her thought she began as follows.

"Since we particularly planned to talk about Québec politics this afternoon ..." she simply said *"... what about Québec's educational system to begin with?*

Let me generalize Antoine, to make the point I have in mind easier and quicker for me to flesh out.

Don't mind my directness or crudeness perhaps at times ... I just want to get to the bottom of things without going through the gymnastics of political correctitude ... it'll be much quicker and far easier to make the points I wish to make that way.

Is that OK with you?"

Antoine Chevalier smiled and simply said *"Look it's about time we clear the air with all the frustrations we've felt over the years about this and other subjects to come I presume.*

Go ahead! ... I'm looking forward to it ... but let me get another coffee first".

Isabelle began as soon as Antoine sat down again coffee in hand.

"Look! You, French-Canadians in Québec, as a group, refuse for ideological reasons, to recognize that the Québec educational system is failing you as a whole, despite all the revolutionary changes you made in the sixties and seventies, ... and after that... along with the enormous and ruinous sums of money you poured into it so far ...

... except for the usual small, privileged group, a privately educated segment, such as the old and always protected inward-looking traditional professions of lawyers, medical doctors, journalists, and university professors".

And now taking a deep breath, as if about to jump off a cliff for a dangerous kite flying adventure, she went on.

"You keep on manipulating at least, if not simply faking your statistics outright to get 'better results', rather than those you had expected to attain at the end of each planning phase.

You average the percentages of tests, whenever students fail expected outcomes, ... you do this to ensure more students 'pass' their exams and be 'promoted' to the next level.

Because of this practice of lowering the bar to get better averages and the appearance of success ... you push this practice to the point of awarding fake ambiguously written diplomas and insist on giving certificates (so as not to make failing students feel bad as one PC objective), to people entering their adult life unable to read, nor manage money, and incapable of functioning adequately in our advanced modern world.

But you really do so, above all else, to protect a system – not the students – despite your pious claims to the contrary.

Always it seems, the educational system must be protected at the expense of students, if need be, ... and nearly always it is the system that wins out.

Your so-called pedagogical standards ... as integral parts and functions of the system and the living bureaucracy that gives it life... reign supreme ... as if an independent self-feeding entity ... which has by now become as a whole __the__ sacred cow – __the__ dogma – of your educational belief system".

Isabelle then stopped for a few seconds as if to contemplate what she was about to say next:

"In fact, teachers with no skills whatsoever in a given subject, say, English literature or math or biology, among innumerable examples, can teach these on the basis that they are pedagogically vetted to teach – a totally insane process, when you really examine this notion.

How indeed can you teach a subject you do not thoroughly master – even when you, indeed officially and in fact, possess teaching skills?

Do you think students don't realized a teacher's limits after a while with this approach?

Look! Students – even those from poor neighborhoods – know when a teacher is faking it usually sooner rather than later.

For example, in many high schools not that long ago, pedagogically vetted teachers were laughed at by their students, whenever these tried to teach aspects of computers science their students had already mastered instinctively without their help ... subjects in which teachers demonstrated an unprecedented ignorance.

Anyway my friend ... the belief that proven teaching skills with little or limited knowledge on expert subjects is a remnant piece of medieval logic ... from a time when subjects were few and general ... while most often unproven indeed ... when any knowledge at such time, however poorly transmitted, was appreciated due to its rarity ... and the population at large was simply ignorant ... intelligent but still ignorant ... since the full effect of the Renaissance, Enlightenment, and the modern world it triggered had not yet taken place.

But today's teaching establishments now ideologically carries on with this dogma in a world where the multiplication of specialized fields and the essence and complexity of knowledge are increasing geometrically.

And yet, the teaching institution in Québec, from teachers along with the massive bureaucracy managing and administrating the education department, insists that 'pedagogical methodology' trumps all, ... and must survive at all costs, ... because you're intellectually and psychologically invested in the ideological view of its superiority at the cost of students' failure ... despite an already predetermined, visible, and somewhat measurable knowledge acquisition fiasco.

That is why; all the reforms of the past decades could not work.

Just remember the 1960, 1976, 1992, 1997 and 2001 reforms.

They failed because the dogma of pedagogical methodology trumped these reforms.

And now what about the ones to come?

That methodology must be eliminated ASAP!

Look! In Québec, we find outdated teaching methods, mismanagement of staff, and an approach to education that is ideological.

A defensive position based on a refusal to seek what's happening in the global accelerated digitization of everything, ... where the teaching staff, valiantly at times, purposely lives within a traditional silo instead ... refusing to observe the future as it races ahead.

You continue to believe and insist on producing – like widgets – obedient inward-looking subjects to maintain a self-defeating status quo.

In fact, the Education Department keeps on demonstrating a complete detachment in their application of new teaching methods, relying instead on many classical methods.

That institution behaves as if totally unaware that the game has completely changed in the of fields of data, information, and knowledge transmission and that this is evolving all the time – doing so now at warp speed.

You, as a people, and everywhere I suppose, ... despite your claims to the contrary, ... desire perfectly obedient 'worker bees' to protect, support and strengthen your community, ethnic group, or nation ... it's a natural reflex. But while you do that, you pay little attention to the strategic and crucial changes demanded by the world your children and grandchildren will be confronted with, ... while you pretend that the demands required by that future will be met ... without planning for it."

This time looking more relaxed, as if she'd just landed from her intellectual flight, Isabelle went on the edge once more, so to speak, and continued her portent adventure.

"Your government never admits it, ... but educational fiascos, whether shown in the open or camouflaged as they most often are, under a plethora of politically correct excuses, are clear signs of this.

*In fact, and to make matters worse, **nobody is ever responsible and accountable** for those fiascos, astronomical costs, shortcomings in strategic planning and tactical on-the-ground operations and experiments.*

*Just think for example of the 'décrochage scolaire' in your high schools especially by male students; or the unnecessary added year of schooling **artificially created** in the establishment of CE-GEPs".*

That my friend, first deliberately camouflages your unemployment statistics by one year – a tactic that also postpones by one year graduating students' entry into the job market. Something you've now done for decades.

Second, it adds an unnecessary cost to your already massive educational budget.

Third, it does not improve the transmission of knowledge that ought to be condensed rather than stretched over a longer period—especially in a quickly demanding world!

In fact, in this last case, stretching time to complete a syllabus that could easily be done in a shorter timeframe, wrongly prepares a student in entering today's work world, wherein all must compete in executing tasks in the shortest time possible – often with targets that seem impossible, or running one's own business as an entrepreneur amid a chaotic environment, rather than leisurely carry out one's assigned duties as those leisurely guaranteed a government job for life with full benefits. Something most other regular folks don't get.

On this my dear Antoine, you Quebecers keep lying to yourselves".

Isabelle took another deep breath, this time as if to re-concentrate her energies and thoughts to continue her argument.

"Everything in the educational system is structured to pass the buck generally, ... and when tackled in an unavoidable situation, it shifts the blame on the system ... and automatically proposes new protocols of execution so that no one in management especially is ever held accountable and fired for incompetence when that is the case.

I'd say that the bureaucratic education machine seems to have a life of its own and for its own sake.

It is as if the system consisted of an independent self-governing entity, separate in some way from those in fact hired and paid to be responsible and accountable, ... and instead feeds that machine rather than shape and engineer it for best results. By this I mean: ... educated young adults ready to face the world as it really is, and not as it is thought to be by so-called State-licensed education experts ... who do not participate in the real world of business competition.

So, excuses have become the pat answer to all ills and purported needs, ... and further training are also automatically recommended to abide by and improve that sovereign system – alleged and real, ... whenever faults or failures of professional teaching staff or administrative personnel cannot be hidden.

And at its best, it is pure management by committee solutions on behalf and at the behest of the educational machine – never for the students – those indeed who should and must benefit from a sound education".

Again, Isabelle took a small break in her argument and after a minute or so continued.

"Either education bureaucrats cannot anticipate the usual types of problems before they show up; ... or are unable in view of their attitude, work practices, and their dogmatic belief to see that the holy sacred mantra of 'pedagogy supersedes all and must rule

all', ... or if they acknowledge a problem, then fail to find a solution to resolve it; ... or if they find a solution to a problem, they simply do not recognize their failure in applying a correct solution, when that is so.

And while on the subject just think of the tragedies, blunders, and other unethical problems unnecessarily created whenever the bureaucratic management by committee assesses these as 'too sub-optimal' to predict".

Isabelle's passion showed her frustration at bureaucratic incompetence especially in this case, since it directly and forever affected those students for which a good educational system ought not benefit the machine running the system at their expense.

While nervously scratching her head as she spoke, she went on some more.

"Your educational system until recently in history purposely shied away from scientific and business fields as prejudicially taught to you by our previous master ... your very own version of a medieval-minded and French-Canadian staffed Roman Catholic Church.

Your educational system was so backward that even the two most famous idols of the Parti Québécois—outstanding separatist stars and leaders René Lévesque and Jacques Parizeau—had to go elsewhere to educate themselves further, one in the United States and the other in England at the London School of Economics, and that my friend took place only a few years ago.

Both adopted English in the process in their international dealings, since they already knew by experience that French was no longer favored in such settings ... and its use sadly has become ever more limited on the international scene since.

And you wonder why, you lag behind most other Canadians". She exasperatedly concluded.

"You must admit" said Antoine *"that we've improved a lot in the last decades from what we used to be before the 'révolution tranquille'."*

"Sure, you have, but not where it truly counts in the advancement of a whole society, if the intention is to bolt ahead and leave your imbedded overly naïve perception of the world once and for all" Isabelle interjected.

"A present perception built in great part still upon the ruins of your previous medieval view of a world nurtured and legated to you by your local Roman Catholic Church". She added.

"Surely it isn't that bad ... we have a lot of educated people" retorted Antoine, a bit annoyed at Isabelle's strong opinion in this case.

"Yea! In the traditional professions where they don't generally need to go outside and compete, remaining with their closed-in local culture and language rather than deal with the real world ... sure ... no doubt".

"Just a minute Isabelle ... we recently had a Premier, for example, ... a highly educated man of the world ... able to see the bigger picture, comfortable in English and gifted to understand the worldwide context in which, we, as a people are living and must live in ... an educated surgeon with an above average ability to express his thought clearly and intelligently ... you just have to listen to him express himself to note clear, precise, and well-articulated thoughts on just about any subject." Interjected Antoine once more annoyed.

"I agree with you ... but as medical professional he's an exception ... he got out of 'le petit monde de don Camillo', so to speak, ...because he lived outside Québec for a while, ... travelled around the world ... and he exceptionally at last joined many other new professionals from other modern occupations, and this in spite of the stifling Québec medical culture that formed him, ... but he nevertheless and exceptionally I admit, feels comfortable everywhere in Canada and elsewhere for that matter, ... but he is still <u>an exception</u> among the medical profession, ... a laudable one but one nonetheless ... from a traditional profession otherwise content to live in its cultural silo and language ghetto my dear Antoine ... far from Montréal.

Oh! By the way Antoine:

> *Didn't he also have a blind spot on account of a stay in Saudi-Arabia, with those fundamentalist god-crazed Moslems intent on forcing their welcoming country, in this case Canada and particularly Québec, to 'accommodate' them with their open hatred of women, the application of claustrophobic compulsory headdress for females of our species, along with a continued attempt to introduce that barbaric sharia code?*

> *Is that because he was well treated, while residing in Saudi Arabia and working as a brain surgeon for its elite class?*

I don't want an answer Antoine ... I'm just wondering ... ... I'm just saying ... that's all ... seriously asking myself ... and moving on with our discussion:

> *Why in spite of his open-mindedness could he not connect with average Quebecers all these years?*

> *In what universe was he living in?*

> *Was it due to the narrow-minded world presented to all those studying medicine in université Laval or université de Montréal?*

Anyway, to carry on with my views on education ... ... many other professions and other fields of knowledge have come along since the medieval age ... because ... let's face it, ... nothing of substance beyond the very few traditional professions really existed before the 'révolution tranquille' in Québec ... and the few outside the traditional ones were generally held by English-speaking Quebecers, ... because no one bothered generally in practice among French-speaking Quebecers to train for these.

Think Antoine!

Look! The 'École des hautes études commercialles' only really took shape after the 'révolution tranquille' ... and a lot of catching up had to be done, because you guys started from scratch 'ou presque'.

Hey Antoine?

Its undergraduates had to study from American textbooks ... such as, say, the old classic ... Samuelsson's basic textbook in economics 101 in the Seventies ... and so on, ... now imagine those at the graduate level.

... and although a lot of progress has been accomplished, much remains to be done ... especially in the field of entrepreneurship, which has not yet been taken seriously despite pious words and rhetoric from politicians and education planners, ... particularly if you are to compete locally – as you inevitably must in Montréal with both McGill and Concordia universities ... before facing up to the rest of Canada, and the USA next door, that most economically powerful country in the whole of human history so far, ... and the sooner in that case the better.

That is why, many French-Canadians, unable to get the best education they ought to obtain in French about business, finance, economics, business management, and entrepreneurship, have since the sixties attended McGill and Concordia (Sir George Williams then) or gone elsewhere in Canada or the US.

You've been playing a catch-up game – especially with new occupations ... including the important domain of business, commerce, and finance ... and retarded your whole ethnic group further in this domain with your idealistic language law ... also a clear sign of your heartfelt inferiority complex and factual fear of becoming irrelevant in this area sooner rather than later.

You have done so for decades ... and until just a few years ago you were still desperately struggling with proper text books and expert knowledge ... including those for advanced occupations until recently unimagined, such as in the field of computer technology, where once more you had no choice but to again borrow American and Canadian text books and often computer dedicated magazines written in the US ... ... even France could not catch up fast enough ... and could therefore not create those essential words and expression on time to help you ... ... so much so ... ... it accepted a great number of American versions for these ... and that is why, you guys in desperate efforts to remain relevant in the Francophonie say 'courriel' and the French say 'email' among many other things in this area my dear Antoine.

Holy shit! Now that I think of it ... you and I know that's not fair to students, who were not encouraged from infancy to learn English in these cases ... and this for ideological reasons, ... but then when you somewhat recognized the issue ...you reluctantly decided to learn it at a later and therefore at much more difficult stage of a student life ... often when attending university, ... while at the same time simultaneously trying to master difficult subjects, ... a double whammy if choosing a degree in, say, business, finance, management, computer science or entrepreneurship.

That is why, I admire François Legault ... at last after four hundred years someone with a business sense to run this important province.

OK! I continue a bit more ... and return to the hurdles your students had to overcome.

The sheer fact, that many did it in spite of it all, shows the brilliance of these students ... but it was still unfair to them, when the same could have been made so easy for them, if they learned English naturally as children ... it's second nature at that stage of their life ... think of the Swedish model for example or any of the other Scandinavian countries for that matter in this domain.

I don't want to piss on the entire educational system here, because there are fields where Québec education shines brightly.

Here I speak of medicine and law, ...but that's because these are already accepted traditional fields usually meant for local applications and consumption, and most are by definition and in fact, although this now gradually includes an acceptance of knowledge from the world at large in the domain of advanced medicine usually transmitted in English first.

Look! By traditional occupations I mean those that never required much entrepreneurship or business savvy, because they rely on government moneys – jobs that were in olden days viewed as vocational callings ... in some ways similar to a religious calling when you think of it".

"You're getting off course Isabelle." Interrupted Antoine

"Ok! Ok!

Getting back to our broad subject here.

Nevertheless, when you examine the real objectives of the alleged mission the educational bureaucracy sets for itself, we find that it does not encourage, nor does it prepare students to look after themselves once in adulthood ... or permit them to view the world as it really is – inside and outside their local ethnic community as adults as well as outside their province and the rest of the world ... and to function as adults once grown up.

As for those alleged successes, the education establishment proudly propagate, I dare say that the Jesuitan approach to prop-aganda never went away in fact, ... and that it has been the prac-tice to use its propagandist tactics in the education arena, ... hey Antoine?

In my view, it merely metamorphosed into a massive secular bu-reaucracy, meant to continue under a new cover, the control of French-Canadians as a community ... at least in this province if nowhere else anymore ... and dare I say it's more so in regional areas of this province.

And finally, schoolteachers at <u>all</u> levels ought to go through a very competitive selection process, be drawn from the best and brightest students, possess advanced degrees in a given specialty <u>aside from a skill in teaching</u>, be given wide autonomy, and be well remunerated.

It has to be viewed by everyone as a valued profession equal to those we presently value as the best.

Otherwise, you will fail to educate your people and again become the 'losers' you were in the good old days of Roman Catholic he-gemony on your territory."

Then, suddenly, Isabelle stopped, as if she'd ran out of gas, and looked at the floor without saying another word for a few minutes ... now mentally exhausted.

Temporarily Hovering Over a Fragment of Discussion 2.
Quebec's Severe Financial Analphabetism

Antoine got up, looked at the Rigaud river for a minute, then turned to Isabelle, and began:

"Yep! 'L'argent et les finances'. That is 'l'autre grande noirceur' I tell you. Look!

I'm often disturbed and feel a great unease on the rather low knowledge and appreciation French-speaking French- Canadians in Québec have about the handling of money in particular, and their knowledge in the management of finances generally including day-to-day personal finances.

Let's see! It is no doubt crucial for anyone's success to be taught at least the rudiments of budgeting, money handling and finances.

And yet the majority of mature French-Canadian adults in Québec still keep on discovering that they are all too often ignorant of the most basic elements in these areas.

A clear majority have never been taught about the intelligent handling of this crucial element to the success of a life well lived ... including many in its privileged segment during their many years of schooling.

Most are ignorant of the elementary rudiments of accounting and budgeting for example.

The notion of compounded rates of interest is foreign to them, so are the ins and outs of real estate investments, market shares, the difference between debits and credits of both side of a balance sheet, pension funding, and the list goes on.

Far too many French-Canadians in Québec suffer from a severe financial analphabetism, simply because it is still not considered vital by, both, the Education department leadership regardless of government in place and its permanent bureaucratic mechanism selecting and setting educational priorities.

And let us not forget that it is the awful original brainwashing against entrepreneurship and the association of money as something evil by the religious establishment embedded in the French-Canadian community psyche for centuries that we still have to deal with here.

That same socially entrenched program continues to weaken us as a society of otherwise intelligent and capable people.

So, while we, at last, got rid of that awful religious death embrace and its associated ecclesiastical 'simagrées', we surreptitiously did not notice that we had kept its intellectual programming intact to a great extent under a secular mask.

No wonder our province is the highest taxed territory in North-America, ... always begging the feds for more money, ... as if this tactic <u>alone</u> would solve the financial problems we create out of our national ignorance in business and financial dealings, ... including all other consequences triggered by our sheer ignorance in this domain.

Just think of the 'Bombardier billion-American dollar bail out' accorded by this province just a while back ... a most unfavorable business contract ... and other future ones to come with other undesirable financial undertakings which ought not be involve in.

Yes! Oh, yes! While we proclaim that 'Nous ne sommes pas nés pour un petit pain' my dear Isabelle, we, as a society, behave that way, because we've been brainwashed that way.

I tell you ... we must get out of this defeatist programming once and for all, ... or we'll bury ourselves eventually.

That is why; an intellectual revolution must take place in education by introducing as compulsory subjects in one's education every aspect of finance, investments, entrepreneurship, business administration, project management, sciences, and technology at the earliest time possible in a student's curriculum, as well as routine personal money handling ... ... and this in addition to other civilizing subjects that are today ignored... rendering us less sensitive to our precarious existence such as philosophy, literature, history, art and music at all levels and for all types of graduating degrees regardless of areas of specialization... subjects currently considered as superfluous ... just about everywhere else for that matter I admit in the case of civilizing subjects, I fear.

That is why further; we must also introduce, both, full and unequivocally English as second language... the language of business and general international communication on our continent and around the planet.

And that this must be done at all levels of our educational system – if we indeed intend to compete with everyone else on an equal footing.

Not an easy task I admit ... with <u>no immediate benefits</u> ... but after one full generation we could compete with anyone in the world, ... and I predict doing so very successful if we bothered.

Having survived as French-speaking French-Canadians in this vast English-speaking continent for four-hundred years, I don't see how we could fail if we cooperatively put our mind to it".

Temporarily Hovering Over a Fragment of Discussion 3.
We All Want 'Our Share' Whatever the Costs - 1

Antoine again began this afternoon's discussions.

"One of the things that has always bothered me over the years, I admit to you Isabelle, was the lack of ambition in my neighborhood in south-west Montréal, ... in that area now being gradually gentrified in what used to be referred to as Pointe St. Charles, Griffintown and the whole St Henri district including the parishes of Sainte-Cunégonde and Sainte-Irénée, where I lived my youth.

And this only to discover, later in life, that this problem was community-wide at one time with French-Canadians across Canada ... with a few exceptions here and there.

A problem that has disappeared in great part today outside Québec, but which has however remained in this province like some crippling intellectual disease of some kind.

An issue too many Quebecers all too often do not or cannot recognize still, ...and if they do, ... have serious troubles managing to this day.

That's about where we were as a people before the 'révolution tranquille' began ... when we were afraid of change and dreaded it so much, ... putting down people trying to do better for themselves ... anyone unwilling to settle for less ... anyone daring to jump on opportunities ... or creating such opportunities for themselves ....

... and it took us decades to catch up ... and yet we're still behind in key areas...

... and I continue to see no national sense of urgency in adopting, say, entrepreneurship as part of a normal education – making it an integral and strategic part of our culture from here on ... along

with the adoption of an attitude to make this an emergent societal goal that could and would easily be agreed upon by the majority ... especially with a demographic that is about to tip over the younger side of the population." Antoine added before sitting down.

"And yet, we still go on using terms such as 'projet de société' to show and add a cogent patina to our societal concerns and interests, ... but parallelly refusing outright to face those issues significantly dimming down our chances for success".

"And what are these issues according to you Antoine?" Asked Isabelle.

"Simply listed in no order of priority, since they're all about on the same level of urgency, if we wish to succeed as a society, I'd say:

> *Fear of business, finance, entrepreneurship and of being overcome by the English language.*

But before we do this, we must first overcome our traditional lack of ambition.

Let's face it Isabelle ... far too many French-Canadians in Québec have no ambition – even nowadays – because centuries of internal religious propaganda have programmed them that way ... the religious influence of older days is still here ... although we never mention this now that we have become a mostly secular society ... the medieval religious memes are nonetheless still working in our now mostly secular society ... and we by ourselves and for ourselves must eliminate these impediments ASAP.

A fact often revealed and highlighted in one easy example, in the dangerously large analphabetism among French-speaking French-Canadian males in our province particularly.

I tell you ... I'm convinced that these memes alone have in great part led us to look for and institute a replacement of our old god figure of yesteryears ... and transmogrified that deity into a Nanny State.

Yes! We now implore, through the secular prayers of separatist-minded people, to be saved from 'les Anglais' as if poor 'victims' of history, life, circumstances and evil sinful individuals – wherein religious scenarios have been replaced by similarly engineered secular ones, and wherein the new god is the Nanny State.

Listen to their rantings against government and business over the years ... and you'll be able to observe the intact religious logic in that ostensible metamorphosis from a religious context to a secular one.

Just follow the growth of labor unions, for example, among others in this province, and note their constant complaints as alleged 'victims' of business and circumstances ... and then consider their part in the destruction of our provincial finances allegedly for a higher purpose ... ... a purportedly 'labor heaven' of permanent jobs for all ... wherein no one can be fired regardless of incompetence or a lack of will to work and earn a living or the logical existence of jobs or skills no longer required ... with ever-increasing salaries based on a sacred dogma of unquestionable seniority ... and the exclusion of a meritocracy in all instances.

That more or less represents the missionary posture of Québec's large labor unions.

It is out of such an attitude of 'me-first-at-all-costs' we created our very expensive Nanny-State.

So, that by now too many people rely on the largesse of that Nanny State for their basic sustenance, while the better off classes ... in spite of their privileges nevertheless also insanely insist on 'their share' of the State's revenues ... regardless of costs to the State and this despite an income well above the average in Québec for them, the health of the business sector, and its governmental financial solvability – present or future.

In this and other self-centered cases interested parties expect without reserve to be supported without efforts by a Nanny-State, the sub-ideology being in my view that:

> *This Nanny-State in all expects must see to their 'needs' <u>without</u> efforts on their part; ... or have others pay for their personalized 'needs'; ... or soothe their emotional desires such as wanting a child at all cost regardless of consequences and in spite of nature paid by the State; ... or getting a top education subsidized by taxpayer money but be unwilling to do one's part in supporting that society such as medical doctor; ... or wanting that their revenues increase to the maximum they can get regardless of present and future costs to coming generations.*

I dare say that it is as if everyone 'knew' that the future could or would end up as dystopian, somehow.

Perhaps that is the reason, why each generation since the 'révolution tranquille' behaves as if theirs would be the last one able to cash in at the expense of all future ones.

Sadly, Isabelle, I truly believe that the Québec Nanny-State has replaced the Roman Catholic Church and the god of olden days ... nothing less ... just as the old god was to purportedly provide all to all ... so ought and must the Nanny-State do so in the mind of these individuals.

In my view that is why, far too many French-Canadians in Québec lack a 'can-do' attitude.

Yet we are an intelligent and socially robust people ... so why do we vote for the first individual promising a yet more pliant and generous Nanny-State, I ask you?

It is as if, this rather large segment of the population had serious problems in getting out of its culturally embedded intellectual lethargy".

All of a sudden realizing the 'can do' attitude of notable groups—exceptional in the Québec context—Antoine made a last point.

"Although, having said that, I must not ignore the creative and entrepreneurial people of the Beauce region and the environs along with a few other small communities and outstanding entre-preneurs such as our present premier, Francois Legault and key ministers he appointed...

... and hopefully with many of today's millennials I note a ten-dency to accept entrepreneurship as natural in spite of the fact they were never taught much in this field ...

... they in my view represent part and function of a generation rejecting the mantra of losers found in the Joual saying of: 'In-venter! Quossa donne'?"

Temporarily Hovering Over a Fragment of Discussion 4.
We All Want 'Our Share' Whatever the Costs - 2

Continuing their discussions from yesterday on that generalized attitude of getting whatever you can from a government whatever the costs, Antoine went on, for a third time in a row, but this time aimed his concerns at the medical establishment which for several years took over the governance of the province to award itself generous financial remunerations <u>without compensating contributions</u> to the health system.

"No better recent example can be found than our medical doctors getting large income increases with the promise of doing their share and contributing in improving the entire health system, which like unrepentant unethical self-centered cowards they reneged ... only to realize that they are significantly less effective and efficient as a profession than their homologues everywhere else in Canada ... seeing less patients ... while insisting on retaining the sacred cash cow of being paid by 'each medical act' performed ... which once translated into practical production methodology ... prevents other competent medical practitioners from doing many of these ... ensuring medical doctors the majority of revenues in this area for themselves ... at the expense of both patients and vastly increased State budgets.

In fact, and as an aside, Isabelle, an average doctor, ... not a surgeon, say, a GP whose regular limited responsibilities and accountabilities are most certainly immensely less than a general in charge and running a massive military base with thousands of people under his command and hundreds of millions of dollars as budgets and in charge 24/7, such as say, in Trenton in Ontario ... yet earns less than a run of the mill medical doctor ... go figure!

A continually pampered class, which after benefiting from provincial subsidies making their training possible, default on their allegiance to their Hippocratic Oath, ... presuming that they, as whole, will not provide their services on a 24/7 basis ... as if people could generally only be sick or approach death during office hours from Monday to Friday.

<u>Purposely and unethically ignoring that the business of medicine is in large part one of timely interventions on a 24/7 basis</u> ... that people in pain or in other medical crisis or trauma, say, at home, or in a clinic or in a hospital, cannot wait until medical doctors are ready to intervene after they've finished their Starbucks Italian-roasted or cappuccino coffee, say, after nine o'clock on a Monday for example.

Medicine is a job 'sur le terrain' and not in some imaginary agenda of a grown-up 'enfant roi'.

Medical doctors are meant to attend to their clients ... the very ones making their high earnings possible ... on the same urgency level as those in police and firefighting forces on duty 24/7; ... or that of those ensuring the movement of all their basic needs (for all of us) also handled on a 24/7 by railroad workers, truckers, bakers, farmers, nurses, soldiers, and so on.

The health business is a 24/7 business and like other 'quarts de métier', medical doctors are duty-bound to deliver their expertise 24/7 ... **there cannot be exceptions** *... otherwise the more vulnerable and chronically sick without means end up in the garbage bin of society ... which I suppose it does not much bother a large segment of the medical class, if I'm to judge their attitude and ethical behavior".*

Antoine stopped for a couple minutes … he was angry by now at the thought of that continuously privileged class now making salaries **without any competition** and yet insisting they be paid and treated as if they did compete in the business world which they do not.

He again gathered his thoughts before continuing his exposé – the usual silent break – whenever discussing difficult or emotional subjects, issues, events, or situations.

***

In the meantime, Isabelle thought as an aside to Antoine's presentation – while on the subject of medical doctors in Québec – that general practitioners of medicine particularly tend to also close their eyes to the accelerated computerization—of everything now in progress everywhere (especially AI and robotization) … occasionally assuming that this would provide them with better tools to do their jobs, which it does, and will for some time, but as she explained to Antoine:

"The irony is that, GPs particularly here and everywhere in the Western world for that matter choose to ignore or simply cannot see that because of their inward-looking perception, and self-inflicted blindness that the digitization of their profession now progress will within two decades or so lose the very jobs they feel so cocksure about right now –… ironic, isn't it?" Isabelle quietly added.

Then another thought came to her mind right after this one. It was a solution of sort that had been percolating in her mind for some time.

"Why not put all both general practitioners and specialists on salaries ... they're State workers after all in fact and every sense?" she said.

Adding: *"This would resolve a great part of the bureaucracy now overseeing and administrating the present complex remuneration system, which requires an enormous administrative effort to manage and automatically and proportionately reduce costs.*

This approach has existed in most countries and particularly in the Scandinavian countries for several decades now. … Why not here? … It's really an easy decision". She said.

Then she decided not to continue realizing she probably took Antoine off his train of thoughts.

*****

Still obviously obfuscated at the medical class Antoine impatiently continued.

"Oh no! Medical doctors as a group in Québec considers themselves a class apart – as if superior to all others ... as if afflicted by a sort of god-complex, ... as if they will not, like the rest of us, also die on time.

A group, which feels no remorse and couldn't care less, knowing all the while that people in pain wait nearly a day ... if not longer ... to be examined by one of them in urgent cases ... an attitude exhibited for all to see on their purported 'rights' to work as they wish, when they wish, under their individual self-designed rules, ... and at our expense – with no regard for sick patients.

Can you imagine the police, firefighters, airline pilots, railway workers, and so on acting that way? ... it would cause riots ... but when it comes to medical doctors... like we did and still do with the clerical class .... we say nothing ... we just bitch, ... but do not elect the right people ... or seriously demonstrate or riot for that matter".

Antoine put his head between both his hands for a minute … got up as if to make another point, but suddenly changed subject again.

"Let's take an obvious instance to show that we now live in a Nanny-State!

Just think of State-paid insemination procedures for those unable to conceive!

*You'd think in this case the couples concerned would listen to nature, which is telling them in no uncertain terms, **not** to conceive.*

No! They prefer to turn a deaf ear to this reality, ... taking a most selfish risk nature itself would not gamble on, ... and insist that the members of their community pay for this self-awarded privilege in addition to the money they themselves provide.

Why don't they instead deliver all the money they intend to spend on such egotistic venture on the poor of this province ... if as they proclaim they are not selfish?

I could show them poor neighborhoods where that money could be better spent ...

An insane attitude indeed I say! ... Don't you think Isabelle?

She nodded quietly.

Temporarily Hovering Over a Fragment of Discussion 5.
Because of Cultural Memes...

"But a considerable number of Québécois have an open mind ... and in fact now travel" interjected Isabelle.

"Yea! But most go the States" responded Antoine *"... especially Florida where they gather into 'Little Québec' ghettos there, ... continuing to speak French in the heart of America, ... as if they were still in Québec, ... without any interest in the country there're in, ... because what they're seeking is warmth rather than spend winter at home ... that's all ... and among these many cannot speak English... and choose not to learn it despite the opportunities given them ... and this again while in the heart of America ... ... It's insane to miss such an opportunity.*

Isabelle! ... ... All too often many of these people are so unsophisticated they even applaud when their plane takes off or lands for Christ's sake ... and many get drunk on the plane.

They have no understanding of the continent on which they live ... most have never visited other Canadian provinces or territories – except for those located on provincial borders of Ontario and New Brunswick – and then mostly to visit relatives close to those borders.

Look! I know I only refer to a segment of the population here, and that a good chunk of Quebecers are better than that ... but my point is this:

> *A much too large a part of Québec's French-Canadians has no ambition, because our culture and the education system <u>still</u> support and encourage that attitude ... and because it makes these people easier to*

control for the moment… like in the good old days of religious hegemony".

After thinking through what he was about to explain, Antoine paused a bit more, and then carried on with his argument.

"Too many Quebecers pretended and many still continue to pretend that Québec is special just because of its language and its isolated culture.

It is not!

It's a red herring simply because the Québec territory is in North-America and not in Europe and certainly not in France, and that many inward looking Quebecers must shed that illusion ... and accept once and for all the territorial context in which they find themselves.

Québec is part and function of the English-speaking North-American continent, whether it likes it or not.

It is located smack against the most powerful, richest and advanced nation on earth, and situated in the biggest and most populated English-speaking territory on Earth – and Canada, if not the USA, is a bloody decent place to live, if I must say so myself".

"But what if Québec was to become a sovereign state as many among you insist or fear?" Isabelle suddenly interjected.

"If Québec was ever to become a sovereign state, then the US and Canada would most likely join forces and ensure the US/Canada border from coast to coast remains as is ... and I suspect it's likely planned that way already—a secretly never-to-be-admitted plan between both countries.

Québec would then become all the poorest, ... its territory would at best shrink to include everything north of Three-Rivers or Québec City to the Labrador border, ... a portion of northern Québec along with the Gaspé area going down south just before the approximate 'border' to but not including the Beauce area and the Eastern Townships along with the Canada-US border then East with a decent strip up to New Brunswick – nothing less ... and let us not forget your Gatineau region.

The most important economic Québec territory in the province would remain with Canada."

Then he stopped and thought about a point that had bothered him … the arrogance of many people from Québec City … by and large civil servants.

"In fact, what you have in Québec City and the environs, for example, are largely government workers—hence non-productive elements to the economy per se—paid in great part by the people anchored in the economy in greater Montreal along with its north and south shores. Québec City has no significant major businesses. It simply lives off the taxes paid by greater Montréal, which in fact include a disproportional number of Anglos and recently embedded immigrants into that community ."

After half a minute or so he then went on.

"I have always thoroughly believed that, both, the Canadian and American governments, would never permit a geographical break of territory of the Canadian federation now sharing a border from coast to coast with them ... because it would not make business and political sense.

*Politically and for security reasons **the US will never permit the vulnerability of its border** with an unpredictable and unproven nation on its frontier. Period.*

The US would see to it regardless of scenarios, that no part of a sovereign Québec touch any part of its border.

Québec would then become a northern nation encircled by Canada and separated from the USA.

As I already said, it would become all the poorer with its present expensive nanny State-based social programs; its weak managerial style; its general negative attitude towards entrepreneurship; its overbearing project mismanagement; its clunky committee method to problem assessment and solution meant to dissolve, if not simply nullify, personal responsibility and accountability; and its frail financial planning practices – especially <u>without</u> the vast majority of its usual revenues coming in from the greater Montréal area, southern Québec and subsidies from the rest of Canada.

All the revenues presently coming out of the Gatineau region, metropolitan Montréal including north and south shores then going east to Sherbrooke among other areas would no longer flow to Québec City ... secured government jobs would shrink by probably 60 to 80% in the Québec City region alone, ... its present social programs would no longer be financially viable, ...its remaining portion of the provincial debt would at best be most difficult to manage ... and borrowing or bond issue would be expensive and problematic on the financial markets ... and on and on ... complications would keep adding on.

This would leave even larger massive debts.

In addition, Québec would most likely undertake clumsy pandering relations with its former country of origin ... a process and an ideological objective based on the implementation of the mythical and so-called insane 'modèle Québécois' of doing things within the so-called Francophonie.

I'm talking about that notion of specialness, which in fact is just a cover-up to hide the inferiority complex of my community".

He paused for about a minute and then carried on again.

"And finally let me say, Québec's separatist minded people must realize that its mission and objectives of total political independence cannot be absolute ... firstly, in view of fusion of everything imaginable presently taking place with the globalization of all activities on earth along with the ongoing centralization of power, authority and resources into ever fewer hands; ... and secondly, French-speaking Quebecer's are already culturally drowning in the vast North-American English-speaking culture and have already begun to succumb to the attractions this presents, ... and also by shear osmosis of the reality that surrounds them ... ... if in doubt all you have to do is ... ... just observe our youth! ... pay attention to what they're listening ... what they're doing on the internet ... and so on ... pay attention to our new immigrants—even those speaking French are already aware of this ... so why isn't the older or the unilingual generations, I say?"

Temporarily Hovering Over a Fragment of Discussion 6.
Substituting Old Ecclesiastical Authorities

A few minutes of silence passed by, then Antoine asked:

"What do you really think of the habit in Québec particularly of functioning and managing everything by committees at the behest of any bureaucratic machine in place?"

Isabelle thought about this for a short while and then replied:

"I suppose ... now ... let me think of this a bit, ... let see ... ... oh yea ... it's an approach to set of administrative tribunals to assess the least harmful decisions and actions with the view of protecting affected bureaucratic stakeholders of course ... along with the bureaucratic system they adhere to.

A sort of secular tribunals replacing in style and logic the ecclesiastical authorities of olden days one more time I would say".

Antoine and Isabelle suddenly got up, as if both had decided to take a short break before continuing another emotionally laden discussion during the afternoon now beginning.

Deciding next to go the small boat deck Antoine had constructed on his property two years ago by the Rigaud River in the back of his house, and where those two Adirondack chairs were conveniently left from May to October, bringing with them scones Isabelle has purchased on St. Lawrence Street in Montréal the day before at the 'Old European Shop', along with one more large mug of that dark French roast Van Houtte coffee Antoine preferred and Isabelle had easily adopted soon after meeting him, probably in view of her already acquired taste for strong dark roasted coffee—a sort of Swedish national preference Antoine had discovered a while back after meeting her on his second date with her.

This time Isabelle continued the discussion that had begun about twenty minutes ago, doing so as if no interruption had taken place.

"The political issue upon which most of Québec agonizes, ... stems, ... and I know I repeat myself again, ... from having replaced the ecclesiastical authorities with secular ones ... ... sadly with the same structural logic and approach ... but never admitting it for fear of awakening some uncontrollable ... lack of resolve ...

... and yet by replicating in many ways the old concept of 'Absolute Obedience' to a sort of an unquestionable 'Immaculate Perception' of sort ... based in a way on their old time religion ... ... they then reintroduced their previous blind faith in ancient dogmas this time metamorphosed into new secular ones ...

...and in their adoption of a new quasi-religion of political correctitude ... quasi-sacred secular administrative protocols were gradually and automatically established during that transition.

These have in fact become the routine 'catechism' of a by now deeply rooted bureaucracy ... wherein, both, unquestionable algorithmic protocols had to be followed and wherein committee decisions replaced local archbishops or 'curés' or even the confessionals of the Roman Catholic Church of older days.

In fact, you could, if you are in an ironic Orwellian mood regard the politically correct language of Québec's institutions and the bureaucratic machines supporting these as the Québec 'newspeak'. ... Yea! ... Think of the totally insane notions contained bureaucratic structures such as silos of controls ... such as those in the Health and Services department – the biggest and most ex-

*pensive bureaucratic money eating monster of the entire provincial government – with ridiculous and unreasonable acronyms and separate missions such as CHSLD. CISSS, CIUSSS, SMAF, RI, RTF, SAPA, DRHCAJ, RPA, SAD, SIAD, CLSC, MSSS, DRHCAJ, PREM, RLS, DRMG ... and I am sure I forget many others feeding the vast bureaucracy in place ... ensuring **no elected government can manage it,** drowning all direct orders by an elected government into procedural cul-de-sac or byzantine ways and means meant for its own bureaucratic continuation and control ... all the while ironically, sarcastically, and arrogantly pretending and proclaiming for all to hear that: 'l'être humain et son bien-être sont au cœur de notre mission.'"*

Suddenly, both their attention focused for a minute or so on a young couple slowly rowing their red canoe down the river as it passed by.

Isabelle then went on.

"Look Antoine!

Once a bureaucracy has installed itself, it remains as is, and whenever given a chance it strengthens itself – unless you kill it.

You know that having worked in a large corporation.

This is especially true, if it is a deeply rooted one that has been part of a culture, ... and in the Québec case, these roots have been there for nearly four hundred years under one dogmatic belief system, ... and remained more or less the same ... as your religious belief system in great part transmogrified itself into a secular one under another ... this time quasi-unquestionable secular one ... ... spreading like a cancer growth into newer bureaucracies ... including new governmental departments and agencies since the 'révolution tranquille' ...

...and this whether, it was once created through a governmental initiative, or simply assigned by a group of interested parties.

It doesn't really matter how it was created in the first place".

"What do you mean?" asked Antoine.

"My point is this..." Isabelle continued *"... regardless of size or logic, once a bureaucracy has been created, ... as you well know ... it is hard if not impossible to dislodge or get rid of ...*

... because the first objective of all bureaucracies is to protect itself as a living breathing entity, as the saying goes ...

... and that is true whether we deal with the blue wall of police unions, or an association of medical doctors, or a large taxation department of a government, or a labor union, or in the case we started with, overstaffed, overpaid and self-perpetuating governmental departments such as that of Education, Health and Welfare or Transportation in this province ... ... and all the others for that matter when you really think of it."

Temporarily Hovering Over a Fragment of Discussion 7.
Le Modèle Québécois - 1

"And the 'modèle Québécois'? ... according to you is what?"
Asked Isabelle.

Antoine stopped to regain control of his thoughts and began his critique for that afternoon.

"Well! Let's see!

In Québec the Nanny State has now replaced in all of its excesses the medieval Roman Catholic Church of a few decades ago, which for several centuries acted as a dictatorial meta-parent ... ... apparently because its population now still psychologically requires the illusive protection of an always correct meta-parent to replace its former dictatorial god.

That is why, the new secular religion of 'Political Correctitude' is the unofficial belief system of the present Québec establishment and is at the heart of its political processes, ... wherein bureaucratic protocols exist as a holy managerial methodology identified as "le modèle Québécois" by Quebecers ... and which forms an integral part and function of the special languages of all professionals and bureaucrats in that province nowadays.

This is routinely characterized with patronizing expressions ... from professionals and bureaucrats that is ... before answering almost anything ... generally framing their opinions and statements ... as if these were meant for quasi-illiterate or an already submissive population with such patronizing saying as: "Il faut d'abords comprendre que ..." ... and so on, ... as if the listeners possessed an intelligence below them or could only with difficulty eventually correctly assess a particular point expressed by an 'expert' or a professional ... unless it was laid out in an almost infantile simplicity ... so that average citizens could 'understand' the selected information transmitted to them.

A situation reminiscent of the condescending parlance of their earlier religious masters, which they in fact replaced, copied, and now emulate".

Antoine paused for a few seconds, squinting his eyes before making one last point on this subject.

"The real issue, however, is that, whenever a group considers itself as special, like Québec does with its so-called 'modèle Québécois', ... added to its self -assigned label of 'société distincte' ... it generally if not nearly always acts in prejudicial ways.

It is in the nature of the attitude and philosophy that goes with this outlook regardless of group or community, whenever a group considers itself almost as a 'Chosen People' or as a victim of past and present geopolitical events".

He stopped talking for a few more seconds, concentrating on the logic he was about to expound, when Isabelle abruptly took the baton and continued the argument she expected from Antoine.

"Among other things Antoine, and sadly I would say, while coming back to 'le modèle Québécois', that decisions by committees are preferred by those intending to spread responsibility and accountability to as many people as possible until in the end <u>only</u> the system can be blamed.

After all, isn't that the very purpose of managing by committees?

With this approach, you eventually reach the lowest common denominator verdict or pronouncement possible ... and you know what appalling solutions are generally implied here Antoine.

Especially when the intent is to ignore debts, the pertinent education of children and young adults, and other effects carried on the back of future generations for the very selfish and narrow interests and benefits of the more privileged segment of today's generation". She emphasized.

"The whole Québec government rules in accordance with this precept ... and the population follows ... like those 'brebis' of religious paternalistic connotations of olden days ... especially by those bent on preserving and promoting the Nanny-State they have now become addicted to.

No wonder your provincial bureaucracies via committees shackled to inflexible protocols for decisions and actions are so deeply embedded in nearly all decisions and actions that should otherwise be taken by someone in the field and truly in charge and in touch with the real world.

No one is permitted to use their initiative in government bureaucracies... lest they be nailed for failing to follow established protocols ... and ruin their career.

Personal initiatives are discouraged in fact and by definition to protect the integrity of the bureaucratic machine.

No one dares to act on their own, ... even if it's to get someone out of trouble, ... for, say, some crazy bureaucratic snafu, ... for fear of stepping outside preapproved automated decision-making administrative algorithms established by the bureaucracy they serve.

You could even say that implanted bureaucratic administrative algorithms have now become the new religious sacred text dictating behavior ... a secular one mind you ... but sacred nonetheless and handled as such ... as if a secular bible of sort if you like.

This 'modèle Québécois' leads to a politically-correct-to-his/her-organization psychosis of a kind, ... and if push too long and too far, ... it will no doubt cause serious existential problems to your community".

Temporarily Hovering Over a Fragment of Discussion 8.
Le Modèle Québécois - 2

Isabelle began the discussion that next afternoon.

"Rather that benchmark the best there is in the construction of roads, overpasses, and bridges in view of our extreme climate, Québec insists on 'le modèle Québécois', which clearly does not work well, since your infrastructure construction projects tend to be of inferior quality and costlier than others elsewhere in Canada ...

... and nearly always contains, it seems, a significant cut for contractors as well as hustlers in the official and unofficial chain of command and approval authorities ... a situation you cannot afford ...

... and increasing your costs apparently by some thirty percent or so at best.

It's as if you were trying to commit financial suicide, my friend.

But what really galls me, and a subject that hardly anybody mentions, is your approach to computerization". Isabelle said as forcefully as she could.

"In the area of digitization, another version of 'le modèle Québécois' made its appearance.

At first and for example, politicians and bureaucrats particularly insisted in adopting already developed computer applications from France under the dogmatic notion that computer programs 'written' in French would be the ticket, since the instructions and procedures would already be in French ...

... and this without ever assessing if these programs were the best to begin with in the first place ...

... unaware it appears that separate computer languages – hence the logic – essential in the creation of such system are independent of one's culture.

They did this in essence for ideological reasons, since the most advanced systems people in the entire world were next door in the USA" and not in France ... an insane strategy.

Secondly, while the superordinate idea blinding their decision-making was that written procedures and panels would already be in French persisted for a long time ... a false positive by the way, ... they continued in their failed ventures in systems development with the help of governmental and private French experts ... until hiring IBM to support them at last ... a good but generally average systems development firm, that spectacularly failed, for example, to see the future ... ignoring the big picture presented by firms such as Microsoft, Apple, Oracle, and all the others ... ...

... ... and as an aside Antoine ... IBM also showed its incompetence with the Canadian government in its extraordinary failure with its created, managed, and operated Phoenix project, which both institutions keep on hiding by using the label "Phoenix" so most Canadians will blame the system rather than IBM, those who specifically mismanaged the project.

Thirdly and getting back to our provincial point here ... ... and most importantly, government executives and directors and their supporting staff could not generally bother with details in the unfolding of their requirements, which unnecessarily costs them hundreds of millions at least due to incomplete planning ... when the success of an information systems is found in great part in the admittedly boring but necessary skunk work of details.

But even if all conditions to systems development were respected in the construction of a given application, clients, (say, departmental representatives and their superiors), to this day kept, and keep on putting, the cart before the horse, ...

... ignoring the most fundamental broad adage and principle of system development of 'garbage in, garbage out', which is exactly what came out for years to this day in most areas. The latest, regrettable, and spectacular example recently being the mess stupidly created by those alleged cybernetical experts and planners from your Québec Transportation department this year.

The fourth crucial failure of systems owners and stakeholders in most Québec governmental system development projects rarely exhausted – as they should have done – in the greatest details possible such as:

1. *What their actual needs really were.*

2. *What the present methodology exactly consisted of again in its minutest particulars.*

3. *Ensure that the project management planning charts were realistic and dynamic in their unfolding and timing.*

4. *Guarantee proper and full costing.*

5. *Assign real specific responsibility and accountability to each task and job created ... and therefore assign employee to each job with specific delivery dates at each step and in the right order following an agreed upon critical path.*

6. *Adopt a task-specific costing process that would respect all accounting principles and applications.*

The fifth and most critical element in the whole process is the hiring of the best expert firm in the area of systems development ... regardless of source, nationality, culture, or language ... if it could not be found in Québec.

Nothing less.

Massive amounts of money have been spent already without significant results, say, in the full digitization of health records, for example, now under development for nearly a couple decades with no results until lately, ...

... and enormous sums of moneys will be wasted again there and elsewhere within government departments and agencies – until a brutal and truly rationalized business approach is implemented" ... nothing less.

And sadly, far more will be wasted in your continued incompetence in the construction of your infrastructure for both digitized systems in all governments departments ... and all the physical workloads undertaken and contracted by the Transport depart-ment". She finally concluded as she wrapped up her presentation.

Temporarily Hovering Over a Fragment of Discussion 9.
Failing Québec's Children For Ideological Reasons

"I'll carry on your argument if you don't mind ... I think we're on the same wavelength here". Isabelle added that sunny afternoon.

"So, relax Antoine! ... and tell me if I deviate too much from your general outlook".

Isabelle took a deep breath, in the style of an Olympic athlete about to make an outstanding gold medal worthy jump, as she concentrated to gather her wits and then began.

"In Québec for ideological reasons and beyond religious brainwashing – although you're no longer religious in the traditional sense – a large segment of your French-speaking French-Canadians still fail to encourage and lead your children to prepare for and live a life in the real world once they're grown up.

You, as a community, still and all too often prefer giving credence to an ideology constructed by granola hippies of the Sixties and Seventies, who had little concepts of the world beyond those promulgated by classical education schooled lawyers, medical doctors, professors, and journalists ... all living and earning a living in their separate ivory towers.

... and this all too often accompanied by an overwhelming separatist presence within the French CBC ... with their obvious parochial political leanings in assuaging and coaxing a then more or less docile Québec population toward an allegedly independent country ... ... a promised land of sort that had been their 'due'

for centuries in their veiled ... if not openly stated broadcasted opinions.

These folks presented their community as a victimized people at the behest of an uncaring English-speaking population ... including those cultural 'turncoats', ... those immigrants choosing English as their new means of communication in Montréal, ... of course forgetting to mention that these people only did so to put the odds in their favor on this vast English-speaking continent ... but shush ... no one among you was supposed to mention this, ... lest you be considered a traitor to the cause ... right?

For decades now, this pipedream of a no-pain sovereignty was shimmered in the eyes of a largely unschooled and inward-looking population, ... as if this bright sparkling goal was soon to take place, ... as if the epitome of a golden age was about to surface, ... as if all could and would inadvertently cooperate to that political end, ... and that we ought to appoint them in the end to run the show of course ... or some similar scenario to that effect.

They would never mention a truism of history of course, which is that ... the elite of your own ethnic group ... as privileged owners and or stakeholders and or professionals ... would by far benefit and profit the most ... and that they would also be as controlling and as self-righteous as those you previously, ... rightly or wrongly considered your masters.

The truth being simply that, ... the old guard wanted to rule again, ... this time more firmly since losing their balance at the onset of the 'révolution tranquille' ... to again once more become the ultimate elite of all French-Canadians in Québec ... and by default over the English-speaking Canadian segment on that territory as well ... to do as they wished ... ready to ensure us all, I'm sure, ... that the phony democratic process of '50% +1' made it morally right and correctly legitimized such permission ... ethically 'forgetting' those in the '50% - 1'.

Then further erroneously assuming that ... original English-speaking Quebecers and newly arrived immigrants in Québec in this case would eventually and automatically abide by and integrate themselves en masse within the traditional French-speaking Québec culture ... and this without regard to the opportunities offering themselves throughout the rest of English-speaking Canada and the whole of the USA.

In addition this was and still is a position blindly marketed and sold with no reference to the massive problems this would create especially by a province financially ill-prepared, deeply indebted, still backward in several respects, with little or no business savvy in fact until a few years ago – except for a small segment of more socially advanced entrepreneurs in some sections of Montréal and the Beauce Region, Eastern Townships, Gatineau, and the environs.

Look! You've accumulated crushing debts since the 'révolution tranquille' at times for valid but also for ideological social programs <u>way before</u> you could afford them.

Several of which were laudable ones indeed, mind you, but which evidently benefited the immediate generation of do-gooders that created them, ... and this again at the expense of those that will follow you ... and which in addition you clearly again could not afford then, now, and will not, for quite some time to come.

But like a stubborn and inexperienced teenager you did it anyway.

This financial and economical blind faith approach to problem solving, I tell you, will no doubt destroy the lives of succeeding generations, if you continue to borrow money at a financially suicidal rate.

What must be done in Québec is to adopt a much broader equality of conditions before promoting an equality of opportunities ...

and do this with a long-range view instead of the usual short term due to the next election.

Indeed, in your bureaucratized, law-ridden, and protocol-intensive governance, you rush into a redistribution of your revenues purportedly to meet in great part a management philosophy you keep on referring to as the 'modèle Québécois', ... and a political ideology that often trumps reasonable logic.

You do so, ... paying little or no importance to the production of wealth in your own milieu, ... while simultaneously still lacking a profound sense of entrepreneurship at the heart of your culture ... a culture that deeply requires a full-scale support for total entrepreneurship, if it wishes to enter what you and I, have been referring to as a possible Québec 5.0.

Another of the fundamental reasons for this is that you do not possess a strong business and industrial infrastructure required to support often commendable enterprises ... ... you in fact make it difficult for any entrepreneur to do business in your province ... you do so through a colossal interference you purposely created ... and by the massive bureaucracies you've established since the 'révolution tranquille'.

That is why;

> *You must grab yourselves by your own bootstraps, so to speak, ... swallow your false pride ... and then emulate the Chinese or Americans – among others – in the domain of social objectives, projects, and programs.*

Obviously, you, as a people, are very minor players when compared to the size of China or the US for that matter, ... but this is no reason for you not to adopt the can-do attitude of both countries for that matter and piggyback on their experiences and successes".

All of a sudden Antoine quickly asked:

"What should Québec's approach be as far as you're concerned?"

"Well! Let me think a bit ...

If I were to sum it up", answered Isabelle *"it would be:*

1. *Assess your situation as it really is, and not as you wish it to be.*
2. *Make a real inventory of all your assets province wide.*
3. *Set long range flexible strategic goal of development, most likely decades long, without ideological shackles to gum up the works ... and then introduce your tactical ones on an on-going basis".*

***

Here Isabelle stopped, as if another relevant thought came up:

"Oh yes! Let me add a note here to what I call 'ideological shackles' before I go on to my point 4.

In my view, I believe that separatists failed to see through the intellectual fog they themselves created by their ideology in that ... absolute sovereignty leads directly to isolationism ... and will especially do so on this North-American continent.

This is especially true now in a world where globalization of everything is in an accelerated mode.

This is particularly frustrating for separatists, ... because of the domination of English in the 20th century and so far in the 21st as the lingua franca of the planet, ... pardon the pun my friend, ... in business communications, computerization, globalization, diplomacy, etc."

***

Isabelle then went on with her other points.

"And so:

4. *Then be intelligent, mature, and humble enough to seek and obtain by all means possible skills necessary to reach your overall objectives ... by benchmarking the best there is in the world, wherever it may be located ... and also to that end use your brightest candidates, who studied elsewhere in the world's best universities, so they can teach at home the skills still unavailable in your province, but which they acquired elsewhere.*

5. *Afterword upgrade your learning institutions and reorganized them in the most realistic way possible – with a mechanism for continuous upgrades ... and please ... not to integrate ideological objectives ... or malfunctioning organization structures ... and most certainly no more than three broad reporting levels at best wherever possible otherwise inefficiencies automatically set it.*

6. *Encourage entrepreneurship in every way possible, because once freed from the fear of self-development and bureaucratic roadblocks, there is no end to what a people anywhere can accomplish ... the rest comes naturally.*

Québec my dear Antoine is no different than others here.

But ... and there is a big 'but' here, ... what is absolutely required before all this can take place is ... a change of attitude, ... which is yet to fully take place as a normalized function in the governmental machine and workplace such as within your provincial education system for example.

In Québec this also means first 'to stop acting like victims'; get rid of the attitude that regards all English-speaking people as uncooperative citizens ... if not simply as enemies of the French-

Canadian community generally and Quebecers in particular ... and grab all those prospects surrounding you all ... to your interests and benefits.

These are everywhere ... simply because at present you truly live geographically and financially in a land of great opportunities ... North America that is.

The rest of the world envies your geographical location and the opportunities there for the picking ... and yet you do little to prepare yourself to benefit from these facts ... it's a bloody shame I tell you my friend.

Yet in my view, there is still hope, ...

... because a segment of the present generation shows itself more entrepreneurial than all the others before, ...

... this implies that despite your communally shared high reticence in this domain, ... you separately and desperately want to get out of that socially preprogrammed fear, ... and grab yourselves by your bootstraps ... ignoring routine critics still discouraging you, ... and joining the global hubris of accepting the planetary language in force, rather that proclaim yourselves as 'victims' of that old nemesis caused by France's abandonment ... I said, and I emphasize ... by France's unethical abandonment of its own citizens once more in the course of its history".

"So, if I can sum up Isabelle" interrupted Antoine "... in this third decade of the 21st century you sense a section of the present generation is fighting hard to disregard and overcome all the roadblocks set by both my community's culture and governmental crazed demands for business conditions and senseless reporting mechanisms ... which are in fact taking place as we speak ...

... and this is probably because the new generation does not want to be left behind ... and that on the contrary it wants to be part of the future ... by being cooperative members of the globalization movement now in progress ...

... and that if this is the case ... gone for them is the traditional French-Canadian inferiority complex. As for the rest, I suppose the objective is to eventually and literally kill the massive governmental bureaucracy presently threatening to enslave us in this province".

"That's precisely what I am trying to convey my dear Antoine", concluded Isabelle.

Temporarily Hovering Over a Fragment of Discussion 10.
A Duplication of Services

"Oh! Oh! Just a minute," interjected Isabelle.

"This reminds me of one administrative stupidity committed year after year by the Québec government regardless of who's in power ... and that's your taxation department.

I can't get over the stupidity of it all.

What a managerially and financially self-destructive measure it has been in this decision to have your own separate taxation bureaucracy!

You act as if a sovereign State, which you are not, and which is pricey, very expensive indeed... with the economically harmful and truly unnecessary additional costs.

Yes! You deliberately choose a more expensive method of collecting taxes, when an already efficient and much cheaper federal machinery in this respect is already in place collecting taxes on behalf of all other provinces and territories for the entire country ... a normal federated service provided by the Canadian federation.

Think for a minute!

You purposely and unnecessarily waste hundreds of millions of dollars, year after year, to collect what Ottawa can routinely and robotically do for you through their federal collecting mechanisms ... and does very professionally carry out for all of Canadian provinces and territories ... except for you guys ... because you insist on doing it separately ... and in addition ... you thereby subject your citizens to double reporting ... one tax report for you and one for the feds.

Are you insane?

This was something the feds were doing for you since the beginning of the confederation ... until you insisted for ideological reason a few decades ago to do it yourself.

Have you guys gone completely mad?

If something can be pointed at for gross financial mismanagement ... that my friend is the most obvious and easiest case for all to see.

You duplicate this department just because you think you're different ... how insane is this, I ask you again?

Where's the accounting logic here ... especially with your debt burden?

It reflects the very attitude and profound lack of fiscal responsibility and accountability which you've been indoctrinated against in the last four centuries.

It's a classic example of financial mismanagement of rare resources ... money which you don't have ... in this case ... and which you sorely need elsewhere in your budget".

"Here Isabelle I completely agree" interrupted Antoine.

"I could never understand this as well.

Yes! ... Oddly enough ... like a fish in water that doesn't know it is wet ... I only became aware of this anomaly, when I move to Manitoba, where I became conscious for the first time that I only had to produce one income tax declaration ... the thought of being different from the rest of Canada in this respect never arose in my mind until then.

Yea, ... I know I should have known better ... but I was buried in for so long in the normalcy of a separate tax department in Québec that I had assumed it was the same elsewhere ... it never occurred to me until I moved elsewhere in Canada.

Silly, isn't it, when you think of it?

*And scary at the same time ... when your very own culture ... **as all cultures do** ... make a stupid situation a normally accepted piece of allegedly 'self-evident logic' – such as a totally unnecessary duplicate taxation department at a dear price to us all in Québec in this case".*

Temporarily Hovering Over a Fragment of Discussion 11.
A Proto-Police State in The Making

Antoine's face now looked sadder as he prepared to make another declaration.

"Another thing that bothers me, more than the enormous waste of money here Isabelle, is the attitude and behavior of the Revenue Department, ... which seems to worsen year after year.

It has become a department that never hesitate to deliberately attack the weaker members of our own society.

It's as if it was on a mission to render those struggling the most ... the weakest unable to fend for themselves ... those most helpless ... completely subjugated to the governmental machine.

At times, I think that our provincial tax department ... and here is the scary part for me that will sound crazy to you ... or anyone else that would be listening ... has begun to act as a State police of a kind in the collection arena," Antoine blurted out.

"It uses its enormous powers to threaten if not bludgeon the already economically weak along with the starting "petites et moyennes entreprises" ... you know ... the so-called PMEs in the Québec jargon ... both with severe economic demotions, if not teetering toward bankruptcy".

"Wow! Wow! Come on now Antoine! Surely, you're exaggerating quite a bit here ... you're going way off on a tangent here," suddenly exclaimed Isabelle.

"I'd like to agree with you my dear Isabelle, but I'm afraid, ... I'm truly afraid that, ... this department has de facto stepped in the area of money collection like a mafia collector... into the role

of a proto-State police ... its methods are more sophisticated I admit than the mythical mafia type... but the end is the same.

In fact, this duplicate and totally financially useless department, as we've already agreed, possesses enormous powers of execution, which it abuses against 'The Weak', 'The Downtrodden', 'The Poor', 'The Quasi-Poor', the small merchants, and so on.

It purposely directs its dedicated financial assaults on waiters, smaller enterprises, or anyone with a 'can do' attitude or someone simply struggling to eke out a living ... rapaciously draining their last dollars, ... doing everything possible to squeeze as much money as possible out of those who cannot defend themselves, ... as well as those at the most critical stage of a developing entrepreneurial venture ... and leading them all to bankruptcy if necessary ... ... in effect picking mostly on those who cannot afford to fight back ... either because they don't know how or simply cannot afford to fight back through the justice system.

*Here you also actually witness taxation collectors, implanting on behalf of the State, **the fear of entrepreneurship** ... ensuring through its operations a continued submissiveness of citizens like the good old days of ecclesiastical hegemony.*

This duplicate and therefore completely unnecessary department contrary to its marketed devoutness of allegedly only obtaining on behalf of the Québec population what is due to the governmental machinery, ... goes on to the point of even making assumptions as to what one's earnings are, when they cannot in fact specifically assess one's or a given small enterprise's revenues, ... using the force of their office to attack their targets of interest financially and separately.

As if shooting at targets one by one with powerful fiscal guns in some way.

But like all bullies they back off, when it comes to major corporations or rich individuals ... because these have a whole staff of highly competent tax lawyers not afraid of their bullying tactics.

To complement the hypocrisy of this department we know that it de facto also refrains from investigating, or at least preventing, tax heavens used by powerful people and organizations.

Oh no! Like a segment of a police State, it concentrates on separately attacking private citizens and small groups one by one – and will continue to do so until no one can fight anymore, which is why:

> *I believe the 'ministère du revenue' was created and the collection of taxations transferred back to Québec to provide muscle – I dare say – as a surreptitious organization to continue to control a scared, docile, and already insecure population at that time, which it continues to perpetuate for, both, psychological and ideological reasons .*

A fascist endeavor of the first order, I say"

Temporarily Hovering Over a Fragment of Discussion 12.
Québec's Evolutionary Steps

"You've got me hooked now with your presentation ... please continue 'my belle' if you don't mind".

Said Antoine with that continuing smile he couldn't shake off at the sight of such passionate performance, along with that emotive presence Isabelle carried with her ever since he first met her in Vermont.

After a little while Isabelle continued from her earlier argument:

"I'm about to say something that will probably make you think I'm bunker ... so just hear me out first ... I simply want to place the various evolutionary steps Québec has gone through so far ... ... as I see them of course".

She then took a deep breath and continued.

"The four-hundred-year old bureaucracy that came in when the Nouvelle France and which disembarked in Québec in 1608, I label as 'Québec 1.0' to use a modern marker for the prepro-grammed culture that naturally came with it, ...

... then at the handing over by France of Nouvelle France to England, wherein Québec merely transmogrified itself into a somewhat hybrid form to encompass its new situation, say, 'Qué-bec 2.0' ... ...

> *... although we could imagine a 'Québec 2.1 and 2.2' respectively in a scenario that would reflect its unfolding due 'The Quebec Act of 1774' and the 'Constitutional Act of 1791'; ...*

It metamorphosed further at the creation of the then Dominion of Canada in 1867, ... say, 'Québec 3.0' to continue my analogy, when a new self-evolving nation could begin to take flight within a safe federal political context.

Québec finally mutated again this time in significant ways at the onset of the 'révolution tranquille' to today, say, 'Québec 4.0' as the present evolutionary step.

At each of the last two political transformation platforms Québec transitioned itself from a fundamentalist ecclesiastical bureaucracy to a secular one ... sluggishly and almost imperceptibly during 'Québec 3.0' ... but dramatically and quasi-instantly in historical time during 'Québec 4.0'.

Yet and nevertheless, the earlier religious skeletal structure of logic stayed more or less intact, and so did the attitude; ... except that in 'Québec 4.0' the bureaucracy became massive, oppressive, more sophisticated, and highly protocol-directed.

Similar to the divisions of the curia of the Vatican in some ways ... but with a costly and ineffective as well as inefficient committee-focused decision-making process, ... as it adopted the new unquestionable secular belief system of a brand new 'political correctitude',... as if a quasi-religion ... ... both as its mentor along with its secular 'holy text' and 'sacred pronouncements' found in all algorithms imbedded in the ever growing massive bureaucracies that have been installed and instituted since the 'révolution tranquille'.

Although the context changed from religious to secular objectives particularly in the Sixties and Seventies, the logical structure remained more or less the same in many ways ... papered over with a brand-new paint job – a new look – so to speak.

The classical medieval view of olden days was thrown on the scrap heap, while honest intents, decisions, and actions, ensured that education of the citizenry had to be upgraded and it was.

The issue nevertheless was that the earlier skeletal structure was kept almost intact, while labels, phrases, proclamations, and alleged targets were renamed, ... the mission nevertheless remained the same.

And that was among other things:

> *The control of French-Canadians in particular by the French-Canadian elite of the day, ... by nursing a continuing control of the population at large ... through the promotion of a disinterest in making money and entrepreneurship, and a continued dread in the questioning of authorities, while instituting a nanny-State to provide an unsophisticated population what their previous god failed to do—as in "god will provide" adage of their religious class.*

With this approach, the provincial elite transformed many religious programs of control into secular one ... I admit in some twisted ways at times ... but it did so nonetheless quite intelligently ... even if in the end, it will most likely bring Québec to financial bankruptcy and political ruin," concluded Isabelle.

Both now stayed silent for several minutes, as if to reflect on what had just been said.

Then Isabelle went on further with her exposé to Antoine.

"And the problem in Québec is that you have institutionalized ... hence bureaucratized to the nth degree ... the tools of your own destruction, by elevating, as in the past, the roles of traditional professions above all those that ought to, can, would, and must otherwise advance your standing as well as your economy in the world.

Look my dear Antoine, Québec approaches these, as if you were afraid of dirtying your hands in unpredictable messy money situations that the accelerating world now demands from all of us ... ... in some ways like your cultural nemesis, Séraphin Poudrier.

It is as if the notion of profits for a job well executed was a dirty concept ... as you were taught ... and illustrated at the end of 'Québec 3.0' and the beginning of 'Québec 4.0' by those old radio and TV programs such as "Un homme et son péché"' ... and I emphasize "et son péché" my dear Antoine ... and all this to the benefit of your entrenched French-Canadian elite.

You de facto continue the Roman Catholic Church programs of classical education in some ways inculcated in our forbearers ... but instead of using Latin or Greek as in the good old days, you've replaced these with a growing bureaucratic language ... a "Newspeak" of your own ... with your own lexicon, grammar, and syntax of expected justifications, pretexts, defenses, validations, rationalizations, ploys, defenses and so on.

And all this in a context of, and to excuse, failures of delivery and shortcomings for realistic planning.

Doing so as if trying to find your own version of a homemade Québec education nirvana triggered with an extreme fear of losing your language, which as intelligent people you know and feel might naturally gradually slip away in this massive and overwhelming English-speaking North-American continent over the centuries ... and all the while insanely refusing to benchmark what's best in the world."

She suddenly stared intensely at Antoine and started to laugh out loud. So loud and so much in fact that tears were going down her cheeks as she ended her argument.

She had abruptly grasped the hyperbolic extent she'd gone through to make her point.

"I did go on and on, didn't I Antoine?"

"Yes, Madame Sundstrom you did indeed, but then I tend to agree with you ... and love to hear you talk, ... call it a weakness of mine."

Temporarily Hovering Over a Fragment of Discussion 13.
An Inferiority That Ought <u>Not</u> Be There.

"Ah! Now that I think of it". Exclaimed Isabelle.

*"Rather than simplify your language, you instead insist on difficult 'dictées' for your students with gymnastics of syntax, problematic grammatical accords, spelling demands and so on, ... just because France does it ... forgetting that the US tailored their original British English to suit their needs, ... and **not** that of the mother country, ... which is why a good part of their spelling and expressions has been simplified among other things.*

In their requirements as a new developing nation able to act on its own terms, Americans became pragmatic with their language by adapting it to the situation at hand.

An approach followed by Canada to a lesser degree but enough to create a sort of Canadian English.

Just check your word processing program for example!

Something Québec should have undertaken long ago but could only reticently begun to define for themselves about two decades back or so.

As a group, you show an inferiority you ought not to have," she emphasized ... *"but feel compelled to display, ... by pandering if not simply showing an unearned adoring awe at France ... and yet on rare occasions you buck the system and assert yourself ... as in the case of your 'stop' signs.*

In Québec you title it as 'Arrêt; a perfectly correct word, while France ignored such a correct word needlessly replacing it with 'Stop', ... just to appear more hip; ... thereby showing their admiration for English, which in fact is accelerating its invasion in that country including such 'holy' places as the Sorbonne, where there is a building and a department called and I quote "Le Learning Centre" ... and pay attention to the total failure of the 'Académie Française' to keep up with reality ...

... and to continue my argument Antoine, ...

... we all know that the UK no longer pretends that American or Australian English are wrong ... nor the English crowd no longer ridicule, nor pretend not to understand their linguistic cousins, because of their accent, different expressions, or words. On the contrary they respect, ... if not openly admire for example, the various American accents, jargons, slangs, and idioms ... and often copy them ... as in the growing use of 'boss' instead of 'gov' and numerous others.

Anyway, coming back to my point, ... you do this while the English-speaking crowd in Québec, the rest of Canada and the United States, use a far simpler linguistic tool that can and does turn on a dime whenever necessary, ... which is the strength of English in the first place and why it succeeds in this fast changing world, ... and one of the reasons it is adopted as a second language by so many around the planet.

You should take pride in Québec's accented French ... like the Americans and Australian did on their own terms, ... as well as get rid of your ideological reason, as if a bad seed, in pushing English out your school curriculum and your Canadian and international dealings whenever you can.

Your attitude in this respect is hurting you as a viable society and diminishing your chance of success on both the Canadian and international scenes," she finally concluded.

Temporarily Hovering Over a Fragment of Discussion 14.
When The Best Cannot Be Found Within Our Midst

Isabelle was now intent on jumping onto the next item she had in mind.

"Let's change subject before I repeat myself Antoine".

"Sure, go ahead" Antoine added quickly.

Isabelle squinted as if to concentrate her efforts for a minute or so … keeping silent with her hands covering most of her face, and then staring at Antoine started her new exposé.

"I fail to understand why Québec as a society refuses to benchmark the best, learn from the best, and hire the best for its projects and programs– if the talents necessary at the moment cannot be found in its midst.

Just think of China in the last four decades!

"China again"? Asked Antoine.

"Yea! I know … I'm back with China again … just bear with me, will you?

After being invaded and fucked time and again by just about anyone who could do so in the last couple centuries – including both England and France among others – and despite their very long history and a continued culture that's longer than anyone else … and in spite of all other roadblocks on their path … … such as a multiplicity of languages, cultures and sub-cultures in its midst

... it nevertheless had and continues to have the wisdom to bench-mark or hire what's best in the world, when what they require cannot be found at home.

That my friend is the sign of a truly pragmatic nation indeed.

Don't you think so Antoine?"

Antoine nodded in agreement.

"They probably had to borrow and at times steal manufacturing creations mind you to jumpstart their economy... and they surely copied the best from everywhere they could as well to that end ... I know I would, if I had to get many hundreds of millions out of poverty ... a perfectly ethical recourse in a dire situation ... be-cause when you're that far behind ... and you want to advance resolutely and quickly and become the leading nation on the planet... you do what must be done to get your people out of pov-erty anyway you can ...

...I know I would have done the same for my family if this had been the case ... that comes in first ethically speaking ... particu-larly if no one else suffers except for the losing elite class of your milieu.

Anyway, my point is that the Chinese in great part piggybacked on anything favoring them ... as I would have in their place with today's restrictive licenses meant to enrich the '1%' rather that upgrade humanity ...

... again, I emphasize the Chinese stepped over their pride and were willing to copy what is best no matter its origin ... thereby benchmarking the best regardless of origin or nationality or lo-cation or belief system.

A sign of immense control, patience, and societal maturity, I say".

Then going back in time Isabelle went on.

"Do you remember the smirks at China's humble beginnings here in the West, when Deng Xiaoping wisely and in non-showy ways launched the 'Beijing Spring' movement, ... and by that event radically changed the founding mission of the Chinese Communist Party, ... and redirected it to a planetary business takeover ... beginning with all possible manufacturing it could handle, ... and all marketing opportunities it could create.

... and China did just that ... didn't it?

... and after a few decades of total cooperation and dedication – inexistent anywhere else ... and a first in world history ... it brought hundreds of millions of people out of poverty ... and made itself a superpower, ... and is about to become the most powerful nation on earth.

An extraordinary feat you must admit.

Because of that enormous national effort, nearly all of us can now afford more things because these are made in China".

You got to give it to the Chinese.

When they set their mind on something ... they get it done.

Why can't Québec adopt a similar attitude?

Chinese don't belly ache like that branch of whining Quebecers bent on blaming their lack of business acumen and entrepreneurship on the Anglos here or in the rest of Canada.

Yea! Look at the extraordinary progress the Chinese have achieved so far ... and try to imagine where they're going to be in the future with that open-ended 'can-do' attitude, entrepreneurship, and excellent managerial skills.

The Chinese also never hesitated to ensure that their best and brightest went to the best universities in the world, wherever these were located, ... although each student had to initially become fluent in another language before doing so.

And then ensure all the knowledge accumulated elsewhere would be transferred back to China ... literally flow back to China by way of these highly educated, best, and brilliant individuals, now imbued with a variety of different worldviews complementing even more an already mature society.

Yet, far too many Quebecers continue, as if a new god figure could or would allegedly again 'provide' them with all their needs ... which of course it never did, ... and never will, ... especially since that imaginary alien in the sky did not rationally exist in the first place ... but nonetheless somehow shows up in the form of a secular ideology this time backed with massive immovable bureaucracies.

An insane notion brainwashed into nearly all societies but particularly for you guys during the good old days of Roman Catholic hegemony, ... with a remaining skeletal programming of that same attitude silently embedded in far too many Quebecers.

As a group, far too many among you still entice your children away from the more remunerative, more creative, more demanding, more rewarding, and certainly more leading-edge scientific and business ventures that ought to be yours, ... unless ... as many among you proclaim, ... there must be an automatic guarantee of a job in the immediate ... for the effort given ... so, you keep insisting.

In fact, doesn't that sound like many members of your own family that you described to me not that long-ago Antoine?"

"Yes! It does". He replied

"No wonder adolescent males especially quit school early, and if lucky will find work at menial jobs for minimum wage ... they do not want to make the effort ... refuse to take chances ... remain financially ignorant ... and entrepreneurially frozen into inaction ... and now additionally they are inoculated into a general mental somnolence playing aimlessly with their intelligent phones or as gamers and so on, ... while insisting nonetheless on an ever-increasing minimum wage with no efforts on their part to improve their situation. Right?"

Antoine nodded again but added, *"although for the next few years, while jobs for 'The Uneducated' and 'The Usually Unemployed' are plenty for now for a variety of reasons, but once the recession sets in for them, and additionally as AI and robotization accelerate with the other workers now feeling safe in their present jobs, it will be quite a shock."*

Isabelle nodded in turn and then continued her train of thoughts.

"Look! You're smack against the biggest economy in the world and most 'vieilles souches' unilingual French-speaking Quebecers still pretend it isn't there – especially those in the classic professions ... I speak especially of your unilingual doctors, notaries, lawyers, living in an inward-looking French-speaking world of their very own, ... all the more secluded from the rest of the world in regions outside Montréal's English-speaking sections ... a group still seeing themselves as superior to the rest of their French-Canadian compatriots.

As a people, you keep ignoring opportunities after opportunities ... ... except of course many of those young millennials and those following them now trying like hell to escape from this conundrum imposed by your educational system, as a good number of them now exceptionally show the world their outstanding skills in digital applications and technology for example.

Antoine was absorbing all that, keeping quiet, continuing to nod at each strong point, and intent on mentally memorializing Isabelle's outbursts out of respect for her opinion and her logic, which had likely been repressed over several decades, and now at last found a safe outlet.

"Think Antoine!

You create control programs meant to discourage the establishment of a business culture simply to ensure that the traditional professions remain on their ancient pedestal, with vastly complicated administrative procedures, too many permits, and other conditions.

That is why you religiously – pardon the pun here – create administrative roadblocks in the establishment of businesses.

Doing so through heavy bureaucratic demands of all sorts along with obligatory permissions and submissions as well as all kinds of reporting documentation mechanisms to organize and do business ... when your very own lack of knowledge in this domain at the governmental level is inferior to the reality of the world at large.

That's crazy.

And you wonder why your real unemployment has routinely been critical in your province until recently, ...and will get worse in the coming decades ... hell! ... people prefer doing business in areas where the government in place encourages it".

"But unemployment level is down significantly right now". Interrupted Antoine.

"It's a temporary blip". Immediately retorted Isabelle.

"your manufacturing is about non-existent except for small entrepreneurs here and there and the real scary thing now in progress but which everyone here especially ignores is the AI technology about to eliminate at least half of your workforce in the next twenty years or so.

Look!

What I'm saying is that you make it difficult to carry out business ventures at all levels, ... thinking you're cool while doing it – simply because you establish bureaucratic procedures for each potential business activities ... and insist on considering yourselves much different from everyone else in other Canadian provinces and the U.S. as well ... rather than benchmarked the best around you to begin with.

You even take business opportunities away by callously and thoughtlessly blocking access to small business, whenever you undertake infrastructure repairs or construction in Montréal where most of your revenues come from ... without regard for future small businesses... or you make accommodations for religious fundamentalists but contemptuously disregard small businesses ... the very blood feeding your governmental coffers at the moment.

You simultaneously as well don't give a shit about your citizens struggling to go to work morning and night, because your transportation executives at all levels and jurisdictions and their support staff are either unable to plan intelligently, or simply don't give a shit ... about your merchants or simply those trying to go to and from work.

Again, I say, you're nuts".

You insist that the Québec method – that so-called 'modèle Québécois' – is unique and special above all others.

Yet, it's not and you're not.

You're just kidding yourselves".

Temporarily Hovering Over a Fragment of Discussion 15.
True French-Speaking American Community

Isabelle went to the credenza this time to pour herself another large cup of extra strong black coffee before continuing her side of the argument that afternoon, when Antoine suddenly this time took the baton.

*"There are moments my dear Isabelle I think that our brand of separatists particularly appears to me as a bunch of culturally cloistered fools disconnected from reality, ... because the general mentality of Quebecers, whether they admit it or not is North American and **not** European ... that is clear to me, ... and the sooner we all accept this the better.*

Yet, our provincial government and our bureaucrats along with our classic professions keep on proclaiming our alleged differences from the rest of Canada and the United States, as if badges of honor.

I know that several differences exist no doubt, ... but when compared to our shared similarities and complementary characteristics they are few and minor indeed.

Despite ideological proclamations we must acknowledge that our tastes and lifestyles are essentially the same as the rest of North America.

We have our own peculiarities that makes us different to some degree and which are to be celebrated, but never to the extent of destroying us financially, or forcing us to pretend we're not located on the North American continent saddled with North-American habits and characteristics".

Here Isabelle intervened.

"If that is the case Antoine, I ask myself:

Why does French CBC or the Québec government, for examples, continue to admire and even brownnose France at every opportunity they get?

I admit to you that this is beyond me.

Yes! Just think for a moment think of your taste in sports from the CFL to NFL football (the type Mario Dumont prefers along with most Québécois for example); la bouffe (and here I don't mean that awful greasy heart-attack-giving poutine with that dreadful industrial brown sauce)... but the real Québec cuisine we've tasted in Montréal, Québec City, Trois-Rivières, Sherbrooke, in the Laurentians, in the Eastern Townships ... and those incredible meals served in many B and B's in Les Éboulements and so on;... and unique first class TV sitcoms, books, movies ... but nearly always addressed to a very small community ... and on and on and on.

Yet, you refuse, ... because of the persisting remnants of your religious brainwashing of earlier centuries until a few decades ago, ... to accept, who you are as you are, ... with all your North American characteristics, ... your strong points, warts, and all.

Instead, you focus on the smaller differences between you and the rest of North-America ... as if such small differences rendered you culturally superior ... or that different ... to the rest of North-America".

How stupid is that ... I ask you?"

Antoine thought about what she had just said and began to underlined Isabelle's point further.

"That's true. We have more in common with the rest of Canada and Americans than we have with France, a country that is still schizophrenically insisting that she continues to lead the world,

... ... you only have to watch their national news to see this ... when in fact it's been left behind through their own mismanagement and plain stupidity since WWI and especially after their collapse in WWII – if we're to forget their previous political blunders ... and this in addition to the progressive evolution of the rest of the world ... ... a world no longer dominated by France and England for that matter but by the United States with Asia in an impressive ascendency and China about to jump ahead of us all".

To which Isabelle immediately added.

"Yes! Oh yes! France with its inferiority complex under the cover of a patronizing superiority over the French-speaking world generally and Québec specifically, treats you as provincial cousins of inferior rank an ocean away – no better.

And I could add, ... as if you are on an equal footing of some isolated Pacific island of theirs at times ... say, Tahiti for example.

They mock your North-American accent, when they should be celebrating it, or pretend they can't understand your expressions, as if your version was inferior to theirs ... as if it has little class or inferior value ... or worse yet ... as if it needed translation, ... instead of recognizing it as simply another rich version of that language.

The French still choose to see you in folkloric settings ... as 'habitants' chasing beavers and moose, driving horse-driven sleigh in the midst of an eternal winter and so on ... and this in 2020 ... and you know I'm not exaggerating that much here

... it's ridiculous to think that way by an otherwise advanced society such as France nowadays...

... and yet you just laugh it off ...

... rather than grab yourself by your own bootstraps and drop them until they beg to get into your fold ... like the Americans did with England.

Its pitiful to watch your politicians and artists from where I stand".

Isabelle frowned in what just came to her.

"This whole attitude reminds me that England also showed a sense of language superiority for a long time over an accented Australian English particularly.

And until recently Australians felt so insecure about their regional accented English that for decades they hired Oxford-accented news readers from England instead of competent Australians ... so ashamed were they of their own version of accented English and expressions.

You told me as I recall Antoine that French as spoken in France is losing its luster, because first it has become fashionable in that country to adopt English words and expressions in lieu of valid French ones for no other reason than they're American or British ... often and despite already preexisting French words.

A sort of snobbishness that goes counter to the evolution of the French language, don't you think Antoine?"

"Yea! No doubt there". Antoine exclaimed.

"Overt Anglicism is rampant in France and a badge of honor in Paris particularly ... and yet they looked down on us ... a people literally living right in the middle of the greatest English-speaking ocean in the entire world, so to speak, ... the biggest concen-

tration of English-speaking people on the largest English-speaking territory on the planet ...and this while we occupy a geographical territory several times the size of France.

*On top of this is the fact that with the speed at which changes take place in this era of globalization, ... and the acceleration of changes expected down the line, ... the 'Académie Française' cannot, and will **never** be able to keep up with necessary, on time, and on target, needed language changes, where and when these are necessary.*

They're already miserably failing at it and will sadly continue to fail by the very logic of its modus operandi".

Here Isabelle wanting to add her two cents to Antoine's comments added.

"Yea! France generally considers you inferior to them within the 'Francophonie'.

It prefers to you, as I said already, in folkloric settings rather than as a modern North American community and still ... ...you continue as a provincial government to pander and cater to them, adopting a sort of feigned sovereignty patina to satisfy the many among you feverishly dreaming one day to address them nation to nation.

It's pitiful for us to watch, I tell you".

***

Then putting her hands around her face suddenly and then staring at Antoine once more with those big blue eyes of hers, Isabelle shouted:

"Oh, my god!

Speaking of France, I just remember!

Do you recall those news reels years ago with that pompous De Gaulle entering Paris, toward the end of the Second World War, as if it was him and the failed, silo-directed, and awfully managed French army at that time that had conquered Paris, and allegedly chased the escaping German army, when in fact it was the allies that stalled their very own entry into Paris in order to let Charles de Gaulle in first for strict political purposes ... and yet most in France still believe this horseshit."

"Anyway, let's leave the French pomposity and their fake hegemony of world leadership for now!" Suggested Antoine with a slight smile in his appreciation of her passionate delivery and logical rhetoric.

Temporarily Hovering Over a Fragment of Discussion 16.
Speaking of Referendums

Isabelle seemed exhausted for the moment and sat down to sip her water on a bright sunny afternoon and had insisted to carry on another one of those political discussions about French-Canadians and particularly Quebecers they had both promised themselves to undertake that summer until the subject had been exhausted.

A good fifteen minutes or so after sitting down Antoine began.

"Look Isabelle!"

Québec's French-speaking millennials, along with the immediate generation following them, want to stay in the North-American context.

They want this at least because of the opportunities this potentially offers them, ... as well as simply compete in the worldwide open-ended globalization game now available to them ... and this include staying in Canada, ... wherein they are not forcefully shackled with a language police ... especially since English continues to be the international language of communication and business at least for this 21ˢᵗ century and probably beyond that.

And let us not forget those multiple roadblocks set by the Québec government for business start-ups ... in addition to the heavy reporting mechanisms once a business is finally established and surviving against an above average taxation.

Anyway, Millennials and Generation Z do not consider English as the language of their British 'oppressors' of olden days as conceived by prior generations, ... but simply as an easy means for *world communications,... triggered in great part by our neighbors to the south and their worldwide influence ... and English being an easy language to learn, they're jumping at every opportunity to acquire it ... since the Québec Education department purposely <u>deprives them of that privilege</u>.*

Millennials and Generation Z want to be part and parcel of the big teams and the big global game now in progress ... and this implies by definition and in fact the USA and Canada as codependent partners ... along with all growing markets and opportunities available elsewhere.

Indeed, our Québec millennials and generation Z are also tired of the usual complaints of alleged unfairness supposedly still valid in this time and place, marketed and sold by separatist factions ... and they resent the idea of an 'us' (the good guys) and 'them' (the bad guys) mentality articulated by separatists.

That is why; I think that any future referendum will deny separatists' aspirations.

Let me also point out here that the only referendum in Québec leading to a 'yes' vote was in 1919, ... and this to get rid of prohibition, ... so that our Gallic population's joie de vivre could at last party as they wished – as proven still nowadays with all the marvelous festivals throughout the summer all over the province.

Referendums directed to political sovereignty led to a 'no' vote, ... implying that Quebecers as a whole had no wish to be a weaker member of the international community ... ... and therefore, be omitted from membership with a much stronger team Canada, so to speak, ...on an equal footing with the USA and Mexico and the rest of the world."

Temporarily Hovering Over a Fragment of Discussion 17.
A Dislocated Discussion

"You make it sound negative Antoine ... but Québec completed three spectacular projects in the past ... didn't it?" Isabelle asked.

"Yes! That's true ..." responded Antoine *..." but only when there was an overall provincial will to do so and the best set of skills happenstances were located right here ... such as the marvelous hydro-electric infrastructure we built ... highlighted by the Manic projects ... a string of meta projects initiated, promoted, and implemented by one tenacious and dedicated Premier, Robert Bourassa, along with Expo 67, which can be remembered as great successes.*

These challenged our provincial pride as well as constitute a massive cooperative effort with Ottawa in the case of Expo 67 ... proving that when we set our mind to cooperate among ourselves or with the rest of Canada, we can accomplish just about anything.

And for the 1976 Olympics we really went into debts with a beautiful but ill-conceived stadium that took forty-years to pay with additional taxes ... and a lot of other shady deals we don't want to face up to or simply pretend never occurred.

Nevertheless, the sooner the world spotlight is off, our provincial resolve withdraws behind the narrow limits, we otherwise tend to set for ourselves, ... and we get right back to our lethargic self.

Beyond that nothing but waffling and ideological pie-in-the-sky projects and programs, usually highlighted under hyperbolic highfaluting captions such as "projets de société", which in the end lead nowhere – except intellectual hyperboles that look like actions, and mismanagement when actions are undertaken because of bungling and unprofessional executive staffs and more unnecessary debts of course.

What I really mean is that our projects and programs ought to be anchored in reality ... I speak of other projects of course aside from these three spectacular ones – proposals that ought to launch us as an important participant within the world's communities.

Instead, we create these so-called "projets de société" meant for an insular community of those speaking French generally within Québec, and which all too often deal with never-to-be-implemented generalities in the real world.

Just think of the Charbonneau commission as a recent and most obvious example.

The real crooks will never be charged and jailed ... and the rare times they're caught as in the case of that criminal, ... that thieving Laval mayor, Gilles Vaillancourt, and that other guy ... from the Italian mafia ... shit! ... the name escapes me at the moment... anyway ... they at worst end up with a slap on the wrist, so to speak when you consider the magnitude of their thefts ... and the incompetence of many, such as ex-Montréal mayor Gerald Tremblay and others, will never be penalized either.

In fact, in nearly all cases of theft or incompetence ... no one is really held accountable and responsible, ... and no fault for errors, or out-and-out mismanagement, or silo-oriented misadministration, or misappropriation of funds is ever made to pay.

And this despite the usual interminable cost overruns embedded within plans if anything ever comes to fruition".

Antoine got up, raised his arms and spread them out as if ready to make a speech to a large crowd.

"This is a cultural trait that is triggered and encouraged by our heavy taxation in many respects ... and I know many people who would rather pay someone under the table than pay usurious taxes to the province just as a matter of principle – including myself over the years!"

"That's a sad statement if you don't mind my saying so Antoine". Concluded Isabelle. After a few seconds of silence Isabelle carried on again.

"Ok! Ok!" Let's look at other aspects of our beef with Québec's approach in its handling and managing of projects, programs and any other task at hand that differentiates it from others".

Grimacing as if he had just swallowed some vinegar, Antoine started on another venue of his general argument in this respect.

"Emotionally directed project management is nurtured by our educational system, which continues to excuse failures and inability to adapt; ... encourages the insularity of unilingual French-speaking Quebecers, ... often blinding them from learning about other realities while denying it is doing so; ... refuses to drill the importance of entrepreneurship as an essential strategy for creativity and success; ... ensures, like our Roman Catholic predecessors, that, say, no financial worthwhile studies or meaningful sexual education are provided ... and failing all these, ... our educational bureaucracy is nonetheless willing to fake the academic progress of its students to protect their alleged productivity under a fake cover of purported progressive efficiencies and effectiveness."

Antoine than added *"... and by overprotecting students, minimizing their weak points and natural errors in the course of a learning process, it in fact avoids teaching them the realities of life ...*

encouraging them instead to rely on the Québec-style Nanny State ... more or less recreating in secular form the previous Roman Catholic notion of a purported benevolent god that ruled the lives of their parents and grandparents.

In other words, I speak of course of an educational system powered by the new religion of 'Political Correctitude', wherein dogmas rule unopposed – in this case and among many others the dogma of pedagogy over the reality of everyday life".

"Hey! Antoine. That is strong talk. Don't you think?" Interrupted Isabelle.

"I know ... I know ... I sound mad. ... Don't I?

Look! I am not referring to the elite – the so-called 1% nor its senior executives along with professionals and managerial staff.

No! These know where it's at generally, ... and attend the best schools and universities in Canada, the US, and England ... ... except for insular unilingual French-speaking ones.

Like everywhere else now and throughout history, our elite class and its executive branch nearly always navigate to be at the helm of the ship of State.

Just remember Voltaire's opinion on this issue, which I think went something like this, if I recall Henri Guillemin correctly:

> *'Un pays bien organisé est celui où le petit nombre fait travailler le grand nombre, et nourrit par lui, il le gouverne'.*

Here I'm speaking of the rest, the majority taught to be docile and obedient – hopefully as in the good old days of Roman Catholic hegemony.

Sadly, since our departure from our centuries-long indoctrination, each generation is still nonetheless taught through its educational establishments to be docile ... under a secular cover this time.

Separatists particularly teach us to fear the future; ... to isolate ourselves; ... to fear those speaking English, because that language is still perceived as the language of our conqueror, rather than the planetary language that it has become ... and this ... not because of England particularly, but on account of American worldwide influence in just about every field in the 20th century ... Americans, who not that long ago rebelled against England, ... and whom we battled against, with and for England not that very long ago, we must also recall.

English is now the lingua franca in just about every field of endeavor ... to ignore it is to disregard the extraordinary privilege for entrepreneurship and the opportunities for business, there for us for the taking, ... especially when located as we are geographically smack against the most powerful and richest nation on earth ... and this from within a liberalized safe country such as Canada; ...

... and yet in spite of that ... far too many among us consider ourselves still as 'victims' of those 'bad' Anglos, ... rather than face the fact that, it was our mother country that dropped us – its own citizens – like excess baggage ... as if of little value to itself and politically unworthy to bother with".

Antoine stared at his hands for a short while, and looked at Isabelle once more, he continued with what appeared to be his summation.

"Look! We're French-speaking North Americans and not Europeans.

Our generalized stubbornness in not joining the international community of business and entrepreneurship, because of a stupid, ideological, and therefore unreasonable attitude toward English has severely limited and continues to limit our development as a people.

In addition, we are not taught to manage our life in general about basic money management and proper budgeting, along with good reading skills and a respect for the written texts exemplified by literary giants and other personages of significance ... we don't even bother with a decent sexual education program for our children.

We keep on inventing excuses for not acting on time, and for postponing the inevitable.

We are trained to accept our lot, because secular experts – real and alleged – be they psychologists, economists, nutritionists, engineers, and so on, that replaced the religious class of older days, purportedly steer us in the right direction.

We mold our students into pliant units pre-programmed for 'Absolute Obedience' to the 'Immaculate Perception' of our version of the new dogmatic belief system – the new secular quasi religion of 'Political Correctitude'.

And yet lately we blindly refuse to recognize religious extremist organizations and communities, intent on harming us in the future, ... because of our own unquestionable manufactured Québec style vision of the world ... and this corseted in a lexicon and a starched grammar of political correctitude.

And on and on it goes my friend".

Temporarily Hovering Over a Fragment of Discussion 18.
Project Management

After discussing the latest bureaucratic snafus that cloudy afternoon, Antoine continued in earnest.

"While we're on the subjects of bureaucracies, let's not forget those thieving bureaucrats and other manipulators demanding kickbacks, and encouraging the construction of inferior roads and other infrastructures ...

... we already know the difference between shoddy work and proper construction and maintenance, when you cross the border to Ontario ... you go from a bumpy and dilapidated road system to a bloody well maintained and serviced one in Ontario ... most of our overpasses were built with inferior materials and are ineffectively and inefficiently maintained and serviced to the point of being dangerous ... each seems subjected to accelerated deterioration when compared to the rest of Canada.

The contrast is evident for us at least living on the Quebec-Ontario border... which were finally upgraded after decades of neglect, ... but still most without proper road shoulders and still without proper maintenance, ... which tells you already that they will degrade quickly.

... once I get off Ontario roads and drive in Québec you observe a road management system that follows to the letter "le modèle Québécois" ... and this mostly with money borrowed at high interests ... and knowing the 'magouille' ... as we guys call it here, ... with engineering firms, the Ministère du Transport as well as those in cahoots with mafia types outside that department, we made sure that all projects cost far more than anyone else in Canada, that the materials used is shoddy, and that the infrastructure end up with a much shorter lifespan, which is why everything deteriorates much earlier than everywhere else in Canada ... ... as

if we were also here again announcing with blind pride that the "modèle Québécois" supersedes all.

No wonder everything costs far more than infrastructure or projects normally would call for ... and little surprise that these projects are all too often put together with shoddy materials, ... and are redone much sooner than later ... so that all those in cahoots can repeatedly feed on taxpayer money.

Hell! The Romans used cement more than two thousand years ago, and their structure still stand up today ... while ours barely last a few decades ... ... the via Appia built in 312 BCE still exists, while our roads end up in pitiful conditions for lack of appropriate construction and proper preventive maintenance.

Oh yea! In addition, each time I travel on a provincial road and enter Ontario in the winter for example I know where I am without looking at road signs ... simply by looking at the road ... in Québec the road is full of ice and snow ... and in Ontario most of the time it is free of both ... and yet Québec is too stupid to benchmark Ontario ... their immediate neighbor obviously doing a better job under the same winter conditions.

"I believe that it's both an intellectual disease of not wanting to know on our part, ... and an ethical failure in literally squandering the moneys gathered by Québec's excessive taxation schemes, ... which we purposely choose to ignore". Antoine, now mentally exhausted finally concluded.

After drinking a sip of water, he veered off a bit to try to explain the system in place.

"And there is the mania of constructing safe bureaucratic protocols of reporting, assessing, and spreading responsibility and accountability to the lowest possible common denominator ... ... usually the system managed by the bureaucracy in place and this

within a silo environment and mentality ... ... so that the system is nearly always at fault, whenever errors are discovered, or calamities surfaced.

It is <u>never</u> the officer in charge.

In such a process, the individual or group otherwise responsible and accountable for a given task or action, can always blame the system ... usually proposing when defaulting ... that further training is required ... or that some fine-tuning must be applied to the system.

Hence in Québec, methodology always trumps personalized accountability and responsibility.

And we still wonder why government bureaucrats and unionized employees never autocorrect wrong practices; ... or fear flat organizations; ... or executives and middle management personnel constantly need assistants to support a given set of tasks at all levels, unable to resist their impulse to overstaff all bureaucracies, projects, and programs ...

... along with their insistence of the specialness of their methodology without regards to other practices elsewhere... just in case a better one can be adopted it seems.

You should look at the organization chart of the Transport Department for example or any other in the Québec government ... and it will astound you with its over-the-top complexities, the multiple levels and of direct, and nodes of, functional reporting relationships, ... as well as a massive need by supervisors, managers and directors, for example, for assistants and more support.

Even in this world of instant communications of all sorts, supervisors and middle managers and directors still require secretaries at all levels for example ... its crazy!

It's no wonder everything cost more in Québec.

No wonder either we're the most taxed in Canada.

We're like adolescents in the handling of cash ... in this case other people's cash ... taxpayers' cash.

We, as a people, can't handle money, ... we can't plan properly, ... we keep on pouring more money as the automated solution to all personal and social problems and situations, ... facts reflected in our bureaucratic organizations ...

...rather than structurally rethink and resolve these once and for all ... or simply refuse to think laterally ... we instead always assume that more money is the only valid solution to problem-solving". He finally summed it up.

Temporarily Hovering Over a Fragment of Discussion 19.
Entrepreneurship versus Labor Unions

After a long pause and the poring of more of that strong black coffee both preferred, Antoine was about to continue, when Isabelle interrupted to make an important point:

"The globalization of manufacturing is in full swing ... it has eliminated hundreds of millions of jobs already, ... and the worse my friend is yet to come now that AI and the robotization of all possible processes has been launched and is accelerating, ...

...this is not a just dystopian view of the future nor a predisposition for such an outlook as some people may be tempted to think ... ... but the logical end result of massive unemployment to come ... if we don't get our head out of the sand ... nothing else ...

... and this is now taking place in parallel to and while major corporations' tentacles in all possible aspects of business, manufacturing, and financial transactions are spreading throughout the planet.

This phenomenon has already and significantly reduced the negotiating strength of the labor movement in the Western world.

It will eliminate it completely in many sectors of the economy particularly here in North America and the rest of the Western world.

Yet, the main labor unions here in Québec continue as if all was rosy ... as if what is in progress here and everywhere was for some mysterious reason not taking place in here ... or at least would not affect us as much in this province.

*Syndicalists continue to pray at the altar of 'negotiated settlements' ... wherein these **can never be undone** regardless of new* *social, financial, manufacturing, business, and other economically related changing realities.*

They deny their responsibility and the significance of their contribution to the massive Québec debts, ... because of exaggerated demands on their part, ... combined with the weaknesses of governmental negotiating teams for decades, ... if not simply an ideological support by government negotiating officers to labor causes ... all of which continues to massively drain government coffers and significantly contribute to balloon the provincial debt even further."

Isabelle thought Antoine was finished making his point on this subject and was about to say something when Antoine although now silent for about a minute raised a finger indicating he had something else to add.

"The strength of labor unions in Québec is an anomaly, which markets will eventually and drastically correct ... unless stalled for a while by ideological protectionist labor laws in this province ... ... but in the end, they will sadly pay dearly ... at the cost of massive job loss because the money will simply run out ... it's inevitable

In the meantime, unions must at last also show to one and all where the money collected from workers and elsewhere goes, ... and what it is used for; ... their financial sheets must be transparent; ... and their negotiating of artificial increases in a decreasing economy must be stopped.

Here, Isabelle, I speak of increases beyond what the market can bear as well stalling the creation of jobs ... because of weak or sympathizing government negotiators, ... or simply because their excessive demands chase away businesses ...

... businesses that would otherwise continue to operate here as well as those willing to install themselves in Québec.

Our general attitude on business ventures, the roadblocks we create against entrepreneurship along with economically blind and powerful provincial unions here in Québec will ruin us, and lead us to bankruptcy, if they are not stopped altogether.

Far too many groups live in their bubble and the labor unions isolated in their administrative and management silos are no exception ... in fact they are the worst offenders in this regard.

Oh, yes my friend ... far too many among local union leaders would rather be a big fish in a small pond than a comparatively small fish in a big one".

Antoine stopped for another minute or so, as if to gather his thoughts one more time, but this time Isabelle continued with the baton before he could go on again.

"You're right in the case of the unions Antoine.

Initially labor unions served a noble purpose and got the workers out of the claws of ruthless entrepreneurs, callous railway, and mine barons along with abusive manufacturers.

But this principled purpose no longer exists nor applies anymore" she went on.

"Now large unions act like parasites, sucking the life out of the economy at the expense of those not yet remunerated at a decent living wage".

"Although unions generally ought to continue to serve a noble purpose Isabelle" interrupted Antoine.

"Yes indeed ... but this is no longer true in most cases as you suggested already". She quickly added to Antoine's sudden idealistic view.

"The large ones as you well know…" Isabelle went on "… especially those associated with government departments and agencies, have blackmailed governments, which did not want to gamble too much when too close to their re-election … and succeeded in extracting egregious inflated salaries, benefits and pensions … and government jobs as we all know do not by definition contribute positively to the economy … they in fact and to its detriment feed from it".

She then took a large sip of coffee from her favorite mug she'd brought in her move from Vancouver to Kingston and now kept on using in Rigaud.

"… and this labor-based belligerence has been carried out at the expense of most taxpayers, who certainly do not have such privileged public financing.

… and not only that my dear Antoine, but they also repeat the same underhanded tactic to prevent taxpayers from fighting back in these grossly inequitable situations … as if to say, … "fuck you" to the rest of the population now bearing a much heavier tax burden … as well as the ones to be borne by the following generations that will have to pay the bills for these privileges, while nothing is given nor guaranteed for the rest and future populations in return".

"Yea! I understand …" said Antoine *"…but they negotiated all the clauses in their labor contracts over decades… although I must at the same time admit; … doing so with governments either lacking negotiating skills, … immature analyses in the costing of demands, … saddled with a lack of appreciation about the then present and future growth and health of the provincial economy and so on.*

Or dare I say, simply by a bunch of mostly lawyer-politicians not really giving a dam about future French-Canadian generations as long as their present generation enjoyed the fruits of high taxes and borrowed moneys to pay for all this".

"And to make a final point here this afternoon my dear Antoine ... the total earnings of provincial and municipal government employees on average far exceed similar and far less secure jobs in the private sectors" added Isabelle *"...and yet they enjoy a level of job security unavailable outside government departments and agencies.*

So, if the trend does not change" continued Antoine, *"it looks like the unions now fully embedded in provincial and municipal government departments, agencies and offices will go on without immediate consequences, ...*

... while in parallel businesses creating revenues for Québec will still go on diminishing ... until only a few mid-size corporations remain ... with the inevitable collapse of our provincial economy ... with no one else to blame but ourselves ... along with our adopted attitude of victimization, taxation greediness, lack of business acumen, roadblocks created to prevent rather than welcome businesses, ... and our fear of the planetary language just because it happens to be English".

Isabelle then suddenly spurted out.

"Here's an afterthought on our subject this afternoon Antoine ...

...wouldn't you think that if these union leaders were looking after the very existence of their organization that they'd be smarter.

After all a good negotiator instinctively nows that, if you alter the context of anything, even to a small degree, you alter the results, while an excellent negotiator instinctively applies this notion as natural as a heartbeat ...

... yet, they appear ignorant of this most basic notion or unable to eliminate their local fiefdoms to increase their 'force de frappe' as a group ... out of that silo mentality ... at the strategically appropriate time in order to combine their efforts as a coherent institution ... and then strategically share the same mission and objectives, ...

... and sadly, labor unions are now losing the ground their predecessors so bravely fought for and succeeded in gaining.

That is why, unless they soon wake up, the remaining labor unions will lose ... likely forever ... their most important and ultimate gains in their struggle with the business establishment ... and then governments".

"That's true" Antoine went on.

"A wise negotiator always settles for what can be obtained in the here and now, instead of pining for some pie in the sky found perhaps in a vaporous future ...

... indeed, a competent negotiator possesses the innate ability to capitalize on the reality of the moment in the context of a whole bargaining strategy.

No wonder, as presently constituted and managed, labor unions vastly harm themselves and their movement, when they insist on ignoring this reality.

That is why, labor unions will lose the battle for fair work and pay, if they continue their silo-style strategic planning and narrow-minded tactical operations ... and this particularly within a planetary labor context—especially with their presently accelerating devolution". Antoine concluded.

"And let us not forget the harm caused by inward looking labor unions within a provincial context." Isabelle reminded Antoine.

"You mean the effects labor unions' attitude cause in different sectors?" Antoine replied.

"Yes exactly." She acquiesced, and then continued.

"Look! In the case of the education department I can't help but note that they are in great part also responsible for the lack of learning by students and the eventual dropping out of school of very many among them ...

... they accomplish this sadly through negotiated clauses .... in keeping incompetent teachers, or competent but low performing ones, or in opposing obligatory continuous training, and on and on it continues."

She stopped for a minute, as if to gather her thoughts on a difficult point to explain, and then stood up with a glass of water as she continued.

"It is a powerful organization dictating their will, protecting imbedded inefficacies and ineffectiveness at the expense of a significant number of students having serious learning issues ... refusing that pedagogic practices be attuned on time, at the required rate, and at the right location in assisting children manifesting problems in personal growth and learning such by means of special methods to eliminate children's learning problems ... as they hide from the reality of not 'disturbing' the static schedule of their membership.

Indeed, the intransigence of the labor unions contribute significantly to both future punitive social and economic problems of Québec." She finally concluded.

Temporarily Hovering Over a Fragment of Discussion 20.
A Paralyzing Fear of English for Many

"I strongly believe Antoine that, if the present language for planetary communication was, ... let's say, Spanish for example, ... French-Canadians in Québec would rush to learn it and be very successful at it, ... and this even in the most remote areas of the province I'd be ready to bet".

"What's your point?" Antoine asked.

"Because of the way history unfolded – wherein English has become the most spoken international language ... and this independent of and regardless of Québec's history ... and most certainly no one at the time could have predicted that the Seven-Year War would lead to this.

I suggest that it was simply and plainly because of the US influence in the 20th century among other major factors that English is presently the dominant language generally used throughout our planet by global elite groups running the show as well as other important stakeholders ... and not because of ideology, ... but simply because the practicality it presents as a common means of communication that would not exists otherwise ...

... an accident of history of sort, ... unplanned but there nevertheless ... like the shared Gregorian calendar by all nations of our world, which in the end became common to us all in great part on account of cumulative international business transactions and treaties among other factors, ... and this to the point where far too many among us forget that there are numerous other calendars widely used still today ... such as Chinese, Bengali, Hindu, Islamic and so on, and many others yet in a more limited

use such as Armenian and Vietnamese for example ... but not for international agreements, global communications and business ... ... since the latter demands commonly understood contractual agreements on the ground, so to speak,

... thus, for efficient communications, a shared and commonly understood language is required ... ... English in most cases has been that language ... and this is overwhelmingly true in our case within the North American continent including Mexico.

And my friend I know this reality about the hegemony of English nowadays sticks in your Québec-style French-Canadian craw ... and this all too often in areas where French unilingualism is the rigueur in rural Québec ... in the very areas where an appreciation of the globalization is low... especially in poor or remote regions of the province.

Nonetheless the savvier people in Québec are aware of that planetary reality:

> The elite and other societal stakeholders here and everywhere else understand there will be winners and losers in the end when that globalization of everything in this world is completed in some far-off future.

Yet, as a society you turn a blind eye to the fact that more and more people prefer and in fact – like French-speaking French-Canadians – communicate in their national language at home as they always did, but at the same time do not pretend that a planetary language does not exist and is not useful, ... and that this language is English for the foreseeable future .

Insanely or out of shear fear of losing your mother tongue ... understandable to a degree in view of your history and geographical location ... you nonetheless and at our expense all too often choose to ignore this fact as a community.

Yet, the Scandinavian countries give us an exemplary model to follow, when it comes to this issue, ... because like them you *should have embraced English for international communication long ago ...*

...to that end you must first admit that the teaching of a second language must begin as early as possible with your children ... or you otherwise create a severe handicap for them before they even start to compete as adults.

My point Antoine is that far too many prefer to remain in their delusional cocoon rather than take the opportunities there for the picking.

There! I said it. Now shoot me!".

Antoine burst in a good laugh, and after a minute of silence or so responded.

"Yea! It makes no sense to accept such a way of thinking as normal and still take pride about an open-ended process ... and yet many in Québec wonder why we lag behind so many others, ... as our children massively drop out of the school system ... especially boys unwilling to accept the challenges pertinent to this 21st century, ... who like previous generations of far too many gutless fathers and grandfathers of past generations would rather try their luck at life without an education ... preferring cultural and linguistic isolation for far too many of them".

Again, after a minute or so of silence Antoine ended his comment with:

"I know these are harsh comments ... and border on quasi racism for the most sensitive among us ... but truth is truth, and it must be said, if not totally accepted as is yet".

Antoine then looked at Isabelle and asked:

"Do you want me to carry on or would you like to continue"?"

"No! No! Antoine go on please!"

"OK then.

As you suggested before, ... despite this we ignore reality, preferring to keep intact the ever-growing and by now massive bureaucracy creating strings of complex problems in addition to normal everyday ones ... allegedly to 'guarantee' our continued existence ... and 'le ministère de l'éducation', the subject that started our debate a few days ago, is a prime example.

It functions as a set of hermetically sealed silo sub-organizations within an organization, which itself runs independently from all other departments in the government.

The bloody secular theology it promotes, is a form of 'political correctitude' protecting all questioning supported by an 'Absolute Obedience' in the face of an 'Immaculate Perception' forming of the present ideology of an alleged dogma of teaching expertise, wherein pedagogical standards trump everything including the very future of students ...

... and that therefore the system, and by default, the bureaucracy activating it, ... and feeding from it, ... rules, ... and that both are allegedly correct and essential ...

... and that if errors take place, ... the system can always be adequately tweaked and recalibrated ...

... but that <u>it must never be questioned</u> ...

... and certainly, <u>never be abolished</u> ...

... since the system and the bureaucracy feeding from it must remain 'as is' at all costs.

The idea in the end is to never lose face, rather than benchmarked the best there is around the planet, ... since the socially sacralized and unquestionable "modèle Québécois" is unique ... and must remain 'as is' ... so goes the catechism of that ideology in this respect my dear Isabelle".

Temporarily Hovering Over a Fragment of Discussion 21.
End-Game for Québec's Unilingual Ideologues

Antoine drank his entire by now lukewarm mug of coffee in one shot, and then took a deep breath, as if to regain a bit more intellectual energy before concluding.

"The Chinese as you have already suggested have done it, without losing face ... and we all know how easy it is to lose face in that culture compared to us ... and this simply because they were mature enough to recognize their dire situation as it really was; ... determined and tough minded enough on becoming the best in the world despite all roadblocks ahead of them; ... intelligent enough to plan, develop, implement and respect their long range plans; ... and disciplined enough to keep their oar in the water until reaching their various societal objectives.

And there're nearly there! ... I'd say in this year 2023 now in progress, ... don't you think?

The Chinese did not lose time dreaming unnecessarily about their past that goes further back than any of us ... nor did they talk endlessly about "projets de société" ... and other castles in the air like we do here in Québec.

No! Since the Seventies they simply adopted the most rational attitude possible; ... prepared appropriate long range plans (often on a fifty-year schedule) each with their short and long range penalties and benefits; ... and used the extraordinary patience, tenacity, endurance, ... and a superior attention to details, Chinese people are known to possess as a whole, ... coordinating, and transforming these into a massive, synchronized, and harmonized national series of efforts that launched them forward with great force and at a prodigious speed ... and not only are they the largest manufacturer in earth, now they're on their way to become its biggest economy if nothing else intervenes.

Yes! Oh, yes! Contrary to us Westerners generally, they approached the dismal position they were in, using the most pragmatic ways possible ...

... avoiding the pitfalls of short returns for efforts delivered to the benefit of long-range societal payoffs ...

... the Chinese did not want to be tied to illusory programs ... exemplified in the compulsive 90-day cycle of returns on investments preferred by Western investors.

The Chinese in fact also avoided pie in the sky projects, by first concentrating on a colossal upgrading of its educational system from top to bottom everywhere with the long-term aim of surpassing everyone, ... while simultaneously and codependently building the fastest, greatest, and most massive manufacturing programs ever conceived in world history.

And it worked, didn't it?

They're also completing the biggest construction of a national infrastructure in the history of the world and will complete it in record time ... the fastest ever in history.

And yet we, Westerners, scarcely mention these most outstanding Chinese successes, ... and this because we already know that it represents an unquestionable superior execution of tasks, projects, programs and so on ... with an efficiency, effectiveness, and massive cooperation and coordination of efforts we have not and will most likely never match ... unless we, Westerners change our attitude and methods.

This fact is especially true here in Québec with our present pissy attitude ... from that segment of unilingual French-speaking French-Canadian ideologues including most certainly its provincial inions ... all insisting they be protected by a Nanny-State without efforts on their part as continuing self-elected 'victims'."

Antoine stopped for a few seconds as if to put a period on the comments, he'd just made and went on again.

"How stupid is it then of us to live in the clouds of wishful think-ing instead of here on earth, I ask you?

The end-game of French-speaking French-Canadians in Québec is cultural suicide with the alleged help of inappropriate, over-stuffed, inefficient, ineffective, and fat bureaucracies that inap-propriately eat a vast portion of the revenues just to feed them-selves, at the expense of taxpayers with nothing to show for it…

… because in the end by dear Isabelle, the ultimate purpose a bureaucracy, say, under the aegis of education … in the case that started our discussions …… like all other bureaucracies … is to grow and dictate as much as possible at the expense of all other departments and agencies … and to satisfy its own self-serving interests and benefits within a silo structure and administrative environment.

***

Fortunately, and contrary to this self-destructive approach … there is an ever-growing enthusiasm among millennials and es-pecially generation Z for entrepreneurial ventures …

… first, because they don't see themselves as victims of history and of English-speaking Canadians like many of their parents and grandparents did …

… secondly, they see themselves instead as fortunately located on a continent of opportunities and freedom amid a global economic growth never possible before in the history of our planet.

In short, they don't want to be on the losing side of reality and history.

They are merely adapting to a new reality … without the angsts, griefs, and pains of that bureaucratic penchant for overstaffing and over-planning, so typical of all bureaucracies everywhere ... and especially here in Québec ... where bureaucratic principles, protocols and other administrative algorithms, trump all ... instead of grabbing all opportunities possible ...

... a significant portion of our millennials and generation Z want to conquer the world with their inventions, creativity, and savoir faire ... nothing less ... as if they're beginning to emulate the Chinese in some way ... good for them I say ... I wish I were there when their efforts succeed in a few decades from now I suspect".

Temporarily Hovering Over a Fragment of Discussion 22.
Bilingual Millennials and Those Following

Antoine took the lead again that afternoon.

"In Québec as in the rest of Canada we do not have heroes of mythical proportions, which is likely why we do not construct ideologies for which we would volunteer to die for ... and not even present-day die-in-the-wool separatist-minded advocates ever expressed such ideas.

Although once ... and exceptionally in 1837... a few bent the most on a French-speaking French-Canadian sovereignty in Québec died for that cause ... under the label of 'Canadiens' as the saying went in those days, ... since everyone else regardless of origin was considered as 'les Anglais' by this insular community.

One of my ancestors in fact was hanged for his participation.

After this brief attempt and failure at independence the Québec French-Canadian community folded unto itself again, until it woke up about a hundred and twenty some odd years later ... triggering the 'révolution tranquille' which resulted into two successive failed referendums.

The dream of sovereign independence of a people considering themselves as a 'Special Group' ... by then calling themselves real 'Québécois' ... came close indeed, but nonetheless failed for several strategic and tactical reasons.

The main ones were that:

> · *Rather than applying a coherent form of rational project management leading to their self-assigned mission – ideology and emotions drove the movement, trumping everything – a strategic error.*

· It paid no attention to the globalization that was just beginning to accelerate in the second half of the twentieth century, which is likely why; it ignored the uncertainty created in the mind of its recent migrant communities – a tactical error.

· It purposely ignored its significant English-speaking communities – assuming they would en bloc vote against a separatist political proposal, rather than truly assuage them with their civilized intent, if that was indeed their resolve – another tactical error.

And now the Parti Québécois and smaller separatist factions are again committing the same strings of errors.

It is as if they could not learn from past mistakes, because a blind ideology always supersedes both critical strategies and crucial tactics in the management of a self-appointed mission.

Separatist-minded individuals as a group tend to have had a restricted view of what the immediate future reserves for us all in all domains, when these are predictable or about to happen ... aside from their traditional infighting and their habit of 'lynching', so to speak, their leaders at the drop of a hat.

Think of it, Isabelle!

The new crop of separatist leaders, is, either out of sheer ignorance, or for reasons of blind realpolitik, purposely disregarding the globalization of everything now obviously affecting all of us around the planet – including the departure of far too many jobs to other nations that we've witnessed for decades by now.

And yet separatist factions and the labor communities are combining their efforts to fight this economic reality, ... acting as if it did not exist".

Antoine now silent went to the window on that rainy afternoon, looked at the Rigaud River for a little while, turned to look again at Isabelle, and continued his argument.

"A reality thankfully seized upon with zest by a segment of the Millennials and Z generations of French-speaking French-Canadians, who have, like other forward-looking generations elsewhere on the planet, adopted English as a second language, ... simply because it is presently the language of worldwide communications among people speaking different national or tribal languages ... ...so, they too could ... like those ancient educated people of the Middle Ages using Latin" as their means of overcoming language barriers to communicate as one single community in their field of interest ... regardless of belief system, origin and nationality ...

... and that is why many from the last generation particularly do not share the ideology of earlier generations, ...

... having by now immersed themselves in the world-wide digital community ... wherein planetary communications reign supreme ...

... and a good chunk of these two generations have no plan to lose their mother tongue either ... it must be said.

They're comfortable with it, as are all others elsewhere on the planet with their own mother tongue.

They're simply practical.

They just adopt the present international language of communication to ensure their participation with the world at large in the brand-new ever-developing world of globalization ...

... and should another planetary language take the lead ... say, Mandarin ... such people would also adopt it as well, ... because their attitude is forward looking with the opportunities available such a move represents".

Temporarily Hovering Over a Fragment of Discussion 23.
Surreptitious Reaffirmation by Renaming

Antoine, somewhat irritated by now went on and elaborated further.

"Another tactic in the surreptitious re-conquest of the lost 'patrie' to the English, entertained by both the clergy and the political class of older times, was what they could have labelled 'Surreptitious Reaffirmation by Renaming'.

In the province of Québec in particular, (although also furtively practiced under one hidden agenda or another elsewhere in Canada on occasion by the local French-Canadian clergy and community backed at times by local politicians), was the practice of eliminating or neutralizing English sounding names where they could.

When that could not automatically be done with already legally identified locations, two practices were then applied.

The first, most often utilized and successful throughout Québec was to add the French sounding name of a Saint to the exiting English name such as, say, "Newton' became 'Sainte-Justine-de-Newton' in the Province of Québec and 'Prescott' became 'Sainte-Anne-de-Prescott' in Ontario.

A practice undertaken whenever a village was taken over due to the presence of many more Roman Catholic French-Canadians into a previously English-speaking area.

Since the name became longer, people generally tended to refer to the part of the name that rolled off the tongue better, ... or could more easily be remembered in the then ultra-religious Roman Catholic world of French-speaking French-Canadians — usually the first part.

In this respect and similar to the example presented here, the name of the saint nearly everywhere this tactic was applied tended to be utilized in everyday life.

As for the second tactic – although less successful – occasionally a secular French name was added instead of a saint as another practice with a tendency to confuse in order to incite people to adopt in practice the French sounding name instead—although with some this practice failed.

For examples, the city of 'Valleyfield' became 'Salaberry-de-Valleyfield' ... and to this day ... aside for legal documents ... both, French- and English-speaking people alike in Québec refer to their city simply as 'Valleyfield'.

There are a few where neither of these two tactics worked, ... such as one-industry towns ... often originally managed by an English-speaking moneyed community, ... which would not have put up with it at that time such as the cities of 'Drummondville' and Thetford Mines."

Temporarily Hovering Over a Fragment of Discussion 24.
A Plethora of Excuses

Antoine began once more after a short snooze that afternoon.

"In the bunch of bureaucratic justifications pretexts and apologies from professionals or unionized employees comes a plethora of excuses – as if these had been engineered by committees, especially created to avoid all responsibilities and accountabilities that ought to come with the acceptance of occupying a job ... any job.

Among these we find routine paternalistic or cowardly expressions such as 'Ce que vous devez d'abords comprendre...'; or 'nous nous devons de suivre le protocole établit...'; or 'les règles n'étaient pas claire...'; and so on.

All typical excuses to avoid responsibilities and accountabilities that are part of the politically correct approach in the alleged solutions to all problems.

With this outlook, nobody is held accountable or rightfully penalized for violating plain rules of conduct, common sense, ethics, and 'bon savoir'.

It is as if, in order to automatically protect the owner and other stakeholders of a given system ... and to a significant extent its support and enforcing staff ... whatever the kind, ... the embedded bureaucracy ensures that 'the system' presented as a non-human bureaucratic machine ... be blamed in fault-finding ... instead of responsible officers and others, ... whenever a bureaucracy is forced to face shortcomings, mistakes, errors, theft, lying, fraud, plain criminal acts and so on.

In this way those humans, making up the functioning of 'the bureaucratic machine' possible, are very rarely at fault, ... while the PR arm of the organization affected reassures everyone ...

that all will be analyzed, ... and if necessary, ... that it all will be corrected in due time ...

... and time here implies the longest possible period during which you avoid comments as a politically correct approach ... a tactic assumed to be morally right for the official or organization being protected ... so by the time the result of an inquiry come to fruition the public at lar ge has largely forgotten what and who caused the problems in the first place ... and the bureaucratic machine will be tweaked so it performs better from now we are on ... we are assured

So, if you steal intelligently; or provide bad service to a customer, or a patient, or a citizen; or hurt someone in the execution of your duties; or complicate the life of clients because of ineffectiveness or inefficiency or carelessness or bad attitude – you'll most likely get away with it in Québec ... in practice your job is guaranteed regardless of bad behavior or incompetence or lousy attitude.

A point never to be forgotten whenever dealing with a Québec bureaucracy ... which as a whole is a North American champion in this domain".

Temporarily Hovering Over a Fragment of Discussion 25.
Education in the Age of the Internet

"Look Antoine!

In this era now beginning, university professors just like high school teachers for example, must dispense with their present job descriptions typical of the 19th and most of the 20th century for instance, as providers of data and information.

Elaborated practices I say that were correct in a pre-internet, pre-massive communication, and accelerated technological applications.

But since the internet, even in this early stage of development, the ability of a teacher to offer a student or anyone else for that matter in this 21st century with current knowledge, is vastly inferior to the one the internet can offer a student ... and this, ... I submit, with more data and information in a single week than teacher can convey in an entire lifetime.

That is why:

> *The role of a teacher must now gradually evolve from providers to that of facilitators and guides in a mentoring approach to education.*

Let's admit out front Antoine!

Schools, colleges, or universities in most instances are already unable to provide many of its graduates with the data, information, and knowledge they will require just a few years if not a few months after graduating ... if they're lucky.

In that sense teaching institutions, must give students an overview of data, information and knowledge leading to ever better skills in acquiring these in the future ... and of acquiescing a continuing education outside such institutions.

As to how the whole thing will develop, I, like you or anyone else for that matter, don't really know where we'll end up in this domain in a few decades from now ... but I am absolutely sure it won't be today's model.

This universal reality must be accepted ... and rationally faced by the Québec education department as well ... and the sooner the better", Isabelle finally concluded that afternoon.

Temporarily Hovering Over a Fragment of Discussion 26.
Senseless Clauses and the Dogma of Seniority

Isabelle began to show an impatience as a once frustrated corporate lawyer that day about labor contracts.

"There are economically stupid labor union contracts, wherein some clauses go so far in the protracting of ineffectiveness as a principle ... say, by guaranteeing a job for life ... therefore shackling the "'patronat" from firing someone for incompetence ... or at least making it extremely difficult to do so.

Check the teachers' contract in that respect?"

"Under such senseless conditions – in this case the education system cannot be improved by definition and in fact – if we keep a bunch of lousy teachers or so-so teachers along with the better ones by osmosis to begin with and most certainly the students with their inabilities or laziness...

... and like the proverbial barrel of apples, ... the few rotten ones affect all the others one way or another eventually ... or using another metaphor, Antoine, this organization cannot be any better than its weakest links.

Don't you think?

And this on top of the various taboo against questioning managerial dogmas already embedded in the education establishment".

With some obvious and sustained impatience, Isabelle continued.

"Another factor that really gets to me particularly is, what I choose to call the 'labor dogma of seniority'.

My contention in this respect is that competence, which belongs to a meritocracy of sort, ought to supersede the 'labor dogma of seniority'... period!

Such a dogma institutionalizes a normalized lack of initiative ... officialized within labor contracts and written job descriptions in large organizations, ... and it eventually shows up in a general-ized cumulative level of incompetence that ultimately weakens an organization". Isabelle finally concluded.

"Yes! Oh, yes, my dear Antoine!

Until the labor unions are out of the picture, the education de-partment will not advance, one iota...

... and once you combine this with the critical need to minimize massive bureaucratic purported requirements, the whole thing can only lead to a catastrophe.

Yet nothing of substance is being done to correct this destructive anomaly", she finally concluded.

Temporarily Hovering Over a Fragment of Discussion 27.
The Labor Movement Is Collapsing Everywhere on Earth

Antoine this time, concentrating on a principle rather than an on-the-ground application of syndicalism, added his opinion on this issue:

While speaking of syndicalism, ... this reminds me of a most important principle of negotiation usually ignored, which is that all good dealmakers instinctively know that negotiation is a euphemism for admitting you will settle for less, once you can identify the real threat of violence waiting in the wings, and about to be triggered by the most powerful of the negotiating parties. Hence by the one ablest, willing, and committed to do you harm for gain.

That is why, divided labor unions in this new global economy are collapsing, especially in view of the fact that they are nearly all isolated into ever-smaller silos of lessening importance at best or of no consequence at all as the globalization of business takes precedence.

That is why also, reality matters little for a labor bureaucracy passed its useful life span, since at such point, it reassesses reality to suit its existence at the expense of everything else – adding new rules to ensure its continuity until it eventually collapses from the sheer weight of its ineffectiveness and inefficiencies, and this at the expense of those it was originally constituted to serve.

That regrettably is what provincially based unions in Québec will succumb to, and seriously hurt both the existential economy of that province.

Anyway, that is why further, the labor movement is collapsing, and its last gasps will take place in areas unaffected by globalization on account of no longer affordable costs to the communities in which they are located.

Temporarily Hovering Over a Fragment of Discussion 28.
Management Ventures and Financial Investments

"Anyway Antoine ... getting back to your provincial undertakings, and in addition to the ossification of the labor organization now in progress everywhere but ... oddly enough a movement still powerful and seemingly for the moment unaffected particularly in Québec, ...

... and ... forgetting this for a while let's concentrate on management ventures and financial investments pertaining to Quebecers.

*Quebecers failed spectacularly in many areas **not** <u>for lack of intelligence</u> but because of a serious lack of organization and entrepreneurship caused by, ... both, your attitude when it comes to the management of business projects, and professional management of money in the immediate as well as over long periods.*

You – as a community – don't seem to make a difference between operating money, capital expenditures, borrowed cash, the true costs of interests on borrowed capital, and so on ... because of your ancestral loathing of money handling taught to you by your previous religious masters ... except of course until most recently for the few more enlightened ones among you.

Let's use the 1976 Olympic to illustrate what I am trying to say.

Look! You honed in on France out of a pure inferiority complex to hire a French architect to design the Montréal Olympic stadium for the 1976 Olympics, all the while pretending to look all over the world for the best ... while ignoring in the process a world class Canadian on your own doorstep such as Moshe Safdie, architect of Habitat 67 and later that magnificent Musée des beaux-arts du Canada in Ottawa among many others around the planet since, ... and this only to meet the then mayor of Montréal, Jean Drapeau's and others' personalized reverence for and idolization of France.

As if Drapeau had to show off that you were sophisticated enough to hire the best allegedly in France ... those, who had in fact again and again left you as a people 'á la derive', so to speak, at the Capitulation of Montréal 1760.

What a financial and planning fiasco this has proven to be ... and more than fifty years later that stadium still does not have a proper roof and no one in practice wants to use it ... ... a huge waste of money sorely needed elsewhere ... and which you continue to need as you still support a group looking after it ...

... and to make it worse yet; ... out of a blind ideology, ... you purposely built it outside the downtown core ... were most of the better-off Quebecers worked and a vivacious nightlife took place ... and still does ...... with the surreptitious intent of creating a new but solely French-speaking downtown further east that would at first compete, then overcome the purportedly English-speaking downtown ...... as the separatist segment of the population kept repeating, ... and in this process be closer to the French CBC building, the so-called Radio-Canada building now defunct... at last abandoned because of its location and costs ... ... and all this with the objective of eventually being superior to present day downtown ...

... Oh no one dares mention it now ... but then Jean Drapeau and his minions often discussed, ... often it in not too subtle terms at times, often conspiring with journalists working for the French CBC.

It has been a total failure according to all rational financial analyses ... and this also because the core of downtown Montréal has not changed much geographically speaking ... despite all that money spent and efforts ... and the stadium remains empty ... silent witness of mismanagement and incompetence".

Temporarily Hovering Over a Fragment of Discussion 29.
Rats de Chancelleries

"It seems all so obvious to me", said Isabelle.

"It is not – and here I emphasize – <u>not</u> the business of a government to create anything, except to truly free its citizens from unnecessary roadblocks, and allow them equal access to opportunities whenever possible, in an atmosphere of total freedom and security.

Hence, the role of government is to simply remove obstacles from its citizens able and ready to plan, develop, create, invest, invent, and implement their favored projects, programs, businesses and so on ... ... doing this through the elimination of bureaucratic barricades as well as the facilitating of incentives along with ease of access to capital, resources, materials, equipment and tools, ... because in the end creativity is never born from the top-down but the other way around, ... since it emerges from the sum-total of the community and the sub-collectivities forming it in general and individuals in particular".

Isabelle went to get herself some water, and once back carried on as soon as she drank her first sip.

"Sadly, my dear Antoine our politicians ... like most politicians ...are like 'rats de chancelleries'.

Among them we find many that are honest and hardworking, but they nonetheless generally provide mediocre results for the public they serve ... it seems almost inevitable.

Many are incapable of doing anything of value for the community they allegedly serve, but their proclamations, like their behavior, border on the simplemindedness of political correctitude to cage in their inaptitude or mask their plain uncaring attitude or simply to cover their laziness.

The cases that created the necessity of a Charbonneau commission as a whole is an example of culturally imbedded politicians' lack of responsibilities and accountabilities in the handling of diminishing provincial revenues ... along with the thieves they hired in the development of infrastructure in the Transport department, among others.

The same can be said about the immense fiasco kept mostly hidden with computer systems development at the service of large bureaucracies in your provincial government ... a nonbusiness like situation that **would have <u>never</u> been tolerated in private industry ... at any time ... for the sake of efficiency, effectiveness, and proper project management. ".**

... but your Québec government ignores them ... hiring corporate losers like IBM, ... yes, IBM which has botched the payroll system of Canada's federal employees ...rather the top guns from the USA instead as well than information firms from France ,,, those very people trying to keep up with Americans and Chinese or anyone who would not be hired by the likes of Google and Apple", Isabelle finally concluded.

Temporarily Hovering Over a Fragment of Discussion 30.
Québec's and Canada's Anti-Semitism Mindset

"I tell you Isabelle, Québec's French-Canadians in particular were brainwashed by their Roman Catholic Church to fear Jews ... often surreptitiously ... as alleged killers of 'their' Jesus, ironically another Jew ... which parish priests and members of religious orders kept on proclaiming from time to time throughout their four centuries in Canada at least.

A national but hardly ever-mentioned hatred grew over that time in my community ...a loathing I also experienced in my own neighborhood – including in my primary school at école Iberville in St. Cunégonde as well as within my very own family.

That same abhorrence of the Jewry reinforced, for example, in the Québec journalism of the thirties – particularly in the veiled articles of our own elite's newspaper 'Le Devoir' ... and at times in not so oblique ways, ... such as when in 1934 it reported on a medical doctor, Sam Rabinovitch, hired by Hôpital Notre Dame, ... a decent man forced to resign, ... because of a strike by French-Canadian internes on the issue of his Jewishness ... imagine not his qualifications ... but his ethnic origin.

A strike that spread to other hospitals ... namely Hôpital Miséricorde, Hôpital Sainte-Justine, Hôpital Hôtel-Dieu and Hôpital St. Jean-de-Dieu.

Other hospitals added their names to petitions supporting the strikers. These came from Hôpital Sacré Coeur, Hôpital Ste. Jeanne D'Arc and Hôpital de Verdun.

In other words, it became a political racial movement supported by practically the whole medical establishment of the day.

A shameful chapter indeed of our French-Canadian history I tell you Isabelle.

In fact, 'Le Devoir' at that time reported that Catholic patients, which really meant French-speaking French-Canadian Quebecers, would find it 'repugnant' to be treated or 'touched' by a Jewish doctor ...

... an awful, prejudicial, and plainly fascist comment from a purportedly responsible newspaper supposedly representing 'la crème de la crème' of my very own ethnic group.

Yea! A statement from an elitist newspaper in effect morally supporting the perceived accepted 'political correctness' of a portion of its elite readers ... in this case young doctors among other privileged groups."

"But this would be unacceptable nowadays," interjected Isabelle.

"Yea! No doubt" responded Antoine.

"First, because we've thankfully evolved since ...

... but second, ... and let's face it squarely ...

... because the Jewish community would not take this shit today, ... and would fight such an attitude with all its might, ... with the whole planetary Jewish diaspora ... as they rightly should."

Antoine looked disturbed by what he had just revealed to Isabelle.

It was something that had weighed heavily on his conscience for years.

Indeed, she in turn sensed the shame Antoine felt at this moment ... at what many members of his community prejudicially truly felt, believed, and acted upon then.

Particularly among educated members of that society – medical doctors as privileged members of that society that ought to have known better – especially with their professional Hippocratic Oath.

Antoine rubbed his eyes to wipe a couple of tears that revealed the rage and emotions this issue had seemingly and suddenly triggered within him.

Isabelle, in an attempt to diminish the apparent guilt Antoine appeared to feel in this case, then told him:

"Look Antoine!

Anti-Semitism shamefully was not limited to Québec ... ... Canadians across the country, for example, more or less carried their hiring quota in their breast pocket.

Look! It thrived throughout English-speaking Canada.

Just think of the open anti-Jewish sayings and opinions of the Social Credit Party, ... or that of the Orange Order ... or that of the Native Sons of Canada.

Quotas and restrictions for Jews were a way of life until recently in our Canadian history my friend.

Industries and universities alike, for example, discriminated against Jews.

And to come back to your case in 1934, ... Jewish doctors before and after that time had great trouble getting jobs in hospitals across Canada, although it wasn't as spectacular as a strike by internes, I admit ...

... anyway Jews were quietly excluded from promotion as judges, and Jewish lawyers were generally omitted as well from most 'good' law firms.

As for all the other professions, say, engineers, teachers and others, Jews had to hide their identity most of the time to find a decent job in their field of work.

Moreover, there was a general unspoken agreement not to sell properties to Jews.

And in many areas across Canada you could find signs telling, if not warning outright, that Jews were not welcomed or allowed".

Isabelle took a deep breath and continued the delivery of her logic in an attempt to dampen Antoine's sadness about his community before the 'révolution tranquille'.

After a little while she then moved on to present the second part of the argument she had just started.

"The Canadian government openly and for all to see, also showed its anti-Semitism, when it refused entry to those Jews escaping the upcoming ravages of the Nazi-managed 'Final Solution', when these refugees seeking asylum from Nazi persecution were denied entrance to Canada.

In fact, as a country we were the worst in the Western world in providing sanctuary for Jewish refugees at that time. A reality that reinforced a national attitude, led before the Second World War by our then Prime Minister, Mackenzie King, of all people.

A man who – after visiting both Adolf Hitler and Nazi Foreign Minister von Neurath – found them most reasonable, civilized, and kind.

Need I say more Antoine?

Hey!

This was a shameful moment of our Canadian history.

And on top of all that let's recall that Canada also exhibited strong discrimination against Chinese, Japanese, Ukrainians, Irish, and Italians".

Isabelle paused for a few seconds and then asked Antoine:

"By the way Antoine, ... now that I think of it, ... didn't McGill University in Montréal, a world class institution by the way, applied an informal Jewish quota of some kind as well in those days?"

"Yea! They did!" responded Antoine.

He then got up.

Now staring at Isabelle and still obviously looking desponded, he continued the argument he'd first started, as if ready to get rid of the rest of that rage and emotional baggage he'd carried with him all those years.

"Nevertheless Isabelle ... while I also agree that what existed in Canada generally existed as well in Quebec, the biases against Jews by Quebec's French-Canadian community was far more virulent than elsewhere.

Even to this day ... and I know I am now an old man ... but still ... whenever using the words 'Jew' or 'Jewish', I emotionally feel that I am insulting someone, so deep are the effects of the indoctrination I forcefully was subjected to in my tender years, ... and yet I rejected my religion when I was eleven-years old.

That's why;

> *Indoctrination administered on a child is difficult to eliminate – even one with an open-mind. It's as if someone had seared a preprogrammed meme into*

your psyche that perpetually leaves a scar even after you've matured.

And that bias against Jews in Québec is without a doubt a meme successfully embedded in the French-Canadian psyche by the Roman Catholic Church over four hundred years of indoctrination, ... as if the Roman Catholic Church at the height of its long lasting hegemony had psychologically branded like a herd of cattle all French-speaking French-Canadians in Québec for sure but in the rest of Canada as well especially in smaller urban areas".

Antoine paused again, and then carried on, while Isabelle kept quiet.

"You could tell this attitude was socially accepted, when in the House of Commons, Henri Bourassa, a Québec French-Canadian, years before that racist, Makenzie King, strongly recommended we close our doors to Jewish immigrants.

The result no doubt of the anti-Semitism sponsored and promoted by the Roman Catholic Church in his youth, which linked Jews with brutal entrepreneurship, unethical business practices, usury, the implementation of modernism, the growth of liberalism, and untrustworthiness, ...

... and I remember all too well in the Forties and Fifties of my youth the connections religious teachers kept making about the Jewish 'attachment' for communism ... an allusion of treachery and upcoming danger.

I clearly recall the Brothers of Christian Instruction telling us in primary school ... grade six if I remember well ... on more than one occasion that ... Leon Trotsky was a Jew and that his real name was Lev Davidovich Bronstein ... there were a few others mentioned of course, but the names escape me after all the years past except for this one, ... perhaps because he was historically more pertinent and famous".

Again, as if in search of some inner strength to spill what he had left to say once and for all, Antoine closed his eyes for a minute, while Isabelle lowered her head in silence again waiting for him to continue.

"And speaking of a religious institution, remember the nauseatingly although then adulated and valued opinions of that French-Canadian chanoine Lionel Groulx, ... and his rants against Jews, ... the silence of his ecclesiastic superiors, ... and the significant influence he and the whole Church allowed him to have in shaping the opinions of politicians and journalists along with the curriculum of Québec's teaching institution, and its own clerical classes among others.

Think also of the yellow journalism then considered normal by many French-Canadian Roman Catholic publications such as 'La Vérité', or 'La Semaine religieuse' or 'L'Action sociale' ... ... as well as the sort of unprofessional journalism transmogrified into an encouraged boycott of Jewish businesses in Québec.

I remember my own mother and my aunt Claire warning me 'not to buy anything from that Jew' on Notre Dame Street in my neighborhood, since the profits Jews made when dealing with them, it was proclaimed, went against us, 'les vrais Canadiens' ... translate this again as us, victimized Roman Catholic French-speaking French-Canadians.

And yet oddly enough my mother would negate her prejudices by nevertheless buying from Jewish stores on Notre-Dame Street in the Ste-Cunégonde and Ste. Irénée parishes in south-west Montréal, where we resided in my youth ... all too often bragging how she had successfully outsmarted this Jew, or that one, to lower their price... and here we were supposed to appreciate her negotiating' skills ...

... but then she was an ignorant woman ... left school in grade two, as I recall her telling me ... to help her mother raised her children, ... while her father, a misogynist of the first order, raped her whenever he felt like it.

Now that I think of it ... boy oh boy! ... What kind of family of dysfunctional misfits did I come from?"

Again, Antoine paused again for a few seconds.

"Anyway ... even the intellectual class got into the act in this province in giving credibility to the many ethically questionable essays of the newspaper 'Le Devoir' during the Thirties and Forties particularly.

Newspapers of the day, including the Roman Catholic backed, say, 'L'Action Catholique' again and 'Le Devoir', suggested Jews were to be feared as potential communists (translate this as enemies of good Roman Catholic French-speaking French-Canadians) – a notion supported and encouraged by the clergy.

A notion also championed by Maurice Duplessis, then Premier of the province, elected by us for many years and shared by many other members of the Union Nationale ... and after your comments on Mackenzie King ... a continuation from and supported at the federal level."

Antoine continued *"And to make matters worse ... at that time, we even had our own little Hitler.*

Our potential dictator, Adrien Arcand, who founded the 'Parti national social chrétien' in Montréal.

I speak of group copied after the Nazi party ... in 1934 in fact ... <u>the same year</u> our doctors went on strike to force the departure of Dr. Samuel Rabinovitch".

***

"Come to think of it ... " interrupted Isabelle *"... wasn't it around that same decade ... that this pompous French-Canadian actor with a fake Parisian accent, ... Jean-Louis Roulx, ... a man who had to resign as Lieutenant-Governor of Québec, ... sported a swastika on his lab coat ... an event considered humoristic then at l'université de Montréal?"*

"Yes! You're right ...

... anyway, coming back to our own inbred outstanding Nazi contender..." Antoine acquiescing with a nod continued without commenting further on Isabelle's observation. *"... Adrien Arcand formed groups of people that organized anti-Semitic rallies,... boycotted Jewish businesses, ... distributed propagandist literature, ... and by their actions promoted the creation of other Nazi-like organizations elsewhere in Canada ... leading to that 'National Fascism Convention' in Toronto in 1938.*

Not a proud moment ... a most shameful one for my community indeed my dear Isabelle".

"Ok! Ok! Antoine ... all that was decades ago ... a lot of progress has taken place since".

Antoine shook his head to show his disaccord, which disturbed Isabelle once more.

"Quebec's history of intolerance still goes on nowadays ... linguistically, socially, culturally, and ethnically, ... but it is better handled, more professionally managed, and far better camouflaged in many ways ... and which still nevertheless quietly finds

expression in its fear of 'the other' with different targets – often against new immigrants nowadays."

Antoine suddenly changed his focus.

"Look! I realize that before my birth and, in my youth, Montréal was an area of many dual solitudes, generally separated:

· *First by 'Les Canadiens' as we called ourselves then (translate this as docile Roman Catholic French-speaking French-Canadians of 'vieilles souches' origin) from 'Les Anglais' (translate this as anyone using English as their mother tongue in every-day life).*

· *Secondly, by the rich (perceived as 'Les Anglais' and especially the Jews) and the poor or and victims (perceived as 'les Canadiens'... nowadays transmogrified further as 'les Québécois').*

· *Thirdly, by Montréal West-enders (les Anglais) and East-enders (les Québécois)."*

And today he finally concluded after a silence of at least two minutes this time:

"The elephant in the room we dare not talk about deals with new immigrants (nowadays mostly identified as a fear of Haitians in the last three decades ago or so ... and anyone of the Moslem faith presently) from allegedly 'real Québécois' (vielles souche French-speaking French-Canadians) ... in addition to our traditional nemesis: the Jews, which we keep quiet about, ... and leave on the back burner, ... for fear this time of being put to task by a mature and self-assured Jewish community no longer living in fear of us."

Temporarily Hovering Over a Fragment of Discussion 31.
Mindset of a Frightened Ethnic Group

After drinking from his second Eska water bottle that afternoon Antoine intent to explain the fright his ethnic group felt without ever admitting it, turned to his new-found soul mate:

"Isabelle!"

He loved to say her name.

"Let me explain further.

Take the case of the Parti Québécois!

More than half of French-speaking French-Canadians located in Québec (especially the unilingual ones) feel a rapprochement toward separatist parties.

Yet, the Parti Québécois organization did and still represents among other things – the significant remnant mindset of a frightened ethnic group, ... as does other smaller separatist oriented groups ... ... expressed through a narrow ... almost theological nationalism ... believing this to be __the__ solution to all of past, present, and future societal problems and issues in Québec ... identifying French-Canadians of 'vielles souche'—without ever mentioning this notion—as innocent victims, ... and therefore morally entitled to be sovereign in every respect ... ... regardless of collateral damage to its English-speaking minority, which in fact ironically provides a most significant portion of its provincial revenues.

And despite this, the notion of being a 'distinct society' with roots going back four-hundred years or so, ... prevents them to acquiesce a diminishing number of believers over time, ...

... a process that took place as more Quebecers got educated; ... got involved in events and situations beyond parochial ones; ... began to be aware and take part in Canadian and US affairs; ...with many slowly waking up to the globalization of everything now in progress.

And yet for a segment of Quebecers, despite these facts and the advent of an ever-increasing number of immigrants coming into the province, ... separatists have not truly gone all out to attract members of these new incoming communities.

And even at this late date, their much too late approach in this respect is lukewarm ... and appears at best ... as a frantic desperate move to sustain their movement.

I'd say, this tells me that believers in the Parti Québécois and other separatist leaning organizations and political parties at this point of Québec's history rightly fear the future ...

... because as intelligent sentient beings, despite their ideology, ... they nevertheless correctly sense their diminishing political importance as a unique community in a pluralistic Québec, Canada, North America and the world at large.

And I presume they also possess the sagacity of recognizing their ongoing, gradual, and almost inevitable absorption into the English-speaking North-American fold in the long run ... even if, say, ... this process will take a long time ... ... a long process indeed ... that will no doubt unfold for decades at least ... and probably a couple centuries or more ... but an ever more inevitable one from now on especially among those with a globalized worldview, ... because of the opportunities represented ...

...and separatists of all descriptions do not want this nor even hear about that possibility. Period.

That is why:

> *Separatist-minded Quebecers are finally willing, although reluctantly to slow down this shift, by accepting*

people from diverse communities from both, first-generation children of immigrants speaking French, along with present remaining long-term resident 'Anglos' into their ranks... but preferably if they possess an 'accent Québécois'.

A desperate move I say, ... what about you Isabelle?"

"*Yea!*" She mumbled.

"But in the world of realpolitik their chances are on a slide of diminishing returns that's for sure, ..." she went on.

"... and aside from this ... I don't really know how they can hope to take over the whole territory of the present province of Québec as it is now constituted ... even if they were to beat the odds now stacked against them ... even with a miraculous minimalist '50% + 1' formula or a much higher percentage.

From my perspective and yours of a few days ago, neither Canada nor particularly the USA would permit it.

Canada would balk at the geographical separation of Canada into two parts and the US would want to continue to share border with Canada and not with an ideologically oriented Québec."

Temporarily Hovering Over a Fragment of Discussion 32.
Problem Solving Founded on a Religious Past

"I will say this in French Antoine:

> *'La 'révolution tranquille' qui pris place au Québec, fut*
> *une bonne chose, ... mal faite, ... au mauvais moment,*
> *... et il me semble sans planification'.*

I believed that many years ago, ... and still see the same failure of intelligent overall planning today.

And this because of the restrictive Jesuitan structural logic retained by the then Québec elite ....

... by a group consisting mostly of the old professional class of professors, teachers, medical doctors, lawyers, notaries, and politicians ...

... until then lectured, conditioned, and psychologically preprogrammed by religious teaching institutions, ...

... including the best learning centers at that time, where the elite was being schooled, such as Jean de-Brébeuf, Jean Eudes, college St-Louis, université de Montréal and université Laval, ...

... an approach now demonstrated in an over the top quasi-religious although transmogrified secular applications of a Québec-defined political correctitude.

This is the reason why:

> *Québec's general approach to problem solving is in*
> *great part founded on a structural logic from its reli-*
> *gious past – a medieval logic I add.*

You only have to examine Québec's fanatical devotion to bureau-cratic procedural protocols and administrative algorithms to re-

alize that these replaced ... and have become as a whole the secular 'catechism' of this now prevalent Québec-styled new quasi-religion of political correctitude.

It is as if, you were still in disguised forms, pleased to adopt, or adapt to, that ancient and not so ancient religious brainwashing along with its 'simagrés ecclesiastiques' ... now adopting the outward allure of secularity.

And let's remember that these same 'simagrés ecclesiastiques, ensured that the so-called 'enfants de Duplessis' were locked up, abused, and most often considered, if not declared, insane by and with the complicity of the most important establishments of the day ...

... and here I blame the direct involvement of the Roman Catholic Church, the Duplessis government that subsidized religious authorities to take care of them, along with the medical and legal classes that supported the process professionally.

Proof that you can easily fall into fascist behavior ... and did, at that time in fact as your history proves.

And to this day no one has done anything substantial to correct this ethical calamity, ... and purge it out of your system.

You simply kept it buried for fear someone see you for what you really were ... <u>and could be again</u>.

No one wants this be brought out ...

... I think it is because it shows your fascist tendencies ...

... which you fear deep down might come out again ... and that scares you".

After a minute of silence Isabelle added.

"This is one case among many reflecting Québec's adoption of a generalized policy of no responsibility and no accountability by your institutions, governmental bureaucracies, and agencies ...

... a tendency to avoid the ethical content of your acts ... or lack of resolve in delivering those that ought to help the citizenry.

And let us not forget your other fascist tendency regarding non-French-speaking 'non-vieilles souches' and especially those born 'outsiders' ... ... in each case you rarely speak of those you consider as 'outsiders' ... yea! ... they're hardly ever mentioned by the separatist crowds.

Yea! You refuse to face this subterranean meme of yours ... and continue in often sophisticated ways to use a subtle language to camouflage your fear of 'the other' ... and this to both yourselves and potential voters.

Except lately with your reactions to the subtle and not so subtle, ... at times reasonable and often not so reasonable demands from segments of the Moslem community.

Yes! In the end that tribal fear of yours nevertheless shows itself for all to see in the 'language police', for example, which you in fact instituted and support, ... thereby promoting yourselves as morally and politically superior to others in this territory called Québec.

It ideologically demonstrates itself in your insistence to demand and enforce by law that all signs throughout the province – when English cannot be avoided – be reduced these in size ... wherein the visibility of English becomes one third of what is necessary for a proper and safe visibility of the French one ...

... a clearly biased application again showing a profound disrespect of your own English-speaking population of about 600,000 people...

... as well as that of your non-French-speaking visitors from all over North America and elsewhere for whom English is used as a means of communication with others across the planet ...

... as well as underscore and exhibit again, your intense fear of 'the other' ...

... in this case the ever-powerful enveloping and developing clout of the English language hegemony of the North American continent and the planetary elite class.

Other frightened communities have made similar moves in desperate attempts to protect their communal language.

The one that comes to mind right now was the move in Ukraine before the Russian invasion to impose by law the adoption of Ukrainian to millions of its Russian-speaking citizens born in Ukraine in an area bordering Russia.

My take on this was then that not only it would not work, but that it would likely end up causing a severe political rift, and did after a short while, and for which Ukraine has already paid dearly, especially with this psychopath, Vladimir Putin.

Here's another lesson to learn by separatists here", finally concluded Isabelle. *"Don't lull yourself in thinking the Americans would not interfere".*

Temporarily Hovering Over a Fragment of Discussion 33.
Forever in The Tentacles of Its Own Ideology

Isabelle and Antoine had been at a farewell show in Montréal by Charles Aznavour, the French singer of Armenian descent, and strong advocate intent on forcing Turkey to admit its genocide of Armenians at the beginning of the twentieth century.

This was followed by a late supper and the inevitable ride back home to Rigaud at around 2 am.

Both were still drowsy having gone to bed in the middle of the night, had not breakfast, and had consumed just a panini for lunch with a glass of milk.

So, their off and on marathon discussions about Québec and French-Canadians started late that afternoon overlapping their usual supper time.

"As far as I can tell my dear Isabelle the Parti Québécois cannot get its act together simply because:

· *It's been drowning in its rhetoric for years.*

· *It keeps on tripping itself on technicalities and ideological details.*

· *It overuses the democratic process within its ranks and files to the point of administrative paralysis ... doing this to such a point that the decision-making process is bogged down, ... with the result of not being able to turn on a dime ... incapable of making timely decisions, ... or take adequate actions to meet political and social realities, ... and this while the world speeds by and ahead of them ...*

· *It seems to be an organization that never learns from its basic mistakes.*

· It appears to forever remain in the tentacles of its own ideology ... remaining an order of magnitude behind from whatever is going on in Québec, ... two orders of magnitude with the rest of Canada and North-America ... and three with the world at large .. ... and that includes other splinter parties and groups still advocating separation from Canada such as the Block Québecois... with others not marketing too loudly their intentions such as the communist leaning 'Québec solidaire' party".

Antoine rubbed his eyes once more, still tired from the night before, and carried on with his argument.

"Take for example... its complete disregard of the new immigrants in Québec ... and the opportunity offered to bring them to its cause ... aside for a few pious words ... ... that would be a one-to-two generation project I assume, ... but one which a good long-range rational planner would normally take on with gusto.

The Parti Québécois in practice catered only to those they identified as 'real' Québécois instead ... here we understand vieilles souches French-Canadians in Québec ... their political base in great part ... ignoring all the while the quickly changing population distribution of greater Montréal and to a fair degree the single-mindedness of that singular and totally French-speaking Québec City community ... ... it is as if ideology nearly always trumps practical applications of realpolitik in this organization of otherwise well-meaning people I suppose, ... but nevertheless often acting as hapless organizers and planners ... yea! ... it's been amateurish in the extreme at times ... all emotions ... no pragmatic applications".

Temporarily Hovering Over a Fragment of Discussion 34.
Traffic Organization and Administration

Isabelle was full of pep and vinegar since she got up that morning … oddly enough getting up before Antoine … preparing breakfast instead of Antoine's usual over the top *"breakfast in bed ma belle madame"* as he loved to say.

So, it was no surprise that afternoon when Isabelle began their discussion, which started that way:

"Québec's political class like its managerial and several other segments within its professional classes, time and again have shown a rather disastrous inability to plan and organize complex work schedules, expert applications of critical path methodology, materials flows, timely delivery of workloads, entrepreneurial imagination, and so on … … and this is not because they cannot do it, …

… but simply because their schooling at all levels rarely teaches them that … … normally training them as a routine in the art of providing excuses for the very failures from which they ought to otherwise learn and improve their skills upon.

"Wow! Aren't you exaggerating a bit here Isabelle?" Exclaimed Antoine suddenly.

"Think of it, Antoine!

From the time, they're born, … from the most to the least privileged ones … children from toddlers to students … … in fact, students at all levels from kindergarten to high school are all too often pampered when failing, instead of being corrected as a practical lesson of life among many others required to survive adequately, ... often rewarded instead ... and thereby disorienting the view they ought to have in observing and appreciating the world as it really is, ...

... the same approach exists when not providing a real effort to get a task done well, ... or for not finishing a report on time or adequately, ... or for incomplete homework, ... and the list goes on.

*These '**enfants-roi**', as you call them yourself ... don't think they need to make an effort to get what they want ... or obtain privileges, ... with the results that ...*

*... those who do not graduate or are subjected to fake promotions during their years attending school ... in order **not** to hurt their feelings for their short comings or negative attitude ... or plain failures ... or lack of enterprise ... really get a life-changing cold shower, when they reach adulthood ...*

... finally understanding then for the first time the hard realities our brutal world reserves for the ill-prepared, the quasi-illiterate, and those culturally afflicted with their Québec-styled financial and practical analphabetism.

As for those, who despite roadblocks nevertheless graduate despite this less than desirable child and student rearing approach, they also discover that despite their education ... that they're generally at a lost, when it comes to live as a responsible adult ... in an adult world wherein no such excuses for lack of enterprise exists.

In fact, they are often terrified once they come face-to-face to planning and executing all the intricacies required in delivering major undertakings, ... something which no doubt often appears to them as incomprehensible byzantine minutiae.

With this thought in mind I suggest to you that no better example exists in Québec for all to see on a routine basis than the hapless, amateurish and most of the time plain incompetence of Québec transport department employees at all levels ... continuing to exhibit their low managerial skills in dealing with traffic flow in planning for or simply the construction one thing or another.

And equally significant is their inability to steer projects to completion on time and agreed upon costs ... and here we see failure after failure after failure after failure ...

... it is as if this was part and parcel of their normal modus operandi.

Oh no! ... 'that can't be' ... executives from that department will say.

And in addition, everybody takes a cut because of all their shortcomings ... a fact clearly demonstrated in the Charbonneau Commission ... and which the Québec government shamefully put on a shelf, so those still benefiting ... including in a not so removed future those who would again benefit ... can keep the ongoing 'magouille' functioning as well as before.

... And to be quite honest, I doubt very much, if anyone fully involved in kick-backs would ever end up in criminal court except in one case to cover those getting away with their involvement in practice or provincial employees be fired outright for demonstrating clear incompetence ... except perhaps for a few expendable small fries ... those unable to extirpate themselves from the trap they may inadvertently be caught into."

Temporarily Hovering Over a Fragment of Discussion 35.
Embedded Fascist-Leaning Memes?

That afternoon both Antoine and Isabelle had been discussing the pros and cons of robotized thinking and bureaucracies, when Isabelle began to make another point – one that seemed more important to her than all the others she'd made so far.

"Wow! ... Now! ... Here's a scary thing", said Isabelle.

"You know what robotized thinking based on bureaucratic protocols eventually leads to Antoine?

Think!

Yea! Think!

Push this logic to its extreme unfolding!

Think of historical events such unchecked robotized development led to, ... and it'll scare you, my friend!"

"What! What!" Exclaimed Antoine surprised at Isabelle's sudden panicky look.

"Doesn't it eventually lead to some kind of dystopian society regardless of size and initial intention?" Questioned Isabelle.

"Isn't that what Hanna Arendt called 'the banality of evil', when referring to the banality of a most ordinary but very dutiful, obedient, and docile bureaucrat in a senior administrative position in this case ... when she wrote that book about the trial of that politically-correct-to-his-organization psychopaths, Adolf Eichmann?" She emphasized.

"Holly shit! Now you're going to hate me now for saying this, Antoine. I just know it.

It just came out.

It sounds awful!

Sorry! Sorry! Antoine.

I don't know what came over me".

After a few minutes of silence Antoine got up and took Isabelle in his arms, hugging her tight for a couple minutes, then passed his fingers in her thick white hair.

"It's ok! I know this seems crazy at first ... extreme even ... ...and it is". He went on.

Now looking straight at her, he carried on with her train of thought, because he suddenly recognized that same secret fear in himself, which he had for a long time felt but he could never share with others and her for that matter – until now.

Both sat down, and Antoine carried on with the theme Isabelle had suddenly triggered.

"Look! Both of us, having been alive during the Second World War, ... the Cold War ... the scary confrontation between the USA and Russia in the so-called Cuban Crisis ... the Rwandan geno-cide of the Tutsi people of 1994 ... and Serbian genocide-war of the early Nineties ... even if we choose to ignore all the others for purposes of our discussion, ... many other real and potentially lethal world-wide confrontations nevertheless still easily come to mind.

Yes! Some of us, older folks, dread the possibility of some sort of dystopian if not plain fascism installing itself within our group,

...or next to us, ... or that it attacks us ... or robs us of our hard-earned freedom somehow ... because there are so many precedents ...and opportunities for such situation to emerge in our day and age are abundantly still present ... and for which most of us pretend do not exists ... along with the barely admitted failed States."

***

After a minute or so of reflection Antoine continued.

"By the way just think for an instant of that ignorant, pompous, and dangerous psychopath, Donald Trump, elected to man the American nuclear button and the mighty American armed forces as 'Commander in Chief' in support of his obvious fascist leanings and extreme biases.

A man elected and presumably reflecting the propensities of large segment of Americans – those who in great part consist of people pushed out of and demoted by their economy; those realizing that their future will likely be one of scarcity, if not plain poverty, with a risk of becoming homeless and totally useless ... with no future for their children and grandchildren ...

People now understanding at last that they are no longer able to compete in an uneven and quickly metamorphosing field for planetary economic survival ... even there in the 'land of the free'".

***

"Anyway, and coming back to the point I was trying to make, Antoine", interrupted Isabelle, *"I believe fascism is probable with the present unfolding of our world history ... especially when we assume, it could take place in our nation ... since it appears to slowly take place with our powerful neighbor next door ...*

... I wonder if we're going to be next after them.

Yea! Without a doubt, it sets fear in us, when witnessing those initial steps leading to what could be ... or at least risks being a dystopian objective ... even if not intended at first or admitted amid emotional ethnic outbursts".

Here Isabelle stopped, got up again, went to the end of the deck, came back, and now standing in front of Antoine, went on with her exposé – as if a lecturer trying to make a most important point to her students.

"The overt prejudices, for example, exhibited in Canada and the actions undertaken by the Canadian government on our behalf against Jews, Chinese, Japanese, Ukrainians and Italians among others until a few decades ago, should have set fear in all of us at that time, as to where this attitude and the acts they engendered were leading us to.

Terrifying for me still is that it did not bother me until now.

And let's not forget the cultural genocide of Aboriginal ethnic groups located on Canadian soil ... and our lack of resolve in seriously handling the poverty our mismanagement of this re-sponsibility has callously created to this day.

We, decades ago, with the intervention of an often disgraced RCMP then and since ... with violence ... removed children from their parents, ...

... doing so to discredit aboriginal cultures, eliminate their mother tongues, and indoctrinate them by force into our Western style culture instead ... ... and all this while religious organiza-tions, charged and paid to look after them, would instead humil-iate these kids, often beat them into submission, and of course as was the accepted practice within religious communities, occa-sionally if not repeatedly rape those considered desirable for such dastardly acts.

I know this scared me when I discovered that in the Seventies ... and you also – no doubt ... and all the more reason for you in Québec in those days, since you lived through the acute disrespect if not plain hatred taught to you French-Canadians in Québec about Jews particularly – along with all those other prejudices you also sadly shared with the rest of Canada generally.

Look Antoine! I think that the reason you feel I went off the rails here, is probably this:

> *What tends to happen when a society with shared prejudices combines these with an ever powerful bureaucratic robotization of protocols to apply its policies in the form of quasi-unalterable algorithms ... then a 'politically correct' outlook is demanded with the inevitable socially accepted contract, approved thinking, and behavior, which must accompany it.*

At such juncture ... a fascist state of mind is set up ... and moral standards to make it acceptable emerge.

As for you ... I'd say ... especially when societal memes have already been introduced in your case by the Roman Catholic Church ...

... with that added sub-meme I could title, say, ... 'a social sacrament of 'Absolute Obedience' to a given and alleged 'Immaculate Perception' of the world ... whether Roman Catholicism in the old days or the present and various 'modèles Québécois' that replaced the religious one in this case ... you and I know Antoine, ... what history has been proven time and again where such an attitude leads to."

***

Isabelle then took a break for a couple minutes or so, while Antoine respectfully kept silent, sensing that her presentation was not yet complete.

She then continued.

"OK! Coming back to Arendt's writing.

"I must admit to you that, I too thought about this after first reading George Orwell's 'Nineteen-eighty-four' at university and later on when I read Arendt's texts.

*Yes! I too tried to understand Eichmann's excuse after that war ... and others elsewhere at other times, ... all claiming they were 'merely following legitimate orders' ... they were ... as if honored to have conducted themselves without a modicum of ethics, ... strictly in accordance to established bureaucratic practices and protocols at that time ... of what was ... and we can now label ... as a dogmatic algorithm of required malevolent conduct ... ... a type of dystopian 'Newspeak' to excuse **The Forever Inexcusable**.*

I too also realized like you that, following established ways and means of doing things outside an ethical context, ... eventually and inevitably leads ordinary people to commit awful things to other human beings ...

... and as uncomfortable as it may be to our present spoiled generation, ... I submit to you that, ... even a small move toward fascism can be seen as vastly exaggerated at first by the most sensitive among us, ... but as it grows over time, ... we get used to it ... a fact made evident again and again in the course of our human history.

Because I too also understand that the morality constructed by the 'politically correct' assessment of the day and location supports a purportedly correct behavior sanctioned by the belief system in place ... and that's what scares me all the time.

***

And coming back again to Eichmann and the Nazis... let us at least consider this!

Let's face it, Antoine! The German-speaking people then as now consisted of a civilized, liberalized, and advanced group of human beings, ... but once a significant part of that nation did not participate in the political development of its governance, ... or despite its suspicions ... was nonetheless willing to abide to a social sacrament of 'Absolute Obedience' to the new unquestionable 'Immaculate Perception' in place, ... thought and believed when not simply assuming to be morally correct, ... especially since the majority had correctly suffered multiple injustices on account of world War One triggered in great part by that nincompoop of theirs, Kaiser Wilhelm II, and the end result of that insanely unrealistic Versailles Treaty ...

... so, a brutal solution to real and perceived problems and issues in such a case appeared reasonable and morally 'permitted' I suppose.

Similar situations that took place in various ways several times in the space of one's lifespan in our case ... hey Antoine!

But let me go out on a tangent again, ... before I continue my Québec argument.

In the first instance the German nation was betrayed by one of their own, that pompous and incredibly immature psychopath, Kaiser Wilhelm II, as the main actor in the launching of the First World War ... despite all the other reasons such as complex interconnected treaties and so on ...

... compounded by the then incredibly stupid 1919 Treaty of Versailles ... especially those unrealistic conditions the French Government pompously, vengefully, and absolutely insisted upon.

***

By the way and as an aside Antoine.

> *That self-anointed nitwit German 'Caesar', the Kaiser of Germany, ... prior to and during the First World War, ... yea ... that man who wanted to outdo*

his other equally psychopathic and socially immature nitwit cousins among others, ... along with them succeeded in triggering the slaughter of tens of millions for the most stupid of reasoning.

A psychopath, we, of the Western world, deliberately chose to retire and support to a cushy residence and easy retirement, until he died a peaceful death during the Second World War, which he had in great part triggered with the first.

He should have been executed for the tens of millions of deaths he caused.

But no!

We protected him, as a valid member of the special so-called 1% within his community, of that select planetary elite class of owners and stakeholders of those days.

***

In the second instance, to come back to the Nazis again and in a different context and timeframe ...

... petty hatred was institutionalized and national policy and protocols of behavior for the implementation of inbred biases became de rigueur in Nazi Germany, ... as it did in England and France in some ways and to some degree as well.

Yet, no one acted in a timely manner to stop the massacres that were clearly being broadcasted ... and being readied, ... not even when it was taking place ...

... and this because our Western reasoning methodology, ... based on our normalized social standards of assessment at that time, ... would not permit it".

***

"Wow! I really just got off on a dangerous tangent here, didn't I?

Ok! Let me now get back to the point I wanted to make at the beginning.

***

Look! What I meant to say aside from all this hyperbolic speculative thinking of mine is this:

> *Once self-righteous foundational algorithms and rules of conduct to an unquestionable belief along with the bureaucracy supporting it are accepted, implemented, and abided by, ... **then massacres become inevitable** ... regardless of the society they emerge from ... and this independent of size and temperament.*

That is why;

> *The sooner we note those first steps to fascism triggered by a massive bureaucracy the sooner we must extinguish it for fear that a political high wind quickly spreads it.*

*I refer of course to **any** highly structured protocol-directed organization for that matter.*

One with a catechism of unquestionable political correctitude, which you suspect my dear Antoine, when speaking of the progressively powerful self-validating, self-governing, self-directed bureaucratic machines of the Québec government feeding itself from the very earnings of its citizens to maintain itself at the expense of these citizens.

Hey! That's another risky statement again.

Hey Antoine? Wasn't it?"

"Yea! That's for sure". Antoine finally said, after half a minute or so, while staring at the Rigaud mountain on the other side of the river, rather than looking at Isabelle.

He then turned to stare at her, and surprisingly continued with the same unusual frame of mind, she had just unfolded before him.

"Look I think that what we're both trying to allude to, and which both our fears have triggered with our obvious dread of powerful bureaucracies is that:

> *Sticking to absolutes, as well as dogmatic rules of decision and behavior, most often, if not nearly always, leads to horrific situations ...*

> *... and that if the Québec government continues in this extreme 'political correctness' of theirs ... along with the brutal attacks it commits for example through its tax collecting measures on the more vulnerable members of its society...*

> *... and especially if all or parts of Québec became independent one day on top of that ...*

> *... a similar danger most likely awaits, since its revenue department would already possess all the data and information required to rule the citizenry with a firm hand.*

Having said that, I add:

> *That if anyone could hear our conversation right now my dear Isabelle, ... or should we openly broadcast it, ... they would consider us guilty of violating some hatred law or other, I suppose.*

Yet we both know, it is not."

Taking a deep breath, he went on.

"We are simply looking ahead at the unfolding controls slowly accumulating by each of the ever more powerful bureaucracies, whenever the use of strict protocols of decisions and behavior are enforced by government ... and out of which a fear of government installs itself in the population at large ... at least among the more awake among us.

I sense that it scares both of us right now for what it could lead to ... that's all.

The whole thing suggests to me that, ... like the highly civilized German nation, ... we too could easily adopt or adapt to a sort of fascist form of government ... and like them despite our democratic institutions, ... and this because that train of thoughts was already and obviously manifest in the Québec of the Thirties, Forties and Fifties particularly... we could, ... given the right circumstances ... reemerge once more, I fear ... with such mentality ...

... although I predict that its effects would be negligible with all those outside of what would be left of the Québec territory then ... and I don't think Canada and the USA would fear us – except to note a sort of insularity of our own design".

***

"Ok! Ok! Antoine!

That's enough with our gloomy thinking. It's about to depress me ...and we may have gone too far here.

I agree with you, ... but just think of what happened a few days ago, ... ".

Here Antoine looked despondent but continued.

"Yea! .... like in a fascist state ... we discovered that the Montréal police and the Québec provincial police spied on journalists to track their sources of information ... allegedly 'legally' ... and

followed their movements with GPS tracking to that end ... and most probably routinely listened to their conversations in view of todays' advanced technological capabilities used by hackers ...

... a situation that made the news around the world!

... and this because a few in their rank and file and the population at large ... fed up with mismanagement, misconduct, mishandling, negligence, and other forms of bungling, labor union frustrations, ... within their organization... informed journalists of their frustrations.

An over-the-top tribal reaction by the police executive rank at the municipal level ... a frontal attack by definition and in fact on all of our 'Inalienable Individual Rights' within a liberalized democratic community without a doubt.

A perversion of police investigation – at times with the approval of incompetent or worse yet participating judges – against whistle-blowers ... ... and now just think of the two scary points this suggests!

> *First, the unadmitted 'legally' authorized spying ventures by a now quasi-militarized organization.*

> *Second, and worse yet, the half-truths or never-to-be-admitted illegal spying ventures on journalists and others for other purposes ... a fairly easy thing to do nowadays.*

You will note that I did not mention the fascist-leaning Québec provincial police of the Duplessis era, ... now sadly resurfacing in our days in a newer form with its new boastful nationalistic ideological label of 'Sûreté du Québec' ... as if a sort of 'proto-armée du peuple'."

"Isn't all this a bit paranoid Antoine?" Isabelle interjected.

"Yea! Yea! Yea! ... I know what you're saying.

And 'yes', I feel like an extremist ... and yet I've been a reasonable man all of my life ... but somehow my gut feeling keeps taking over ... and I fear ... and understand that ... my view of Québec, in a not too distant a future, risks to be eventually dystopian...

... but these so-called initial fascist-leaning memes we spoke of before keep on showing up, ... and this troubles me intensely.

I feel down to my bone marrow that, there are crucial questions that must be asked and answered as soon as possible in view of our past behavior toward other communities – especially the Jews ... an historical fact that contributed in no uncertain ways in showing our inbred tribal biases.

What I am in fact strongly suggesting is another fear of mine.

I suspect that a trigger-cause of some kind might activate that old tribal intolerance again.

Here! That's it! I said it".

Antoine's eyes now opened wide as he suddenly recalled.

"Boy oh boy!

Recently I heard the news about the creation of a new political party in Québec ... a fledging group mind you ... but reminiscent of Adrian Arcand, ... you know, that Hitler wannabe of the Thirties ...

... a political party fashioned as a reaction from the desperate outlook sensed by Parti Québécois turncoats in 2016 initially to be at first called 'Front National du Québec'...

... a carbon copy of that fascist-leaning political party from France, ...

... which then changed it, after being ironically rebuffed for adopting that ultra-right French political party's name without its permission ...

... a party it nonetheless intends to emulate and benchmark.

I don't know if the seeds of hatred to be sown by that new party will eventually bear fruits, ... but the reactive process of fear of 'the other' continues in my view, ... and so do the potential consequences such an attitude contains.

I also believe that one of the seeds for a reactivation of those intolerance-infected memes that surfaced in the Thirties, Forties and Fifties especially, ... embedded long ago and kept more or less under control since within my community, ... are being revived once more, ...

... and as the perceived danger intensifies from the point of view of hard-core separatists, more people blow on the burning coals of intolerance, as Premier Couillard once said ... and it scares me.

And even if this attitude was only to affect a reduced independent Québec territory in the end, it would still be a dystopian life for its residents ".

Antoine eyes now opened wide once more as he suddenly recalled an article that had disturbed him greatly in the last few days.

"Of yea! ... There's this new group called ... let's see ... my memory's going to shit as I age ... of yea I remember ... 'La Meute' ... or 'Wolf Pack' if I were to translate it.

These people apparently have attracted more than tens of thousands at last count to a secret Facebook group in little over a year according to a newspaper ... but I can't recall which for now.

A group that is among other things against multiculturalism; ... hopes to become a lobby group; ... is dedicated to making Quebecers aware of the threat posed by Islamic fundamentalism with a fear of living under sharia laws in a sort of totalitarian Islamic regime ... although here in this case;

I can partially understand their fear, if we are to pay attention to extremists in Islam causing havoc everywhere, and bent on establish a planetary caliphate intending to abide by the hundreds of broad commands and direct orders contained in the Koran.

Nonetheless this 'La Meute' has drawn up plans for a hierarchical organization modelled on a military background, already copied in France and Belgium by groups that have adopted its name and organizational structure ... ... we refer to people here connected nevertheless to strong veins of opinions in our case throughout Québec ... especially outside Montréal.

Like separatists-leaning Quebecers, its members believe that French-speaking Québec has become disconnected from its history and culture ... making us vulnerable to the designs of immigrants generally.

Look! We can only ignore the feelings of Quebecers in this area of concern at our risks and perils, ... because the danger with a group such as 'La Meute' and others like it ... is that it is not that far removed from the Québec mainstream, ... because extremist congregations highlighting this state of distress are not the only ones adhering to this conclusion... it has in fact become part of the platforms of the province's opposition parties moderated by the fear of being judged as 'politically incorrect' .... always mindful of the heavy price to be paid, if judged anti Francophone in this secular province ...

... although they continue to rightly believe that ... the very survival of Québec's culture, which it presents are under fire by the English hegemony ...

... translate this as American influence and all those Canadians everywhere insisting to speak the other official language of Canada ...

... as well as other surreptitious and supercilious attacks including the present challenge to Québec's values ... whatever these may be ... by outsiders ... especially a gradually self-affirming Islam".

Isabelle interrupting Antoine said.

"It's just a very small group my dear Antoine ... why worry so much?"

Surprised at her comments a befuddled Antoine responded.

"Don't you recall the size of the group Adolf Hitler had been sent to assess ... that so-called 'DAP' ... the original 'German Workers' Party' had seven members at the beginning ... and soon after Adolf became its 55th member ... to eventually become its leader ...

... eventually transforming it as the murderous 'NSDAP' that 'National Socialist German Workers' Party' with millions of adherents.

I know I sound crazy ... maybe ... well probably ... I'm overreacting ... yea no doubt ... but that crazy feeling eats at me ... and I don't know why it does ... although I know neither you nor I will be around when this takes place ....

And now we have this ignorant, narrow-minded, and foul-mouthed bully Rambo Gauthier ... a guy that would have felt most comfortable with those Nazi oppressors at that time ... and yet people from the lower St-Lawrence region and others outside major urban centers think he would be a good leader ...

... the older I get the more discouraged I become with these developments.

Here, I supposed the 'politically correct' crowd would jump all over me for saying such things ... or accuse me of some so-called 'hate crime' for speaking out if not incarcerate me at some point I suppose" Antoine finally concluded.

Temporarily Hovering Over a Fragment of Discussion 36.
The Secular Religion of Political Correctitude

Antoine began the discussion that afternoon.

"We, in Québec, tend not to go beyond what is uncomfortable, because our rigid 'politically-correct' philosophy, belief system, and attitude, do not permit it.

Our analyses and syntheses of events and situations, considerations, opinions, morality, evaluations and so on, have now metamorphosed from an old-world Abrahamic religion to a secular one – the new world of 'political correctitude'.

Let me explain to you what and why I consider the 'politically correct' verbiage and attitude generally everywhere and the particular version that has infected the French-speaking segment of the Québec culture.

This approach promotes a physical, psychological and economic dependence of artificially infantilized human beings on State-sponsored programs, previously administered by the Church on behalf of the State, in whatever form ... as therefore normal and right, ... since it keeps such psychologically shackled people at bay, encourages self-censure, and ensures a minimum of questioning about the existing orthodox way of doing things.

A system of thought wherein 'disobedient' people to the political correctness diktats in place are often considered guilty of a 'hate crime' every time they communicate thoughts contravening social acceptability for public consumption ...

*... such as proclaiming that religions **ought not** take precedence over other forms of thought ... ... simply because, if we want to*

be intellectually honest, ... a liberal-leaning community continues to ensure that these unfounded dogmatic belief systems be excluded from scientific examination".

"What are you getting at with that point?" Asked Isabelle.

"Simply this. That 'political correctitude' concerns itself with evasion of consequences in a language of guilt and failure ... promoting a systemic erosion of responsibility and an automatic denial of accountability.

That it is in my view an Orwellian 'newspeak'.

That is why ... the latest politically correct generation now emerging is gutless, filled with dread, and saturated in a paralyzing fear of everything ...

... except of course for that segment among the Millennials and the emerging Generation Z with an entrepreneurial spirit.

***

Now think of the following facts to illustrate my point:

Just think of those outstanding cases of obvious data, information, and knowledge manipulation, witnessed daily in the media ... although no one it seems, questions its gobbledygook.

Or consider the case of psychology ... here I speak of those high priests of the new secular quasi religion of 'political correctitude' found in the texts of the DMS ... that sacred encyclopedia of saintly interpretations and appraisals for the control and management of American minds ... and ours by default.

*This quasi-dogmatic book, a holy text of sort, supporting this contemporary new secular quasi religion is above all **the** 'Bible' of meanings and values of our construed and expected contemporary human behavior.*

It represents the worldview of this antagonistic and argumentative organization, licensed to evaluate our sanity, ethics, and intentions with the alleged and snobbishly presumed self-awarded certainty of a scientific field of knowledge, which <u>unequivocally it is not</u>.

Oh yes! Psychiatrists and psychologists, those modern clerics of our contemporary meanings and values, use this publication as their holy scriptures—insisting we accept their self-assigned, self-justifying, hallowed, and immutable self-serving sacred proclamations.

Arrogantly doing so with axioms and theories examined by committees, voted on officially or through self-serving literature ... rather than enforcing the application of the full scientific method, which they cannot effectively undertake at this early period of their evolution.

Nevertheless ... because we let them ... psychology and psychiatry continue to deliberately add new chapters to the socially sanctioned 'Immaculate Perception' of America and elsewhere ... all the while refining their quasi-unquestionable 'bible' ... their proprietary dogmatic belief system ...

... and thereby imitating the style and broad managerial objectives of Council of Nancaea of 325 and others that followed afterward.

Accredited, as they thus are, ... and based on their 'sacred' texts ... their operational manual of saintly interpretations if you prefer ...

... they can officially render judgment on your state of mind ... and label you psychologically unfit with what they consider sacred pronouncements.

Therefore, you can effortlessly become a non-person, if they choose to brand you a neurotic or schizophrenic or psychotic, ... whether you are or not, ... and that regardless of anything else ...

these categories should be part of our human ethical rationaliza-
tion project."

Antoine paused for a while, went to get a drink of water, and continued his exposé.

"Then it is fair to conclude that; Ronald D. Laing would still be
painfully ashamed of the catechism of our contemporary psychi-
atry and psychology.

***

I also dare advance the notion that the "missa solemnis" of 'po-
litical correctitude' found in the rituals of self-centered yuppies,
and the modus operandi of dying governments found in predatory
tax collection processes, are, both, procedural approaches lead-
ing to coercion and violence as well as shortsighted but eventu-
ally otherwise intelligent forms of surreptitiously applied barba-
rism.

My overriding thought on this subject Isabelle can be summed up
as follows:

> *Dare attempt to express a free thought, or simply ob-*
> *ject to things outside the parameters of 'political cor-*
> *rectitude', and you will unceremoniously be branded*
> *an out of control artist, or a racist, or a misogynist, or*
> *a liberal in a US Republican connotation, or an anti-*
> *Semite, or an Islamophobe, or a fascist, or a Marxist,*
> *or a separatist, or a terrorist, and most certainly a*
> *traitor, or otherwise sued or imprisoned for a hate*
> *crime ... and the list goes on."*

Antoine now looked perplexed, removed his glasses, and rubbed
his chin, as if to gain time before summing up his rather negative
assessment of what he had just conveyed.

He then carried on.

"Instead of being proud of the supposed open-mindedness 'political correctitude' allegedly brings, we should be trembling before this fact, as we meticulously worship the punctilious rules of thinking and behavior it represents, ...

... indeed, as we sanctify the correctness of either our personalized or shared social order, ... as we create eclectic liturgies, ... manufacture ersatz theologies, ... and create commands of 'Absolute Obedience' to an unquestionable 'Immaculate Perception', ... we gradually suffocate the freedom valiantly earned since the Renaissance and Enlightenment by our predecessors.

Yes! Both, political correctitude like its primeval parents, Abrahamic religions, insist on punishing anyone, trespassing the taboo against questioning the inherent logic of its manufactured self-righteousness.

Once we intellectually bury ourselves in such a dramatic and admittedly stupid intellectual straitjacket, we demand devoted radical apostles, unethical militants, and willing martyrs to bring 'outsiders', to accept and abide the 'right way' in the understanding, observing, and living of a fabricated purported reality, wherein adherents are morally entitled to coerce others onto that 'right path'.

Ultimately a fascist attitude emerges out of a 'political correctitude' molding a behavior that promotes silence in the face of 'The Unethical', often by shying away from disapproving, or condemning, or passing judgment on dogma promoters including as ultra-conservative politicians or religious extremists for that matter.

Indeed, I'll go so far as saying that once we lose the right to question and criticize entrenched beliefs, ... and the violent acts these potentially or kinetically permit, ... we de facto recognize that totalitarianism is quietly if not openly settling in ... ... often under the cover of an alleged reasonable process of accommodation ...

... and in the Québec case it is clearly demonstrated by a refusal to abide at least by those reasonable recommendations made by the Bouchard-Taylor report to cite one obvious example. And always, I despair when thinking of the stalling techniques of Québec government administrations ... regardless of party, ... when an ethical act of great significance for the future of its community must be done in time and for the right ethical reasons.

Finally, my dear Isabelle we both know that:

> *A democratic process without a total respect of all 'Inalienable Individual Rights' of all citizens at all times is simply a sophisticated form of fascism by another name ... often mild at first but growing over time, if left unchecked.*

And yet in spite of this we allow the demotion of women by indoctrinated Moslems within our mist ... afraid of making these women truly equal in practice to the rest of us ...... and this for fear of being accused of intolerance of religion, which is in fact a set of truly idiotic dogmatic belief systems, ...

... while we should be keenly aware that such obligation comes directly from edicts and diktats of misogynist imposition by clearly narrow-minded men and the intolerant indoctrination by religious groups ...

... we should be ashamed of ourselves for covering our cowardice with the new cultural excuse of political correctitude, in this regard as well as in others".

After smiling ironically Antoine added further:

"This reminds me, as an aside comment, on the 'politically correct' language, which I'm sure also applies elsewhere.

The purpose of a 'politically correct' language is to ensure we water down real events and situations so that they do not offend our ingrained sensibilities, while also minimizing our notions of responsibility and accountability.

That is why:

> *We in Québec say 'aggressions sexuelles' instead of 'brutal rapes' to tone down the emotional content these represent for a victim, while minimizing the criminal content and the barbaric context for the perpetrator ... nearly always a man ... another fascist leaning I suppose".*

After being silent for quite a while, Antoine made one final point – in an attempt to somehow forecast the ultimate consequences caused by that widespread quasi-analphabetism of far too many unilingual French-Canadians—in great part young males in a 21ˢᵗ century context.

"Look Isabelle, I think our schools – like many others elsewhere – are both ineffective and inefficient in providing a taste and an urge for a basic education ...

... and fail to prepare our children to face and handle life as it really is, ... in our quickly changing ever-advancing society ...

... especially now that we must contend with a highly competitive digitized environment ... in a highly competitive digitized global world!" Repeated Antoine.

"Anyway, the future is quickly catching up with us.

To begin with, ... for the last few years the internet triggered the ongoing destruction of all traditional educational systems as we know them presently ... and this whether we stubbornly choose to deny or not ...

... and only a handful of the most prestigious learning centers around our planet will in the end survive ... and this only after major adaptations to this reality has been completed... and this most certainly includes Québec.

As far as I can see, knowledge has become and continues to be ever more preeminent in all activities pertinent to this new age since the advent of the internet, ...and that preeminence strongly suggests to me, if not simply announces that...", here

Antoine stopped for a few seconds, as if to weight his words carefully before continuing.

> *"...the present cultural set up and its various promotional programs assigning credits for officially acquired and socially recognized portions of that knowledge, diminish in direct proportion to the use and accumulation of knowledge provided by the internet."*

He, all of a sudden, became silent ... then went on with ...

"Wow! ... That was a mouthful! ... Wasn't it, Isabelle?"

"A bit I'd say!" She added with a smile.

Antoine, encouraged nonetheless by her smile carried on.

"In my view this implies that data, information, and knowledge heretofore provided by a socially established caste of knowledge dealerships and stakeholders – all teaching institutions in fact – has begun to give way mostly against their will ... to a redistribution of data, information, and knowledge as well as move away from several of its present sources, ...

... wherein everything will ultimately be available to all and shared by all ... even when and in spite of desperate attempts to control all by those previously in charge continue to insist on retaining the status quo ... such as school boards and administrative university staff.

In addition to this convenience, access to data, information and knowledge will no longer be subjected to market conditions set by the data, information and knowledge merchants and owners known to us nowadays, ... it is instead gradually becoming a choice made by each individual".

"So, if that is the case, Antoine" interjected Isabelle *"all education departments everywhere must begin to adapt ASAP ... suggesting that those, who do not adapt, will fall behind sooner rather than later ... and ultimately become irrelevant if they do not adapt"*.

"Yes! That's exactly what I am suggesting". Intoned Antoine.

"And that other fear, you did not mention here, is what?" Asked Isabelle.

"You already read me like a book, I see" Antoine retorted.

"Well! The issue in Québec is that roughly 50% of French-speaking French-Canadians within that province suffer from one form of analphabetism or another ...

... that's bloody high for a First World community.

A condition of quasi-analphabetism about people barely able to function in everyday life because of this handicap.

Now ... ... project this reality within our ever-advancing digital world ... and you already see a disaster in the making for that afflicted segment of the population and the society that must support it.

An affliction, as we already agreed last year engineered and caused by the rigidity of the ideology imbedded in the Québec Education department."

"So, the question remains ..." intoned Isabelle, *"What's the solution?"*

"I obviously don't have all the answers," responded Antoine, *"and not an easy task indeed, I admit, ... but it must be done, ... because ...*

... if we keep the present direction based on present results – no matter how we mask them with statistical mumbo jumbo and politically correct ideological jargon in support of the classical view on the dogma of pedagogical applications ... the whole approach can only lead us to disaster ... ... and the end of our community as a valued member of Canada and the world for that matter.

Therefore, the education system must remove itself from its classical model and metamorphose into a totally relevant one, ... one immersed in the full technology and digitization of the moment at each instant of its existence from here on end.

Our classic classroom model must be changed to better integrate our quickly changing world.

I believe we can do it.

That the intelligence is there for this.

The creativity of my people must be released from its preprogrammed shackles – and here I speak of those memes seared in our communal intelligence by our very own French-Canadian staffed Roman Catholic Church from older days ...

... and presently imbedded in the professional class that worked in tandem with it ... ... and which in turn has taken over that way of thinking since the 'révolution tranquille' under a secular mask, and re-labelled it with the secular title of "le modèle Quebecois".

That is, we must eliminate our fears of non-involvement, non-entrepreneurship, non-business, non-financial immersion, and those other cultural urges for insolating ourselves from the world at large; including from our other fellow Canadians.

So, a psychological 'surgical operation' of sort is required and this ASAP.

My gut, common sense, and reason at least tell me to scrap the present education department in its entirety.

Look!

I don't mean to destroy competent, well-functioning and crucial training programs meant to teach and hone mechanical skills such as dentistry, construction skills and so on ...

... Oh no! ... no! no! no!

... What I suggest is that digitization is bound and about to and will eventually eliminate many present-day occupations that can be computerized ...

... and will at least and this to a significant degree alter these and others, ... including the way all other occupations – regardless of their level of sophistication ... presently function.

Here, I also refer to professions such as GPs and pharmacists in the medical field among others ... along with most lawyers ... who most likely and erroneously assume that far less significant jobs compared to theirs would be eliminated first ... especially with their view on all those occupations without extended university training, ... which would be affected by today's ongoing computerization of tasks ... but not theirs of course ... since theirs required intense sophisticated training

*... ... a **crucial error** my friend...*

... all the while ignoring the extraordinary easiness with which the decision-making and action process can be routinized and successfully implemented as imbedded algorithms when their turn comes in the not too distant future precisely because of the

detailed applications of their profession already known and ready for computerization".

"If you're right ... and aside from certain groups of professionals for the moment" interrupted Isabelle, *"...you must gradually re-design – starting right now – a brand new education system, based on today's knowledge access realities, ... with none of the present employees whatsoever now forming existing bureaucracies automatically considered, ... because to keep the present staff at any level, ... would be tantamount to retard ... and at worse ... try to eradicate the metamorphosis, which must and will inevitably take place ...*

... otherwise, the reintroduction of the present **'ideology of a sacred untouchable pedagogy'** *on top of the heavy bureaucratic machinery of which it is an integral part ... will trump all in obvious and surreptitious ways and means, ...*

... and would continue under a camouflage of alleged changes or superficial ones, which would nevertheless inevitably lead to an educational disaster with dangerous repercussions within your society.

Indeed, without a sound education based on today's quickly changing realities" Isabelle added further, *"Québec will not survive as a distinctively well-functioning community – just like any other maladapted community for that matter.*

In fact, I would add that:

> *All other inefficiencies and ineffectiveness presently augmenting the costs of running your Québec society will dangerously worsen much sooner, ... if you do not completely reinvent your educational system from scratch".*

Here Antoine made a confirming assumption on what she had just said.

"That is why then, I presume:

> *We must stop our race to irrelevance dead in its track, as we speed up toward our self-made social insignificance, ... because many more victims will suffer in the short life allotted us by the incomprehensible system that created us all, ... and that would be a terrible shame ... since we each have only one crack at this precious life of ours.*

Nevertheless, I firmly believe that we in Québec, have the capacity and the communal intelligence to efficiently and effectively revised our entire educational system, ...

... but only once we collectively make up our mind ... instead of building castles in the sky, as the saying goes ... and that gives me hope" Antoine finally concluded.

Antoine, however, abruptly looked gloomy, soon after expressing his enthusiasm for a future activated by future-oriented Quebecers.

"Nevertheless, and unless we do something drastic, the vast education establishment and its bureaucratic machine will continue to feed themselves on the inefficiencies and ineffectiveness of its membership, ... and will go on growing ever fatter as time goes by, until the whole institution ultimately collapses under its own weight, I fear.

***

"Oh shit! ... I hope we do not pander to religious groups as special exceptions ... because we will otherwise continue to create second rate citizens for those trapped with their dogmatic shackles in a world that demands first class openminded people – nothing less.

That is ... in philosophical terms ... we must reverse the very foundation of our national attitude reflected in our societal decisions and acts, into one reflecting open-mindedness on all fronts.

This demands that we no longer include the opinions of and objections from stakeholders and owners of dogmatic belief systems of which religions easily and obsessively appear the most obvious and the most destructive.

As for the engineering of a brand-new educational system I cannot pretend to be an expert because I am not, ... but this fact does not preclude that what I perceive is not there.

Anyway, aside for this anomaly, if we make up our mind on time, the future can be very bright for us all".

"By the way Antoine' Isabelle suddenly intervened with raised eyebrows.

"Why does your provincial government regardless of parties make it so difficult and often nearly impossible for already trained and qualified immigrants to work in their field of expertise?"

And without giving time for Antoine to respond she at once followed with.

"You're the worst in this area as far as I can recall in the Western world ... in the Western world I repeat, ...Why? Why? Why? ... I ask you".

Antoine thought about it for a short while and proposed.

"I supposed that each profession and other expert groups acting within an enclosed silo organization does not want to allow immigrants within their ranks, ... or at least postpones that decision

as long as possible ... and by default I must admit that such behavior reflects the intention of such groups to scrupulously insist that Quebecers ought to remain in their traditional social cocoons, rather than promote their community into 21st century realities.

With legislation to eliminate corporative biases, the process of exclusivity will nevertheless continue to exist – although admittedly to a lesser degree".

Temporarily Hovering Over a Fragment of Discussion 38.
Must Be Run as a Holding Corporation

Isabelle started the discussion this time.

"Ok! I'm a lawyer, ... but I nonetheless worked for years as a corporate one in a large organization, ... and I dare say that ... I understand the ins and outs of a corporation's absolute requirements for the continued rationalization of its operations.

It's a most basic application among others of corporate survival, where investments must provide a continuing return on investment.

That is the reason d'être of any profitable organization ... the zero-sum game being the lowest possible common denominator in the case of a non-profit one.

And since the Québec Transport department meets all the major attributes of a construction holding business, it goes without saying that ... ... it ought to be run and managed as a sound business corporation with all the conditions, situations, benefits, and consequences this implies.

Otherwise, you end up with what you keep on referring to as 'magouille' ... something that is obviously widespread in all public works everywhere on the planet ... wouldn't you say so, ... hey Antoine?

This department should therefore be constituted as an independent holding corporation with all of the freedoms and restrictions this implies with all various independent companies it ought to create and list on the Dow-Jones, where their performance could and would be easily observed, ... and assessed by active and potential shareholders and not just one untouchable owner.

This solution of course applies to all Transport Departments eve-rywhere ... not just Québec ... so, what I am saying in other words is this:

> *The actual construction business branch of a Transport Department should be separated from it and reconstituted as construction businesses on the stock market independent of interference from that de-partment with the condition that it is owned by many shareholders with the governmental share being no more than 49.9% ... and managed by 'top guns' from the private sector under the control of the minister of Transport and a renewed staff ...*

...and wherein only thoroughly vetted contracts with the approval of two separate accounting firms ... should be approved within a Transport department ... and this ... never by the same account-ing firms for a given construction company ...

*... and all contracts awarded ought to have been subjected to worldwide competition ... Yea! **A worldwide competition** ... in-cluding its own separate companies forming the construction arm of a new thoroughly reorganized, ... and fully rationalized Transport department ...*

*... because **<u>only</u>** when worldwide competitors can bid on given projects will the bidding process clean itself out".*

Temporarily Hovering Over a Fragment of Discussion 39.
Mitigating a Financially Destructive Impact

Antoine smiled at the much-anticipated taste experience Isabelle had promised him about what she called her special hot chocolate recipe, as she walked into the living room with a large tray on which he could already see two large mugs and a plate of their favorite fresh baked big blueberry muffins.

After a good twenty minutes of quiet enjoyment, while they once more appreciated the view from their large living room window, they turned to face each other.

Isabelle then triggered the start of their conversation that leisurely afternoon.

"I think it's your turn to try to articulate a solution to one of Québec's most serious impediment for its financial health ... Isn't it?"

"OK!" Antoine responded, ... and after a few minutes or so began.

"I think we ought to see what can be done with a labor union movement that is seriously damaging and continuing to worsen Québec's financial stability and viability as it continues to resist performance improvements, enhanced technological advancements, and managerial enhancements.

The labor movement has become a solidly implanted rigid institution that acquired extraordinary powers and privileges in the early stages of the 'révolution traquille', which it now interprets and believes to be eternally correct and forever theirs ... and therefore remains unaffected in its view by a dynamic world economy and social changes now evolving at warp speed ... along with the present on going globalization of everything as well as the accelerating application of AI and robotization in all fields possible.

... a movement I say ... seemingly removed from what is happening here and everywhere else ... as if immune from all this because of the purported purity of their ideology and the contained provinciality of their movement.

A movement still in the throes of its self-assigned self-designated heroic role as a once rightful crusader for the so-called 'little people' against 'big business'.

A crusader now at a time and place when such a need no longer exists ... and ... when industrial barons no longer pay starving wages or set desperate working conditions for workers.

Labor unions purposely continue to ignore the symptoms and overt signs of Québec's diminishing sources of revenues, waning manufacturing industries, the financial abyss of ever-increasing debts, and an ingrained robotized limited performance in terms of efficiencies and effectiveness of bureaucracies, locked-in establishments, and workers therein represented by these labor unions.

While the labor movement now operates in a society where 'Inalienable Individual Rights' exist as an everyday reality in a context of a liberalized community ruled by decent laws along with, multiple protections for citizens of various kinds, they now nevertheless behave still as crusaders this time against fictional enemies.

The labor movement must finally recognize that there is a willingness and a direct involvement by private companies to adapt to an economic global participation ...

... and that this will gradually leave the labor establishment only with captive clients such as government ministries, departments, and agencies along with municipalities ...

... a captive local economy that cannot be transferred such as local firefighters, police forces, hospital staff and so on ... therefore with people removed to some degree from the effects of the world economy ... physically removed that is ... yes ... but still connected to the rest as digitization of everything continues nonetheless its devastating effects.

As for the rest, ... the moveable jobs ... accelerated developments of technology, ... instant financial transfers and investments contribute to the movement of hundreds of millions of jobs along with massive workloads, ... whenever and wherever the quality of work and the labor costs can be maintained or better yet improved upon elsewhere.

Québec has not been immune to that fact and hundreds of thousands of jobs have already disappeared from the province; ... with an ongoing transfer of jobs that continues to hurt us financially; ...

... and this province will be severely affected in the future to the point of endangering its financial solvency ...

... and yet labor unions are still functioning as if they were still operating in the Fifties and early Sixties.

That being the case then, I state that the labor movement in Québec, as presently constituted, has become not only irrelevant but financially dangerous if not simply ruinous to the economy.

Let's face it, Isabelle, signals of an overall economic transformation started decades ago, but which became obvious for us all to see, when the Chinese began their extraordinary metamorphosis into the biggest manufacturing nation on earth ... ...has been a fact among others totally ignored by the labor movement here, ...

... and this although factory after factory kept closing, ... moving to China and later on to Mexico and various South-American and Asian countries.

Labor unions went on nevertheless demanding and obtaining strings of salary increases and working conditions our factories could not afford, if they were to survive financially ...

...and let's be clear here ...

... I'm not talking about the brutal capitalism of heartless business owners, ... but those willing to stay ... but no longer able to survive within the Québec economy".

Here Isabelle added.

"And this includes I suppose ... now that I come to think of it ... those companies that simply moved mainly to Ontario or occasionally elsewhere in Canada, because of both union demands as well as real or anticipated heavy rapacious provincial taxation schemes and other nonsense put together by various Québec administrations regardless of party since the 'révolution tranquille'.

She then got up suddenly to get a bottle of cold water and continued as if there had been no interruption in her presentation.

" ... such as your provincial government's insistence that worldwide or Canada-wide corporations conduct their business in French ... despite the fact that the language of business in North-America especially and internationally is English ... a political process superciliously established with a language police to boot ... trying to force business into this both arrogant and self-defeating objective ... and in this situation my friend the unions are not helping their cause either."

Abruptly, as an aside comment, as if to reinforce Isabelle's presentation Antoine added.

"That reminds me.

Do you also recall the extraordinary '23hours-59minutes" efforts made by the Québec government of the day, when corporate giants such as Sun Life and BMO, each in turn for example and among many others, decided they had enough, and moved everything in practice to Toronto ... or when CPR moved its entire headquarters to Calgary for the same reasons ... and then later when the Montreal Stock Exchange was incorporated into the Toronto Stock Exchange.

In each case, the labor unions paid lip service to the situation ... and did not alter by one iota their money grabbing tactics ... ignoring each time the signals sent to everyone else by such departures—and this on top of the arrogant enforcement of French as if the language of international business and operations. It was as if both the provincial government and labor unions existed in some alternative reality".

After Antoine's comments Isabelle moved to another labor issue but not before remaining silent for a few minutes of reflection once more.

"Québec's labor unions possess a legal foundation that makes it easy to force employees to join and pay dues to this now massive and imperative bureaucracy beyond a ridiculously low set of legal conditions to oblige willing and unwilling workers alike into its ranks ... at the cost of losing their job for all those refusing ... and beholden in addition to continually pay for that 'privilege'...

... and this while union members or anybody else for that matter cannot examine and analyze what's being done with all the massive revenues labor unions collect from workers ... or analyze expenses incurred by these organizations".

Now looking at Antoine with that penetrating look of hers, she went on.

"The world of brutal business and mean administrations that characterized manufacturing, mining, and others in the first half of the 20th century and before that time, no longer exists in Québec ... and pretending that it does is dishonest.

Not only that, ... while factory after factory moved out of Québec, as well as large corporations fed up with your pettiness toward the world of business, ... the labor movement concentrated its efforts with captive occupations instead – especially governmental and municipal jobs.

Occupations that could not by definition and in fact be anywhere else other than local.

Here I mean all provincial and municipal bureaucrats, police forces, fire fighters, construction workers, provincial, and municipal blue color workers, and so on.

It is with these captive clients they get their biggest source of revenues ... and this against the financial health of both levels of governance.

And let us not forget again the sheer lack of negotiating skills on the part of government delegates along with agenda-driven conciliators at all levels favoring the union movement of the last five decades.

Both contributed enormously at the over-the-top costs of all provincial and municipal services in Québec.

Sadly, and despite everything taking place with job movements, job elimination, job transformation, brand new high-tech occupations, and so on, the arrogance of unions for some insane reasons got worse".

"Alright! Alright! Isabelle ... and your solution is?" Interjected Antoine after her short monologue.

Scratching her head Isabelle thought about it a bit, although it was clear with her quick response that she'd made up her mind years before.

"In most cases labor unions should and must be abolished ... ... because they represent another historical time and place in the evolution of societies ...

... a time and place when and where they were necessary and within which they accomplished much ... generally raising salaries, working conditions and benefits to an acceptable level, ...

... and in view of our presently evolved society we must at once revoke the right to strike for <u>all crucial services</u> at least such as hospitals, health clinics, nursing home, surgery theatres, fire-fighting, and police forces.

Yes, my friend, decent working conditions, benefits, and salaries have long ago been reached for all government employees and large municipalities in Québec ... in fact going well beyond average working conditions, salaries, and benefits for comparable jobs everywhere else in the rest of the business world ...

... and these I insist, are superior to the rest of the working classes in regular corporations – big and small – that earn less while still living comfortably – especially when compared to most of the nations of the world – including the USA".

"As far as you are concerned aside what you already proposed ... what must now be the process with unions in Québec?" Inquired Antoine.

"First, you must completely de-unionize the public service beginning at once starting with managerial and supervisory jobs ASAP and on with the rest after that.

Secondly, you ought to ensure that only meritorious appointments and promotions reign supreme ... otherwise the sacred cow of seniority will rule, and incompetence will set in again, ...

Thirdly, by retraining and retooling vetted unskilled employees to avoid any future lack of skilled workers ... along with an un-negotiable clause against nepotism regardless of logic proposed.

Once these steps are implemented than a reset of your economy can continue, since efficiency and effectiveness can only exist in a world wherein the aim of an organization predominates on a basis of meritocracy ...

... and wherein, as in the Québec case, we are not living in some underdeveloped society but in an advanced, liberalized, and privileged community already enjoying all the safeguards of freedom for all ...

*... then all the more reasons to do without now **parasitic bureaucratic organizations** such as no-longer-required labor unions bleeding hard-earned provincial revenues ".*

Temporarily Hovering Over a Fragment of Discussion 40.
Project Management and Business Acumen

Isabelle was on an intellectual warpath again.

"Separatist-minded Quebecers could not even intelligently manage their way out of Canada, when the odds favored them decades ago… so enamored with the 'Laurentien' dream drummed into their psyche by that xenophobe, Jew hater, general ass hole cleric, chanoine Lionel Groulx, …

… they never paid the least attention to all the logic necessary to legally take over the very territory they claim as eternally theirs …

… as if an absolute and unquestionable truth …

… when in fact it was and continues to be also occupied by a significant group of people most unlikely to agree with their proposition, … because of the natural sense of intense insecurity it created …

… I of course mean most Anglos, new immigrants, and Aboriginals … … unless they make an effort to explain their reasons and real intentions to them first …

… in other words, unless they become transparent in their dealings with these groups instead of hiding behind some highfaluting rhetoric difficult to interpret.

On the contrary, they continue to scare many of them away … … and go on with this tactic against those remaining and in surreptitious ways create more anxiety for them … making them feel as if they could no longer expect a decent and safe future for themselves …and especially for their children".

As if to highlight a first basic tactic in a new direction to be undertaken, Isabelle then suggested the following as questions:

"What are you waiting for, ... I mean you, voting French-Canadians in Québec, ... to naturally keep within your province and your economy all citizens within your province into your social fold?

I refer to Québec graduates from English-speaking universities, ... people who must go outside the province to make a life for themselves, ... because they don't feel comfortable ... ... and take for granted that a career in Québec is not to their advantage?

You do nothing ... and yet you invest tens of millions each year for their education ... I tell you this is an insane way of planning a decent, workable, and ethical society!

By the way, now this comes to mind.

Why are there so few – to the point of non-representation – employees whose mother tongue is English within the Québec government offices ... although they represent a significant minority?

Why do you discourage them in fact ... or at least ignore them ... from sharing their aspirations and life with the rest of you, ... <u>as if they do not matter to your society</u> ... <u>as if they did not belong</u> ...?

... are you just stupidly pretending you can do without them?

Why indeed do you act, as if they did not live side by side with you ... and ought to not become an integral part of the citizenry of your province not just legally, which they are but, in your mindset, and culture as well?

Why pretend they do not contribute in fact to the largest part of your revenues in both absolute and relative terms?

Why intellectually exclude this significant group from our economic planning, just because they generally tend to be federalist – politically speaking – <u>and this because you offer them no other choice</u>?

Why have let over 600,000 English-speaking taxpayers leave Québec in the last thirty years or so, because of this lousy ill-planned attitude of yours?

Why encourage this enormous economic hemorrhage by doing next to nothing to prevent it?

Why get rid of this enormous brainpower that could have given you much support and guidance in many respects on your difficult ascent in acquiring that sense of entrepreneurship and business finesse, ... which you so much needed and still require?

Why indeed I ask you Antoine, if not for ideological purposes ... with the coarse intent of chasing out of the province as many Anglos as possible?

Thereby leaving a greater pool of French-Canadians in relative terms ... and supposedly and illusorily manage just as well if not better without the cooperative support of Anglos ...

... and this in accordance with that so much over praised new 'modèle Québécois avec des valeurs Québécoises' as you guys keep on saying.

The answer obviously for many is because of a narrow minded navel-gazing ideology proposing that:

> *Québec belongs, regardless of consequences, to French-speaking French-Canadians of vieilles souches origin first, and then to the rest of French-speaking Quebecers – Anglos being last on your list, if at all.*

A notion not clearly mentioned in your 'politically correct' atmosphere by nationalist-minded political parties, but there nonetheless since the beginning of the 'révolution tranquille' to this day".

Now Isabelle after this string of pertinent but loaded questions and statements, and now wanting to get back to her opinion on project and program management, returned to her previous argument.

"As a group, those managing projects and programs as well as those engineering and building work schedules and systems requested, so essential to the functioning of an effective and efficient organization, ... first tend to over-think ... and generally don't deliver on time, and as it should, ... what was initially agreed to and contracted for.

*Planners within the government must refrain from dreaming in colors, ... get down to earth, ... and once having thoroughly laid down their **real** needs in all possible details, ... then look for the best people to get it done on time and as requested.*

To do this they must first look around to find out if their proposal has already been undertaken with success by someone else on the planet ...

... and if so, ... whether it would be advisable and economical to benchmark it ... and this <u>regardless of origin</u>.

With such an approach, no more money is likely to be wasted by involving incompetent government-based directors, managers, engineers, systems analysts and so on, for vetted projects and programs already developed elsewhere".

Secondly, if a project cannot be benchmarked ... than a search for the best on our planet must be undertaken to get it done ... and all efforts must be exercised to get the best group available and equally able to carry it out.

If such a group is Québec-based all the better for the province, ... if not then all the better for Quebec's future and maturing entrepreneurs to learn from outsiders.

Then Isabelle got up to draw a classic organizational map of sort on that white working board they both used from time to time during their discussions. A board they kept hidden most of the time in their rather large mud room in the back entrance.

Once she finished her map, she then turned toward Antoine and said:

"Here is my pet peeve with governmental organizations anywhere ... a subject all government organizations never want to hear ... and abide by ... and if obligated to consider ... simply it pays lip service to ... rarely acting on real improvements ...

... and that subject my dear Antoine, as you already guessed as an ex-human resource professional, is a flat organization with functional transparent connections to all stakeholders ... wherein lateral connections encourage silo-breaking and where hierarchical authority is flatten to no more than three levels if at all possible.

An organizational chart in each case that must consider today's ever accelerating communications nodes, devices at the disposal of all, the digitization of just about everything – especially systems applications, and so on.

This implies the robotization of an ever-increasing number of tasks and jobs, which by default already demands the elimination of most 'secretaries' and so-called 'personal assistant', various other so-called 'assistant' and 'assistant to' by these or any other highfalutin title allegedly created to facilitate the works of those already in charge of a specific group regardless of level ... ... because ...

> *... 'assistants' whatever the kind and title only underscore the inability if not the shear incompetence of the person in charge of a given project, program, department, area, region and so on.*

And by implementing this first and most basic rationalization – a rather simple job – you will save a good quarter of salaries and benefit expenses without affecting efficiencies and effectiveness ... ... on the contrary it would likely reduce unnecessary coordination meetings and eliminate silo comportment by underlings.

This is made all the easier nowadays with all the technological support provided with the digitization of just about everything ... and in the case of critical reports the head of a team can easily do it and immediately send it to his superior and other stakeholders if necessary ...

... no intermediary personnel is required with such things, for example, as, say, with the help the now ubiquitous Microsoft Office along with internet ... available in the cloud on all sorts of digital equipment, devices, and applications.

Flat organization also eliminates the creation of jobs meant for political party hacks, friends, and family members and so on, because an overblown organization cannot with this incumbrance bring efficiency and effectiveness to a mission-oriented group ...

"... and when more people than necessarily are purportedly needed to do a good job, than the whole project slows down and becomes costlier ... more adjustment meetings are required ... more steering committees are needed ... and so on.

More micro silos are then created ... because everyone creates little empire regardless of size ... and generally everyone wants to enlarge the group one is responsible and accountable for eventually ... thereby artificially and psychologically augmenting one's self-importance in the process.

That's a classic organizational characteristic of government departments and related establishments and administrative arms, I say".

"So, what you're saying, to make it short and sweet, is cut the fat ASAP as you would in private business". Summed up Antoine.

"Yea! That's right … do so immediately!" Answered Isabelle.

"You must run all departments and especially service centers like you would, if you owned them, … as if it were your own money at stake, …

… and unless you do that … you'll never get out of the financial hole you're in … and this is especially true for Québec. Period". She said in concluding her argument.

"… and before I shut up my dear Antoine, … let us remember that none of this can take place unless Québec's education department impregnates its entire educational system with a true spirit of entrepreneurship … and this to a level wherein Québec can compete with the best in North America and the rest of the world – nothing less".

And then all of a sudden, she said:

"Hey, maybe with François Legault, a businessman, now at the helm of the province … your chances might have increased … who knows"?

Temporarily Hovering Over a Fragment of Discussion 41.
Provincial and Montréal Police Forces

"Antoine, did you hear about the provincial police constables' routine rapes of aboriginal girls and women in Val D'Or, Schefferville and other areas controlled by the Québec's provincial police force – that so-called 'Sûreté du Québec'?" Asked Isabelle.

Antoine's face suddenly showed revulsion.

"Yes, I did, ... and it makes me sick ...

... it's the behavior of a fascist police force ... this time exercising its self-assigned prerogative against a vulnerable segment of the population ...

... and if the actions to correct this are merely political papering over for public relations purposes ... than I think that it will surreptitiously and not so covertly legitimize it taking root elsewhere without a doubt ... ... that is how, after all, seeds of totalitarianism start ... ... by excusing criminal behavior ... ... or pretending it does not exist ... ... or doing nothing to prevent it ... ... until it's too late.

I admit to you Isabelle that my instincts tell me that not only has this practice existed, exists right now, and will continue to exist in the ranks of that organization, but that it is a practice in all police forces everywhere, whenever they can get away with it ... ... history throughout the planet is witness to this reality ... and this for two reasons in my view.

First, a police force in great part and just about anywhere attracts far too many of those in need of feeling superior to others – often those with a profound sense of inferiority eager to demonstrate an image of their self-importance to fellow workers, and especially over private citizens. I presume it is caused by a form of psychological and social immaturity or other ... and let us not forget what the assignment of authority and power over others vested in them legally does to such a personality... ... it all too often leads to a psychopathic profile of one kind or another ... never admitted by those in the know of course.

Second, police forces generally see themselves as more important than other citizens – except of course those who could do them harm such as politicians, judges, lawyers ... oh yes ... and motorcycle gangs or mafia types ... ... in these cases, they almost shit in their pants ... making sure they don't overstep their authority ... and are generally most lenient, when accidentally dealing with them ... ... as for the rest, it's a free for all ... because they know the system will protect them in nearly all cases and not the citizens brutally attacked ... ... either by agents of their department, prosecuting attorneys (always looking for a judgeship), politicians (especially when close to an election,) and the so-called blue wall of theirs.

That is why; their unethical evaluation of a crime committed against a police officer in the line of duty, for example, in their mind consists of a crime of higher priority and significance .... almost one of 'lèse majesté' ... a crime above all others ... and that extra efforts in such a case are spent and coordinated to find a culprit ... efforts that <u>would not be spent</u> on crimes committed on regular 'civilians' ... as we are often referred to by police forces.

In fact, I have nearly always considered police departments as semi-fascist ... like seeds waiting for the right environment to emerge ... on the verge of expressing their fascist tendency".

"Aren't you exaggerating Antoine?" Interrupted Isabelle.

"No! I am not". Shouted Antoine at once.

"Ok! Ok! Let's see what else you have to say". Isabelle retorted with some surprise in her voice at Antoine raised tone.

"Just recall our contemporary history ... and examples of police brutality will jump at you .... and in this case, I suggest that Québec is no different than all others.

The first that comes to mind is the gendarmerie de Paris, which cooperated in the arrest and delivery of tens of thousands of Parisians designated as Jews by the Nazis, thereby serving as a conveyor belt, so to speak, feeding the ovens at Auschwitz and elsewhere ... insanely or malevolently doing so with some professional pride, ... because they met the schedules and quotas assigned to them. Somewhat like that psychopath, Adolph Eichmann.

The second ... let me think a bit ... oh yea ... is the traditional attitude of police forces around the planet from the best to the worst, ... which is an attitude from mild to the worst psychopathic behavior ... ... that these jobs tend to attract people with a self-righteous attitude leading in too many cases of abuse of the power delegated to them ... especially when cultural biases are imbedded in a given society ...ask those with a darker skin color how they feel in North-America for instances about police behavior.

Look! There are many cases that could be cited ... but let me add a couple personal ones of mine within Québec.

Let see! ... ... oh yea! ... ... I remember most clearly as a youth in my neighborhood, those members of the local municipal police in the St-Henri area of the Forties and Fifties in south-west Montréal, who routinely raped sex workers from Workman Street where I grew up as well as those in the environs ... it was considered fringe benefits that came in with the job ... mostly in the form of blowjobs.

A fact known to most of us in these neighborhoods, which is why no one ever complained, for fear of reprisals from that group of criminals with a gun, a stick, and a badge ... ready to terrorize you ... and whom we knew would in turn be protected by the authorities.

As teenagers, we avoided them like the plague, because once they zeroed in on you for whatever reason, you ended up guilty of whatever they said you did ... and paid for it dearly.

If you insisted on your innocence ... they simply beat you up or assaulted you in various ways ... in the end those arrested confessed, just to end their fears or beatings.

No one spoke of this reality, which quasi-dictator Maurice Duplessis protected and the Roman Catholic Church almost blessed as its enforcing agents.

So, no!

I am not surprised at criminal police behavior in the case of rapes of these easily victimized Val D'or, Schefferville and other areas controlled by the Québec's provincial police force against Aboriginal girls and women for all the reasons you know, ... and for which these females are all too often subjected to in the world at large and even at home ... and this even if it is never proven in court ... ... because the odds are stacked against native women ... not only here but in the rest of Canada". Antoine finally said as he ended his categorical monologue.

''And the solution is....?'' Isabelle asked as she opened her eyes larger than usual.

Antoine then went on. *"In a real ethical liberalized democracy, wherein 'Inalienable Individual Rights' reign supreme, because police officers – whatever the rank – are sworn to act on behalf of the State that authorizes them to ensure all uphold the laws of the land, ... then such officers, ... if found guilty of a crime ... or misdemeanor ...while on official duty, ... should be subjected to a fine ... or a prison sentence ...* **at least twice** <u>the one allowed by</u> <u>the laws of the land,</u> *...* <u>because of the extraordinary privilege</u> <u>and license accorded them.</u>

Otherwise police forces everywhere will slowly for most and much faster for others become more oppressive – as can be seen in the militarization of police forces around the planet at the moment ... a process for example that first became evident with SWAT teams followed by tank-like military vehicles, materials, and other equipment".

"Is there hope at all with views like these?" Asked Isabelle.

Antoine reflected in silence for a few seconds and came out with following:

"At the most basic entry level each constable should possess at least a bachelor's degree in humanities or sociology or psychology on top of a police academy diploma—nothing less ... ... and be rigorously tested psychologically for biased attitude and comportment ...

...and above all, the macho arrogance, conceit, and self-awarded sense of superiority, generally brought about by a government-

warranted license to inflict violence on real and perceived recalcitrant individuals including death, if necessary, ... should excluded...

... this demands someone able to handle conflicts with a human approach about exhibited emotions, tantrums, and aggressiveness found in localized human conflicts and situations." Antoine finally concluded.

Temporarily Hovering Over a Fragment of Discussion 42.
Police Forces in Québec, Canada and the USA

"While we were on the subject of police behavior yesterday, I should have pushed our discussion further," Isabelle said, *"about this nasty habit by police forces everywhere in the USA and Canada to systematically zero in on people with a darker complexion ... as if programmed within their training specifically or at least as if reflecting the 'White population's propensity to think that way".*

'Yea! ... let me think!" Antoine responded.

"OK! ... In the capitalist system now running the world, those in charge, those with the most money, resources, and authority, must see to it that their wealth and power are protected ...

... so, the capitalist system demands by definition and in fact and therefore by default, total security from uncertainty as much as possible including possible if not eventual rebellion by the 'have-nots' and or the 'have-less', ...

... so behavioral algorithms have to be naturally and routinely implemented and activated.

On the north-American continent this implies in a disproportion-ate way, what we usually refer to as 'White power', that that pref-erably English-speaking 'White men' of European origins are, if at all possible, elected or appointed to all important posts, ... or at least 'White women' acting as if they were 'White men'.

Anyway, such persons then see to it that, police forces representing their meanings, values, and standards are constituted to protect them from the rest of potential if not active political opponents from outside the so-called 'White population'...

... although, ironically, a significant part of the 'White middle class population' are now becoming ever more desperate at their very own economic situation and beginning to form part of those who might be considered enemies of the ones in charge.

Anyway, in the context of capitalist system on our continent the police institution is constituted to protect and serve the 'White population', their authority, resources, and properties ... and this my friend requires and at times if not often demands violence.

In the meantime in order to cage potential enemies in into psychological, social, and physical ghettoes, 'non-Whites' are devaluated as human beings, citizens, and competitors, ... and generally harassed by police forces throughout North-America in our geographical case ...

... especially those with a marked darker complexion ...

... as well as those from groups producing, so to speak, religious psychopath such as Islam, proud of their murderous ways for what is to most, vaporous purposes that can only exist in deep states of insanity.

It also includes those bent on proclaiming ancient tribal territories in spite of losing these to immoral but nonetheless far more powerful invaders, Europeans in our case, ... here of course I speak of our multiple Aboriginal nations.

Temporarily Hovering Over a Fragment of Discussion 43.
Police Forces Definancing

On the third succeeding day discussing immoral and at times psychopathic police behavior Antoine spoke first that afternoon.

"I would say that no reform will succeed in transforming immoral and at times psychopathic police behavior ... ... because such things as proposed body cameras, and sensibilization on systemic biases and social prejudices along with the recruitment of people from so-called minority groups ... can only provide partial corrections at best, ... since imbedded biased beliefs are nearly impossible to dislodge, once inculcated in someone early in life ... as proven by our recent history, say, ... in the last two hundred years or so.

*Chocking police forces' growth and especially its ongoing militarization through significant budget reductions is the most powerful political and economic tool we have ... **but only if** and we redistribute every penny to vetted endeavors truly meant for the 'épanouissement' of repressed minorities ... and this toward the improvement of our own society wherever we are located.*

That is why, at last, the notion of de-financing police forces and reallocating these funds to the interests and benefits of on-the-ground programs truly favoring and encouraging everyone's security is productive, reduces violence, and promotes ethical behavior.

Indeed, this is absolutely required, simply because police reforms otherwise do not work, ... and we ought to realize at last that:

> *Far from being an aberration ... police violence is the normalized routine behavior of an average cop regardless of position, type, or rank ...*

... history proves this point over and over again.

The mythology sold to us that police forces are there to protect you applies only if you are those selected ones for which these work for ...

... if in doubt, simply think of disappeared in Latin America ... or murdered Aboriginal women in Canada and the USA ... or ask yourself why the majority of prison population in Canada is made up of Aboriginal people especially in on the Prairies ... ... and this in spite of their rather small number when compared the total Canadian population.

Evidence of the racist attitude of our police forces has been around since the beginnings of Canada ... and indeed, accusations of law infringements in this domain began with them ... as they did so on our behalf for many among us.

Although we cannot be proud of our police forces, it is far worse in the USA where laws made by the 'White establishment' is all too often openly used to target rather that protect 'Blacks' especially, and get them out of the way into prisons often for minor things such as marijuana possession ... as long as they're locked up somewhere ...

... and we continue as well to see police harassing people of color, as we love to say, as they routinely go to work, buy a burger, go to an ITM machine, or simply fall victimized to some psychological event they find difficult to control, etc., ... all excuses are good for a cop to harass these people, and when the opportunity presents itself to simply assassinate them.

Yes, my friend! Imagine what the billions of dollars now spent on repressive measures from police forces could and would provide if spent on social programs meant to improve society instead of harassing targeted citizens.

Temporarily Hovering Over a Fragment of Discussion 44.

Health and Welfare Services: The Aged and The Sick - 1

"To select the most recent thing, which jumps at me right now Antoine, is the way your provincially administered nursing homes operate and the intellectual gymnastic they go through to explain operational mishaps.

What bothers me the most in fact is the way these centers ... and this ... whether they admit it or not ... treat those most vulnerable older citizens ... ... as if leftover debris of recent history, ... seen as no longer of use to present day society, ... considered a burden, ... and all too often thought by some as about ready for the garbage heap.

The easiest and most obvious example of this, is the way Québec treats those no longer able to have normal bodily functions, ... left in diapers full of urine and shit, ... just because it is not filled up to capacity, ... or now that I think of it ... serving them unappealing meals to boot, if not simply disgusting ones a good part of the time ...

... your well paid dieticians are more concern about the appearance of good nutrition in their reports than in reality ... their ongoing excuse being budget restrictions and an extraordinary lack of both initiative, creativity, and imagination in the construction and assembly of meals ...as well as a bureaucratic machinery preventing the few good ones from seeking suppliers outside those authorized.

I remember the ubiquitous unappealing steamed fish, served still on Fridays in this ex ultra-Roman Catholic province, covered with a revolting white sauce reminding one of semen with its uneven distribution ... truly unappetizing and unattractive I tell you,

... but let me go out on another tangent for a few seconds here ..." Antoine added "*before I carry on with my overall thoughts on this issue.*

> *When using the unethical logic of my ancient reptilian brain ... and imagining a despotic dystopian world, wherein revenge is the norm, ... I sometime secretly think that ... people contributing to this situation ... whether directly or administratively ... abiding to a notion of 'Absolute Obedience' to the 'Immaculate Perception' of the bureaucracy in place and which they blindly and bureaucratically served ... ought to be subjected to the same conditions for a while as those under their charge ... condemned to a wheelchair 24/7 ... and forced feed those awful overheated and ill-constituted unappetizing meals in some imagined alternate reality.*

I admit to you that this thought keeps jumping at me from time to time, whenever I enter a provincially managed nursing home – a so-called CHSLD or its equivalent in the private sector".

Antoine then dejectedly concluded.

Any way you look at this ... it's a fucking shame indeed ... when it is <u>deliberately</u> committed ... because it is reasoned as politically correct and <u>normal</u> to leave people sitting literally in their urine and shit for hours and on purpose, ... and feed them unappetizing meals ... just like prisoners ... just because their victims cannot fend for themselves anymore ... knowing all along that most have been dumped there just to past the responsibility of purportedly taking care of them to a bureaucracy provided by a Nanny-State government to that effect ... which in order to meet internally rationalized administrative and planned budgetary ob-

jectives ... ignores that <u>they too</u> will end up there ... or find themselves in a worse place if the provincial government—regardless of administration—don't put its act together soon.

A totally unethical approach in the treatment of human beings ... especially those most vulnerable and no longer able to look after and fend for themselves because of age or accidents of life".

Here Isabelle I have nothing to add except feel a profound shame..." quickly confirmed Antoine. *"... although I must also conclude ... and not to excuse Québec here ... that this same logic exists everywhere in cases like these throughout North-America, ... when and where people cannot fend for themselves ... either to increase profit margins or simply remain within budget allocations ... although we seem at the worse end of it".*

Both kept quiet for a good ten minutes, while Isabelle fiddled with one of Antoine's fountain pens, which he favored for reasons he could not clearly rationalize to himself.

Now sitting Buddha-style in her big black leather chair closed to their large living room window, she changed subject, as she added her contribution to Antoine's remarks on the health and welfare issues in Québec, ... as she perceived them of course.

"For many years ... your health and welfare department was managed by medical doctors ... no doubt medically knowledgeable physicians each in their field of competence ... but medical people nonetheless ... saddled with Québec's embedded bias against entrepreneurship and business acumen more profoundly programmed in them than all other occupations ... as one of the old professions forming its original elite in the last four centuries or so ...

... a fact made all the more evident when listing all academic subjects required of them to reach their level of competence ...

and when considering the hermetic silo in which the medical culture sees itself as a most special group ... and which it has always assigned to itself and functioned as such to this day.

Hell! ... even nowadays my friend Monique, a GP, tells me, many doctors are so afraid of not being at once viewed as superior to other hospital staff that, they parade around with their stethoscope around their neck or sticking out of their pockets, so the rest of the staff immediately recognizes their status ... so afraid are they to be taken for 'mere' nurses or nursing assistants or administrating staff.

That having been said my dear Antoine, I suggest, that the organizational problem is not one of intelligence in the Health and Welfare Services Department but one of managerial and administrative competence ... in a context of financial relevance, critical path management and so on ... ... and even when someone with foresight suggests a significant improvement ... the 'white wall' of the medical establishment blocks him every way it can ... even when largely benefiting from increased revenues and benefits and diminishing working hours.

Instead of cooperating in the provision of increased efficiencies in a difficult to steer and manage enormous department, ... medical doctors, both GPs and specialists alike, generally prefer to play silly rearward-looking games by not surrendering routine medical decisions and acts, for example, that can clearly be done by others, qualified at different levels and fields, such as pharmacists, nurses (especially the super nurses with master degree in hand), etc., ... just so they can maintain their pedestal a bit higher and a bit longer ... or otherwise feel offended when their traditional authority is either questioned or reduced to the interests and benefits of the people they allegedly serve in the medical domain, ... while continuing to expect their high earnings nevertheless for comparative accountabilities and responsibilities in other professions or occupations.

It's a shame I tell you ... and you and all other taxpayers else-where I suppose ... let them". Finally concluded Isabelle.

Antoine got up to get a glass of milk to go with those biscottis they had bought in Ottawa a couple days ago and went back to his chair with a discomfited look, thought for a little, and summed up his thoughts on this subject.

Temporarily Hovering Over a Fragment of Discussion 45.
Health and Welfare Services: The Aged and The Sick - 2

"The insouciance and plain lack of empathy demonstrated in the summer 2020 reveals that no one is truly scandalized to discover that the oldest generation is scheduled to be imprisoned more or less into CHSLDs or similar places at the private level ... that no one give a shit about forebearers in the winter of their lives ... those who not only gave us life but cared for us for many years at their expense ... our attitude toward them remains unethical and immoral but we deep down don't really care.

Through our governments we created 'storage hangers' for old folks ... so we don't look at what we will inevitably become" decisively said Antoine.

I think ... well in fact I believe ..." said Isabelle continuing Antoine's argument *"...that the negative attitude we develop as individuals and eventually as a society is reflected as you near, say, 50 years old.*

Yea, from that time on begins a slow and humiliating descent as fully participating citizens of society ... younger people generally lose their interest in you as if 50 years of age and up gave a license to the younger crowd to gradually begin to diminish your importance by automatically assuming and even proclaiming you to be less 'cool', less 'hot', less 'with-it', not as fast nor as efficient nor as effective then younger people

... ... you are then, once going over the threshold of 50 years of age, considered less attractive and less believable ... you are no longer part of the in-crowd ... or left behind in technological applications and understanding ... or worse existentially speaking, ... you constitute a roadblock to their emancipation.

Translate this as allegedly blocking a younger person from a good job ... you know! ... the one our sitting on."

Whether you're just a few years over fifty or in your mid-eighties or nineties those below the fifties put you in the same group ... it's easier that way ... less difficult than rationalizing an insensitive and unethical attitude.

This negative attitude, however, worsens once you reached 65 years of age... and from that day on we prefer not to have to deal with you or even see you because you are now indelibly part of the useless bunch ... you will from now on be grouped in the '65 and over' in all feedbacks, responses, comments, surveys, medical summations, and all other statistical databases, analyses, syntheses, and reports ...

*... exceptionally you may get a temporary reprieve if you are still autonomous (self-sufficient enough **not** to require help), ... often condescendingly at such time to be only good enough to, say, doing yoga exercises ...*

... unless of course you belong to the so-called '1%' with a vast fortune or became an icon of your society ... in other words an exception among the exceptions ... more or less."

I agree wholeheartedly with you, acquiesced Antoine.

"As a distinctive ethnic group, we like to brag that we are, as we say, 'tricotée serré', ... but this is not true in many cases, as we, as a society, let more and more responsibilities and accountabilities go 'à la dérive' ... by now believing that it is no longer our ethical duty to behave responsibly and be accountable for our acts ...

... in our mind and as a society we seem to have transferred that concern and ethical duty to our Nanny-State ... beginning with our attitude with our oldest generations ... particularly the oldest.

This attitude is further reenforced by the entire economy here and elsewhere, which is geared for – almost entirely – to the younger generations ... with a fake concern for our older generations in order to attenuate our guilt and mitigate all responsibilities and accountabilities in this regard... among those aware of what is happening.

All that was more or less hidden for decades from the population at large and the journalist class whose job it is to underline such issues never truly bothered with the revelations and the alarm bells this should have triggered ... so, ... in 2020 we discovered the enormous lie and our manipulative fake concerns about the aged ... with the advent of Covid-19 ... in all CHSLD and their equivalent at the private level ...

... and here I would like to be elephant in the room nobody wants to see ... all more or less ready to denigrate, vilify, malign, libel, or even violently attack, if possible, the messenger of what I will now make two statements about:

> *First, whenever old people are gathered in designated areas specifically designed to park them away from society until they die, we in fact and by definition create 'concentration camps' of a sort, to ensure we don't witness their deteriorating and normal physical and mental processes—lest we otherwise admit that this will eventually and similarly happen to us all.*

> *Second, we continue to mitigate our immoral management of the aged to the point of leading to a larger than normal rate of death due to our actions or lack of them, ... such as our deliberate unpreparedness,*

*and mismanagement of these 'concentration camps',
... wherein we in fact and by definition commit a deliberate and well thought out a distributed genocide of sort ... although this concept is never admitted by any of us ... remembering always that a genocide is directly or indirectly, or by deliberate neglect, or otherwise ... causing the death of a specific group for ideological reasons ... absolutely defenseless and vulnerable people ... especially relevant with the most vulnerable among us in CHSLD and other nursing homes in the private area, ... with the goal of excluding them from our daily lives and passing the buck to our Nanny-State ... but this we refuse to consider and even less acknowledge ... yet there it is."* Finally concluded Antoine.

Antoine got up once more and repeated verbatim with the same discomfited look he had thought but not expressed the day before:

Sadly, Isabelle no one will be blamed, ... nor be held responsible, ... nor considered accountable, ... nor fired or otherwise punished for unethical or illegal acts committed ... no one ever is.

The promotion of incompetence goes on and on ... that is why, we blame 'the bureaucratic machine' ... the bureaucracy in place ... under Québec's present secular religion of political correctitude ... you know that blind faith dogma of bureaucratically approved behavior presented as morally sound in our contemporary Québec 4.0'.

In both Ontario and Québec, the Canadian army reported that, for most old people they cared for in nursing homes in both provinces, medical care from mediocre to terrible, was the rule with many patients afflicted with bedsores; as well as a generalize unfamiliarity, when not simply an acceptance in not using preventive hygienic protocols; a dangerous lack of personnel to care for these most vulnerable people; with heavily physically and or psychologically afflicted residents caught like rats in a trap, often with the smell of urine and shit permeating corridors, ..." exclaimed a furious Antoine.

After a little while he continued his exposé.

"We also had from other sources explicit reports of patients – because these are in fact patient in dire need of receiving hospital care among other things – drugged to keep them quiet, being insulted or roughly handled, left for hours and all too often days in filthy diapers, soiled beddings, and all this in a total atmosphere of disrespect ... handling these most vulnerable patients as if inconsequential widgets ... ... and this by either uncaring or neglectful workers as well as simply caring but burned-out or ill-trained staff ...

*... whatever, the reasons the dignity of patients is generally **never the priority** of such establishments ... ... their mission being in all appearance to obey without question the diktats of the bureaucratic machine in place in the case of the CHSLDs ... the augmentation of the bottom-line in the case of private nursing home*

...

*... in both cases patients are merely a means to end, **never the raison d'être and priority** ... underscoring the delinquency that lead, for example, to so many deaths in these establishments generally but particularly in Québec." ... finally concluded Antoine.*

"That is why ..." Isabelle interrupted *"... there is an urgent need to overall ASAP this awful 'modèle Québécois' ... don't you think Antoine?*

Look this province is behind everyone it seems in the handling of the aged ... rather than warehousing the aged in semi-ghettos today called by that awful bureaucratic 'newspeak' of CHSLD ... away from regular societal life, we ought to and must, if indeed we are managerially logical as well as ethical people, provide homecare ... ... in fact, ... I read lately that Québec only provides 17% of its budget in this regard and is far behind such places as, say, Denmark, Sweden, and France for that matter.

Temporarily Hovering Over a Fragment of Discussion 47.
Health and Welfare Services - Dogma of 'OMERTA'

That afternoon Isabelle took the lead and began.

"The 'Omerta' concept adopted by the Health and Services department proliferates as the weapon of choice in the control for recalcitrant employees tempted to report unethical or criminal behavior on the part of management ... with people needing to survive – in jobs generally occupied by women and all too often single parents – makes it easier for management to control them ... which they routinely do ... so that a culture of fear permeates their every hour at work ... and yet this result in a sort of accepted bureaucratic bullying of employees"

"I heard a lot about this in the last few years ... ", added Antoine, *" ... but the supervisors in the field responsible for this embedded attitude and comportment in turn also dread their superiors for fear of transgressing some punctilious rules or some algorithms of operation or other ... so that in the end those at the very top of the pyramid never get the information needed to make adequate decisions or find out too late to do anything constructive ... if they are the rare type to take action , that is ....*

... this culture of fear implies by default one of reprisal and intimidation ...

Temporarily Hovering Over a Fragment of Discussion 48.
The Language Issue

Isabelle began with something not that important to the world at large but which nonetheless bothered her and which she'd noticed in Québec.

Something she thought was both revealing and completely unnecessary.

"Antoine! There's no better example for all to see about your un-admitted opinion and fear over the weakness of the French language now and in the future, than in the laws controlling the use of French signs in public places and roads in Québec.

As you enter Québec from Ontario by the 401, for example, just before you get on the 20, you see a large well designed panel on which is written 'Bienvenue' ... and underneath, contemptuously for all Canadians, 'Welcome', ... only one third the size – along with it equivalent in Spanish and Portuguese underneath – the same size as the English sign.

Again, rather than make the whole of Canada and the US next door feel welcome, ... you pretend they are less or no more important to you than, ... say, Brazil, and the rest of Central and South America... and tell me Antoine,

... who the fuck drives from these places to get on the 401 to enter Québec ... I ask you?

Pardon my language Antoine and the pun, while I'm at it ...but it's a fucking insult to an English-speaking Canadian like me or an American for that matter.

And if I didn't know about the extraordinary fear and sense of inferiority inculcated into your community over the last couple centuries about your mother country losing to England, ... I could not forgive your classless arrogance toward us here".

Now Isabelle reflected on what she had just said and came up with a proposal.

"The truth is ... you don't have to lose your language to adapt ... saying that you will lose it in such a case is a red herring benefiting the separatist-minded only.

All successful businesspeople, scientists, entrepreneurs, traders, manufacturers, airline pilots, diplomats, national politicians, and sea ship captains throughout the planet ... all communicate in English for a multiple of reasons of security and business transactions, ... and keep on utilizing their mother tongue at home ... with no fear of losing that capacity, ...

... but they make bloody sure they learn as soon as they possibly can the international language of communications, which for the 20th and 21st centuries so far, has been English ...

... and the fact that, English was the language to which your country of origin abandoned you to, has nothing to do with this reality.

We're all living in a different historical time ... and international communication languages have come and gone ... they have changed from one period to another.

Everybody should be taught the predominant language from the earliest time possible ... especially when young ... when learning a language is instinctive, ... requires little effort, ... and permits one to become flawless with its use.

So, why not copy the best of the bunch ... the Scandinavian countries ... the population of Sweden for example is about the same size as yours ... and that of Norway is even smaller than yours ...

and there, three languages are encouraged including one's own ... anyway you know what I'm getting at.

"There it is ... the solution is so easy to implement ... all you have to do is get over your victimization complex".

She stopped for half a minute or so and then carried on.

"Ok! Ok! I know it's not easy for many still indoctrinated Quebecers ... but it must be done ... or you're toast.

Your bilingual French-Canadian elite has understood this already ... and are racing ahead of the rest in your province.

They're leaving behind those either refusing to learn it for ideological reasons, ... or in the impossibility of learning it because of social conditions are set against them, ... or those in any group unable to adapt for a variety of reasons ...or because your education department insanely or for ideological reasons refuses to teach it to children under the best conditions possible, if at all.

*Whatever the reason: **adapt or sink!***

Not a kind comment I know ... and no doubt easily perceived as politically incorrect ... but reality is reality Antoine ... right?

Just like, say, calling a crippled man 'physically challenged' is pure bullshit, because in plain language he's still crippled ... and being crippled in one way or another is not a crime nor an immoral state of being ... just a goddam inconvenience making life harder ...

... and so is not being able to communicate easily with the rest of the world <u>especially when it is to one's advantage</u> ... and this on account of some inbred victimization complex and ideological expectations from some real or imagined treatment."

Temporarily Hovering Over a Fragment of Discussion 49.
Québec Education and Artificial Intelligence

Isabelle always eager to start first, … began the discussion that afternoon.

"It becomes ever more obvious that the effects artificial intelligence will offer at first and will eventually impose upon everyone an overall application of machine learning procedures that are bound to clash against present day sense of equal opportunity among the more liberalized societies such as Québec …

… and thereby create a sort of continued and increased feeling of injustice in among many people in view of its quasi infinite capacity to improve itself at the expense of our species, …if we are not very, very, very careful.

Although we must admit we have no specific idea as to how we will handle this problem as a society, which is already affecting us to a significant degree, … although we find ourselves merely at the beginning of its application … the business establishment however appears ready and bent on its accelerated application assuming that they will dominate societies …

… AI also announces an upper super-class …

… I refer to those usual owners and stakeholders supported by artificial intelligence specialists who will benefit from it, … while lower classes will be negatively affected by it to various degrees.

The fact, that we are at the beginning of a universal application of artificial intelligence in all aspects of human life, demands of us to immediately consider all new automatically applied algorithms, which will by necessity be part of all activities integral to its functioning.

That is why. my dear Antoine this inevitable model-building process must be addressed not only by a government but especially by its education branch as soon as possible ... or the rate of failure and severe social problems will skyrocket.

In my view, with the present attitude in the Québec Education department, it will likely postpone that decision as well as retain its present modus operandi regardless of upcoming events ... unless a forward-looking leader representing a wide-awake public does what must be done.

I must admit to you Antoine that, ... with an extensive analphabetism in Québec the odds are against unilingual French-speaking Quebecers ... and this simply because most of these people are already buried in their increasing poverty and ignorance, ... or soon will irremediably be ...

... while the younger ones, now blinded by and addicted to the multiplicity of digitized devices, ... especially their easy to use digital phones, ... among other things, ... will probably wake up and realize the precarity of their dire situation only when it is too late".

Temporarily Hovering Over a Fragment of Discussion 50.
Québec's Old French-Canadian Inferiority Complex

"Québec's purported French-Canadian specialness is a useful tool to control the anger of its poor, vulnerable, and unilingual classes", Antoine stated that afternoon.

"Whenever social frustrations, political roadblocks, lack of opportunities, and low economic prospects, are viewed as imposed by an uncaring mostly Anglo federal government to a 'victimized' people, separatist-minded elite ensure that an illusion of injustice is created, and then nurtured as a victimized people of Canadian history ...

... a tactic used to channel away the lack of enterprise and entrepreneurship of far too many ...

... all the while never admitting that it is caused by an educational system structured to produce non-performing adults along with a dangerously large segment of analphabetism.

I point my finger at a separatist-minded Québec elite that pretends that, it, and its predecessors, where not the authors of the situation endured by underprivileged unilingual French-Canadians ... ... thereby callously and hypocritically pointing others ... English-speaking Canadians that is ... as the source of their purported oppression.

Today's unilingual French-speaking Quebecers' idea of specialness continues to adopt the language of the oppressed, as if still subjected to some colonial rule, ...

... although it hides a serious inferiority complex expressed as a list of entitlements unavailable in other provinces ...

... as if more authority, power, and money would miraculously remedy their systemic fundamental problems of organization, management, financial responsibility, educational upgrade, and so on.

Many among fundamentalist separatists have adopted a sort of paranoid theory that immigration and multiculturalism will de facto wipe out the French-speaking culture of Québec ...

... preferring to see a conspiracy by the federal government, rather than adopt workable and positive welcoming programs of integration to this beautiful liberalized secular society of ours.

After all, despite our diminishing influence in Canada in view the increasing population outside Québec, we still remain an important member of the confederation ... and nearly always function in cahoots with Ontario to exercise a sort of veto power on crucial Canadian issues... or continue to act in tandem with Ontario in promoting matters pertinent to both provinces.

That being the case ... I ask myself:

> *Why do unilingual Québec French-Canadians still concern themselves with such things as the aftermath of the surrender of French held territory in North America.... including Québec ... by France in view of its loss of 1759 ... until the 'révolution tranquille' of the Sixties?*

> *Why did they choose and keep reelecting a near fascist premier, who instituted a sad period of our history?*

I speak of course of the Duplessis period ... as if we possessed a need to identify with a strong and authoritarian leader to protect Québec's French-Canadian interests.

> *Why do our underprivileged and fundamentalist-to-the-core separatists often blame Québec's Anglos, or migrants, or racial groups or fundamentalist religious types, and especially Islamists?*

Although in this latter case Islamists really pay the price for the overt inflexibility and aggressiveness of their belief system ... a fact intensified at times in the extreme barbarous acts of its extremist god-crazed membership around the world.

Anyway, as a liberalized democracy with broad economic prospects, we can improve our situation and stop this self-defeating creation of an alienation due in great part as well to an inferior education system. Another 'modèle Québecois' that can only produce a large underclass of unemployed, uneducated, and analphabetic citizens ... with little prospects in future Québec, and next to none elsewhere.

The private sector, tired of and faced with the public sector's incompetence, has taken matter in its own hands, attracting people, who insist on succeeding in life, ... those bent on not being subjected to the massively bureaucratized, inefficient, and ineffective public education system.

So, our hope now rests with the best of the best. That much smaller section of the education department from the private sector now separately producing excellent French- and English-speaking education.

That is why for example, ashamed of its anticipated low performance at the international level, the majority of our public schools refrained from participating in it lately".

Temporarily Hovering Over a Fragment of Discussion 51.
Combatting a Contemporary Ignorance

It was Antoine for a second day who began the afternoon discussion.

"We in Québec must start combatting the growing analphabetism and general ignorance settling in within our French-Canadian society in our province.

I speak here of an ignorance that weakens a society, wherein a good half of students – especially its masculine part – barely function in a world that demands a good foundation of ever-increasing data, information, and knowledge ... in a world commanding a continued ability to analyze and synthesize the world as it really is... in an ever-more sophisticated, technologically advanced, and politically complex environment.

That is why, of all governmental expenses, education must come first as a priority, if we intend to advance in all other domains and create a strong and successful society.

This begins by reducing the supreme importance the Education department here in Québec gives to its idealized and frankly sadly 'sacralized' pedagogical theories by concentrating instead on the reality of everyday life ...

... doing this with an obligatory internship in as many fields of expertise and knowledge possible by all teachers ... a policy that must be implemented as soon as possible ... so that teachers end up knowing the subjects they're assigned to teach rather than rely solely on their teaching abilities.

Indeed, no one should teach without thoroughly understanding the subject imparted without having experienced it – nothing less.

Look! You **cannot** *teach, say, math, swimming, or biology, ... among an infinite number of subjects for that matter, ... regardless of your ability to teach, ... if you do not thoroughly know a subject ... period.*

To otherwise believe you can base everything solely on a pedagogical expertise is ideological ... which is the case with the Education department ... it is to dream in colors ... it is as if they existed on another planet.

That is the reason the curriculum of all teachers must be meticulously, and scrupulously reviewed, ... and also the role of teaching promoted as a most important one within our society ... but not before professionalizing it properly in all aspects of the role to be played ... ... a role that ought to incorporate people from all fields of knowledge.

For example, people properly educated in the public school system, should at some time in their career provide a compulsory assignment ... as payoff for their free education, say, ... a two-year stage in a teaching institution ... similar to an obligatory military service ... as a rite of passage in a liberalized democratic society... a responsibility that ought to be looked upon with respect and gratitude by that society.

A role that ought to also be staffed with an equal proportion of women and men to counteract the already embedded bias between the two genders with nearly all societies on earth ... including ours ... to counterbalance today's gender inequality in this domain.

This of course demands that we set an entirely new way of selecting and assigning teachers, since our teaching methodology must first be completely transformed.

While education must produce an expertise aimed at the job market so that one can live a pleasant life, it must also with an equal effort and priority include a larger understanding of the world in which we live – including such areas as history, philosophy, economy, finance, politics, the arts, music, and so on.

*That is why; teachers must become **envied roles** within our society, ... in view of the importance and essentiality assigned to it by our society for the success of our whole community ... all the while keenly aware of the strategic and non-negotiable priority of <u>equal mastery</u> of pedagogy and an inevitable in-depth knowledge of the subject or subjects taught.*

No one indeed should be authorized to teach without thoroughly knowing the subject imparted even if in possession of a degree in pedagogy.

That being the case then, the more competent teachers are, the less the executive and managerial groups will have to worry about the engineering, managing, and supervising of education systems, programs, and projects.

Above all teachers must believe to be and act as professionals, while recognizing that their education must continue in perpetuity ... like everybody else in this new ever evolving world of ours.

There is no shortcut to this.

That is why, we must attract the best candidates possible ... giving priority to those showing an evident ability to express themselves, a curiosity in many fields, and a tendency to observe reality as it really is in the context of the world at large.

Our society and the government that represents it, must therefore put the Education department at the top of its priority – as the critical priority for the entire province if it intends to ensure a better future.

Rather than preach form an elevated platform ... like the 'curés' of old-time religion, ... teachers must now work as team leaders and provide meaningful empathy with their students.

That is why further, potential teachers, once promoted by a university, must be selected before being appointed to a specific job, ... and this only after being vetted and completing their 'internship' stage – as done with highly specialized professions such as medical doctors, lawyers, and aircraft controllers for example.

Last and equally important, ... a teaching establishment must be a pleasant area with agreeable surroundings leading to a longing and a pride to be there ... at locations wherein knowledge, impulse to learn, and contemporaneousness simultaneously exist", Antoine finally concluded.

Temporarily Hovering Over a Fragment of Discussion 52.
Quebec's Charter of Values, Revisited

That afternoon it was Isabelle who began expressing her frustrations.

"Québec's charter of values and its codependent so-called 'modèle Québécois' in this case, both imply that its citizens ... here we really mean French-speaking French-Canadians in Québec, often considered themselves as a 'special people' over the years ... as if a sort of 'Chosen People' usually presented as a victimized community ... an outlook marketed especially since the Plains of Abraham by their previous religious masters.

This earlier self-promoting propaganda programs used and indoctrinated into your community by its own Roman Catholic Church has replicated itself to some degree in the secular arena ... subtly embodying foundational fascist leanings of a people saddled with an inferiority complex, which it has had difficulties getting rid of.

In fact, separatist-leaning Quebecers frustrated at the evidence of two failed referendums, and now in this early 21st century witnessing a movement toward an unstoppable global involvement by an increasing segment of its Millennials and upcoming Generation Z taking part in that globalization, want to redouble and unite their efforts in convincing their compatriots to become a country ... as if all of a sudden a 'de-Canadianizing' of their self-created issues and problems would suddenly make these disappear: ... as if by miracle ...

... a rather immature way of understanding realpolitik ... don't you think Antoine?

That is why, such desperate attempts as 'Osez repenser le PQ' and 'Faut qu'on se parle' projects of a few years ago lead nowhere except fancy rhetorical arguments and pronouncements.

In the meantime, the crucial and strategic issue of a thorough reform of the education system to bring it to date to the realities of the 21st century is still discounted, ... and your level of analphabetism has augmented for a liberalized democracy, ... while your economy slowly continues its slide into a dystopian future as far as I'm concerned, if you don't change direction ... because you have much less industry than Ontario ... all proportion considered ...

... and yet ... far too many of you guys continue to push for a referendum or tightening language regulations which borders on paranoia ... and your political masters walk around like perambulating zombies ... as if nothing was wrong ... and as if everything was unfolding as it should.

I despair for you guys at times", finally concluded Isabelle.

Temporarily Hovering Over a Fragment of Discussion 53.
Québec's Taboo About Self-Criticism

Antoine waited until past two o'clock that afternoon to begin the day's discussion. After sipping on a cold beer, he'd just took out of the frig, he took a good sip, smacked his lips, and began.

"There exists in Québec a taboo no one it seems dare talk about, lest you be considered a traitor to the 'validly moral cause and mission' of French-speaking French-Canadian in Québec.

From a systemic tendency for self-depreciation to its opposite notion of overvaluation of our self-assigned and self-promoted 'modèle Québécois', both, lead us avoid true rational debate with all those concerned in resolving our societal issues.

Indeed, if criticism or embarrassing questioning come from a French-speaking French-Canadian Quebecers – especially one considered 'vielles souches' like me, he is not tolerated by the 'bien pensants', as if such a person was a traitor to the cause, so to speak, ... as if afraid that such discussion might reveal or diminish their chance to become a sovereign country of sort.

And when criticism emerges from outsiders (other Canadians outside the province) all possible rational discussions are automatically eliminated with the debate ending 'magic' expression of "Québec bashing"—especially when dealing with the 'modèle Québécois'.

That very model that made us the worse managed and least prepared lately in the Covid-19 pandemic to name only one example."

That 'modèle Québécois' also created in another recent and classical example, the mismanagement situation of a major snowstorm in 2017 leaving at least 300 people in their vehicles all night with no plan for such eventuality, and truck drivers refusing to help these people, and where two persons needlessly died ...

... of course, the outsider that criticized that event was severely punished for it ... having to resign his job at McGill simply for telling the truth. .... when he said that Quebecers were filled with "un profond malaise social", which they generally are.

Temporarily Hovering Over a Fragment of Discussion 54.
Québec's Ecucation Startegy with Millennials and Generation Z

Antoine talking as an old man much closer to his end than his beginning, decided to go all out, as he put his faith into that emerging segment within Québec's Millennials and upcoming Generation Z.

"My hope for French-speaking Québec is that our educated portion of Millennials with the upcoming support of Generation Z, both, refuse to follow the politically correct methodology of previous generations since the 'révolution tranquille' ...

... and at least reject the politicking of the last fifty years or so, ... and embark on a more rational national undertaking favoring knowledge above all else, at the expense of a dogmatic ideology ...

... ensuring the whole community is endowed with a world class education ... in view of the globalization of everything now unfolding ...

... and if they definitely adopt such an approach their success would indeed be assured ... and by default that of the community they represent.

That is why their outlook is and must be planetary and not local.

A segment of our two new generations inspires a win-win attitude methodology demonstrated in ambitious projects, entrepreneurial undertakings, and professional management of everything, wherein decisions are no longer taken by committee but by whomever is in charge ... in the case of the Education department it is the Minister of Education.

Segments of these two generations, although forming just a fraction of what it ought to be, nevertheless purposely goes beyond the narrow-mindedness of local politics with a view of a broader background of events in which all must eventually operate.

I see this in their rejection of traditional religions, which have for purpose the control of people's thoughts and behavior implied and ordered in our old dogmatic and violence-based Abrahamic blind faith-oriented belief systems ...

... the very reason that prayers of any kind has no place in an education establishment ... a tactic used everywhere whenever a religion can get away with it ... history is proof of this—including our own here in Canada generally and Québec particularly.

These generations like similar ones elsewhere are instead concerned with gender equality, planetary ecology, ...

... and view themselves as most vulnerable earthlings first and therefore ...... take on the role of stakeholders and maintainers of our planetary wellbeing.

For them there are no frontiers and no political borders anywhere.

We are in their view all members of a same tribe of Sapiens, ... human beings first and above all else ... ... trying our best not to divide ourselves by dogmatic belief systems, damaging economics, and harmful cultural characteristics.

The only 'B mol', as I often qualify many of my outrageous statements, is that ...

... all too many still among the educated and non-educated alike right down to that large group afflicted by analphabetism, are those tending to act like 'enfant rois' ...

... a role they carry on as spoiled kids, spoiled consumers, and spoiled citizens into their entire adulthood ...

...insisting all along on having evermore state-guaranteed benefits ... ... thereby copying their parents and grandparents at a cost to be dumped on the next generations ... and as always it seems never being quite satisfied.

***

Nevertheless, let me say this ... French-Canadians in Québec are generally a happy and resourceful lot, ...

... and finally, their creativity – at least for many Millennials and those from the Generation Z right now ... are breaking the restrictive bounds that held back previous generations for so long.

In my view, Isabelle ... without a doubt in my mind ... significant segments among my people now clearly see themselves as versatile French-speaking North-Americans able to take on the world using the opportunities available to them ... and no dogma and or no ideology will cripple their communication skills with the rest of the world by refusing to integrate the present international language of our planet, ... English at present, or perhaps Mandarin in some future" ... French-speaking Quebecers are indeed capable, willing, and flexible.

But first a sound education based on world standards wherever these can be found, and imitated when these exist elsewhere must be adopted ... and a thorough restructuring of the entire Education system must take place.

However, employees' union are likely to kill any logical and reasonable restructuring that would advance such a massive project ... and this for narrow, self-serving, local, regional, and provincial purposes.

Regrettably employees' unions must be legally suspended – at least temporarily – if no true cooperation exists ... otherwise no improvement is possible, and the Québec dream of a strong future will remain just that: a dream—no more.

Temporarily Hovering Over a Fragment of Discussion 55.
The Ticklish Case of the Much Necessary English

Here's a case in point! Antoine began that last afternoon.

While an increasing number of French-speaking Canadian citizens in the province of Québec rightly claim the opportunity to learn English to participate on a leveled playing field in the world of business, many yet are generally unaware of that need in this area until they're adult, ... in view of the near silence by the education community about a sound knowledge of money, commercial ventures, markets, and financial investments and other fields of specialization required to function within their own society, the rest of Canada, the USA, and the rest of the world for that matter ..."

He stopped for a few seconds still looking at Isabelle and carried on as if he hadn't stopped.

"... and in this era now progressing ahead at an accelerated pace ... our participation in the globalization process is all the more essential ... if we wish to survive as a viable entity with the rest of the planet,

... where the international language, among other factors, is generally English ...

... yet, we still hesitate in making English compulsory in school ... which is why ... a majority of Quebecers, find this out <u>only when it is too late</u> ... ... that such crucial overall knowledge goes hand in hand in negotiating one's way in the present world of global business, entrepreneurship, and education.

"The Scandinavian countries are most practical in this area while keeping with pride their much smaller languages in normal routine everyday life when compared to us French-Canadians" Antoine concluded. *"So why don't we do it? Period."*

Part 2.

MORE RATIONAL BUT WORRYING VIEWS

*Daring to mention issues contributing to the dwindling importance of France's once planetary hegemony—and by ricochet the French-Canadian continuing conundrum in view of this fact, ... along with the destructive religious operational **meme** transferred during 'la révolution tranquille' into the secular arena known to us as "la méthode Québécoise".*

Ad Hoc Thoughts on the Québec Case

Les Enfants De Duplessis.

In the province of Québec in Canada in my lifetime, the medieval-minded Roman Catholic clergy and their acolytes in cahoots with equally unethical psychiatrists, psychologists, social workers, physicians, lawyers and politicians then directed by the xenophobic dictatorially leaning provincial Premier Maurice Duplessis, ensured that children born out of wedlock were evaluated as mentally deficient, so *'sinful'* mothers (i.e., they never penalized responsible fathers) could be punished I suppose and the clergy could make money through government subsidies, and additionally obtain free labor out of these unprotected, despised, deprived and rejected children, as well as <u>punish them for a crime they never committed and which never existed</u>. Yet, decades later, present leaders of this now weakened regional Catholic Church, callously, cowardly, and arrogantly retreat from recognizing the true harm done to these still unprotected, still despised, still deprived, and still rejected people. Yes! Here is a local chapter of a planetary totalitarian organization still adamantly refusing to make amend, never mind provide some well-deserved recognition and compensation. And so, I proclaim:

1. Shame on you Cardinals Joseph Charbonneau, Maurice Roy, and Paul-Emile Leger, and all the religious orders and support

staff that took part in these acts of disgrace, humiliation, mortification, and degradation. Acts committed for ideological purposes and financial returns.

2. Shame on you Cardinals Jean-Claude Turcotte, Marc Ouellet and Christian Lépine for continuing to belittle what happened and deny justice to the victims of these acts of infamy as the third millennium begins.

The *barbaric* and medieval mindset of your perception is indeed still shamefully and viciously visible today. These cowardly and callous acts still disgracefully disparaged, if not denied altogether, are now forever recorded in Québec, Canadian and world history!

Pompous Heartless Misogynist.

In 2010 cardinal Marc Ouellet, shamefully from my province and ethnic group of origin, still showed his deeply inbred hatred of women and his uncontrollable obsession in wanting to control them at all costs, by proclaiming for all to hear that and I paraphrase; *"even a woman,* we include girls as well, *" who became pregnant by a rapist,'* and I add regardless of harm and pain committed during that rape, *"had the moral duty to give birth to that child"*, allegedly because of the respect for life we must all possess. What a crock of manipulative bullshit. Among other things, this thought alone exhibits the mind of a mean-spirited sexual sociopath buried so deep in his delusional world and compulsive needs to control those he fears the most, women, that his pomposity probably blinds him to that fact. Shamefully, this *barbarian* is a member of my tribe and ethnic group, and a most senior executive at the Vatican. And lately rumors of compulsive sexual behavior are emerging about his past behavior obligingly and automatically dismissed by Pope Francis.

Betrayal of Québécois - 01.

Many people of French extraction in Québec rightly or not proclaim their political independence as all ethnic groups and sub-groups throughout the planet do at a certain stage of their development. Sadly, many of them also irrationally believe that such a successful undertaking would free them from their real or alleged oppressors, forgetting all those lessons recorded throughout the annals of history. Yes! Many such politically committed Quebecers still assume that their own *Special Group* and its accompanying petty bourgeoisie would be kinder to them, overlooking of course that the bourgeoisie everywhere on Earth forms the most importantly integrated group in the planetary-wide daily application and management of social and political controls everywhere at the minuteness levels and has done so throughout history. I speak of course of the special role played by the class of *'Planetary Managerial and Professional Support Groups'*— whatever the specialty — in their active involvement toward the implementation and maintenance of the status quo on behalf of society's owners and stakeholders.

Betrayal of Québécois - 02.

In early Québec history the slow development of Quebecers of French extraction began with the premeditated betrayal by their clergy along with their political masters in France; then the same clergy again associated itself with similar allies from a victorious England; and after that for the third time the Catholic clergy of Québec did it again with the continued coercive implementation of the Catholic doctrine with those who could profit the most within their very own culture, such as lawyers, doctors and politicians. So, I say, let us not fail here in Québec and elsewhere for that matter, now that we've finally begun to overcome that gang of scoundrels; that older subset of dogmatic belief system administrators for society's owners and stakeholders. I refer of course to the local chapter, or if you prefer the Québec franchise of *'The Planetary Managerial-Professional Class'*.

I Remember Very Clearly.
I remember very clearly our local priests in the Ste-Cunégonde parish of my early childhood and their cohorts, the Brothers of Christian Instruction from the Iberville primary school, which I attended, as well as those from the Juvénat Mont-Lasalle, where I stayed for two years as a Juvéniste (a first level training to be admitted into

their novitiate), telling me more or less that, there were us Roman Catholics, those truly *"chosen and enlightened people", who had* the privilege to go to heaven, if we were really, really, really good (if we obeyed without question); while all other non-Catholics would end up in limbo somewhere, especially the Jews they insisted who had not recognized him as the *"savior of the world".* That he was another Jew was never mentioned. Yes! And all others would be left out of this grand and unique scheme, because of the *"errors of their beliefs",* we were told. The militarized, totalitarian, genocidal, and warring Romans, were rarely mentioned of course. This sounds medieval, doesn't it? Even in those very early years, despite the intense brainwashing suffered in a medieval-like Québec at that time, and in spite of my extreme naivety and my being a child, I still thought of this to be a crock of manipulative shit.

Vielles Souches Bourgeoisie.

Those 'vielles souches' notions of the Québec bourgeoisie about proper French grammar and its alleged correct pronunciation are among other things motivated by inbred snobbery and perceived class difference, since this specific class of bourgeois have elected themselves, and insists on being identified with their 'exclusive' European ancestry. In this self-assigned context, it then considers itself as the educated segment of the chapter of *The Special Group* that ought to rule that particular section of Earthly landmass called Québec. Most from readers of "Le Devoir" newspaper being members promoting this vision still today.

Victimhood: Québec Style.

While I readily admit that Quebecers were treated as inferior beings by the English conquerors in cahoots with their very own French-Canadian Roman Catholic clergy along with their own politicians, lawyers and doctors, it worsened even more after the creation of Canada, when this same clergy cooperated with its own bourgeoisie, continuing their intense control of a rather docile religiously brainwashed population to their interests and benefits. What astounds me today however is that Québec's separatists still behave as victims at the beginning of this 21st century—faced as they are with an incredible array of opportunities most people can only dream about elsewhere in the world—such as the biggest set of potential customers for any business smack against their political border. And still refusing as a decreasing

North American minority of about 2% to fluently speak the number one language of the continent as their second language to facilitate their North American communications (wherein 98% speak English) and on a global basis as well. So, instead of capitalizing on their incredible freedom of thought and behavior along with astonishing economic and business opportunities among numerous others offered them by living smack against the most powerful country in the world at present, with all the advantages this provides any good entrepreneur, aside from being an integral part of a steadily growing highly democratic Canada, too many 'vieilles souches' French-speaking French-Canadians do nothing but complain about the good old days when they were truly victimized. Yet, effective religious and other social controls ceased several decades ago, but many independence-minded Quebecers will not admit it, or worse yet cannot see it, and do nothing to get out of their psychological cul-de-sac. And this while pretending that their own elite would be kinder to them and would also spend their regular and new revenues if any to the greater advantage of the population they allegedly serve, forgetting innumerable historical lessons, so blinded are they with their ideology.

Seeds of Québec Fascism.

Not so many years ago in the province of Québec, Canada, in my lifetime:

1. Divorce was nearly impossible.

2. Pétain was considered brave.

3. Chanoine Lionel Groulx's xenophobic ideologue logic and profound anti-Semitism seemed correct and so laudable it seems to nationalists that they dedicated his name to a metro station, streets, schools, etc.

4. In my primary school classes, we accused Jews of the vile crime of 'crucifying' our godly figure, himself a Jew, and anti-Semitism was quietly and not so quietly de rigueur. The invading Romans were rarely mentioned.

5. The world was divided into Catholics *(i.e., the 'Chosen People')* led by god's chosen elite (i.e., the Roman Catholic Church as *'The Most Special Group'*), and all those who were not part of this group 'but really wanted to be' of course, according to those indoctrinating children through Catholic catechism and stories purportedly based on holy scriptures.

6. Many French-speaking Québécois of French origin liked and considered fascism a worthwhile alternative, having been in a form of intellectual medieval totalitarianism themselves from 1608 to the 1960's.

7. Le Devoir newspaper, the one favored by the Québec elite, supported, encouraged, and rationalized xenophobic outlooks, as well as seriously flirted with, if not adopted outright, a penchant for fascism, through pompous supposedly scholarly exercises or blunt articles written at times under pseudonyms—always with a proclivity for authoritative solutions under the cover of elitist intellectualism combined with a despicable attitude over democratic British style institutions.

8. "Les enfants de Duplessis" happened because it was considered reasonable and a normal procedure by the Québec elite and its Québec style Roman Catholic Church of the time.

No better than the beginnings of Nazi Germany in its first years, I sometime conclude. So, from time to time, I ask myself this scary question: When will those seeds of hate, and others not mentioned, germinate further in my land of birth? I admit to shaking in my boots at that very question. That is why: Courageous Esther Delisle is reviled by diehard Québec separatists, treated as a traitor by the "pure laine" Québec elite, and ignored or ridiculed by its inbred academic community, since she dared to openly bring into the light of day the unconscionable and shameful Québec history of the 1930's and 1940's particularly. She forced us to clearly see our cowardice in the face of an undeniable Holocaust in Europe and our unadmitted quiet glee in some respects over its execution by many of us at that time among other things.

> **Although....**
> It must be admitted, however, that Esther Delisle's presentation
> was rather clunky, but she was nevertheless accurate.

Yea! I know there existed a strong anti-Semitic current throughout English Canada in those days as well, but it certainly did not become the mythological affirmation it did in Roman Catholic French-Canadian circles in the province of Québec at that time. I know. I was there. I witnessed it. I lived through part of it.

Recent Semi-Fascist State.

Recently in their history Quebecers rejected en masse their isolation from the rest of the world and distanced themselves almost completely from the domineering Roman Catholic Church, that had shackled them spiritually, ethically, politically and every other way for so long in a quasi-medieval mode of life. Oh yes! Not so very long ago in my younger life and much before that, the province of Québec in Canada functioned more or less under a sort of Canon law at home, school and church—having done so first since the foundation of New France in 1608, then again after its defeat at the hands of England in 1759. During, in between, and after these two events, it operated as a more or less semi-fascist religious State until the so-called "révolution tranquille". If in doubt think of the following easy considerations among many others:

1. The British and the Québec Roman Catholic Church reached an agreement to control the French-Canadian population of the day that would benefit both these stakeholders and protect their interests. Both State and Church combined forces again to suppress the freedom of French-Canadians, especially in Québec with the pernicious involvement of their petty bourgeoisie: attaining a high point during "la grande noirceur', just before its collapse following the death of its xenophobic Premier Maurice Duplessis and his era.

2. An invasive program of violent interference was created throughout that time to protect the interests and benefits of the

Roman Catholic Church and special laws were created to that effect.

3. Communism, the Church's sworn archenemy at the time was hailed enemy number one with the so-called *"Padlock Law"*, which was used liberally against groups and individuals the Québec government or the Roman Catholic Church proclaimed as "heretics" of one kind or another.

4. In many quarters including my neighborhood as a child before and during the Second World War, Pétain was considered a "reasonable man" and Mussolini a "strong leader".

5. Priests in nearly all villages, towns, and cities as well as newspapers generally, surreptitiously when not openly supported and promoted fascist ideas.

6. That sanctimonious *self-righteous* rag of the day called "Le Devoir" rationalized the wearing of the yellow star by the Jews of Germany among other things.

That is why still, we, French-Canadians, tagged as so-called "vielles souches", are not supposed to recall these things or if we do, dare not mention them, unless be considered traitors to the cause of political independence.

The Parti Québécois Is Racist.

The Parti Québécois is racist. The reason shows in its exclusivist undercurrents legated by its Roman Catholic 'vieilles souches' and 'pure laine' notions, while never admitting it and upon which they imagine Québec's future decided strictly by such specifically identified French-Canadians. In this idealized scenario, the Parti Québécois ignores the will and aspirations of all other Québec citizens in principle and in fact. Except lately out of desperation. Indeed, with it more than a million non-French Canadians consisting of English-speaking residents and newcomers located in the province of Québec, were out of the formula envisaged by separatist-minded Quebecers. As if those people could not be part of their proposed political end. Oddly enough all the while ironically ignoring that tax contributions from non-French-Canadian

Québécois 'pure laine' exceeded at least for the last two centuries a per capita income superior to that of their French-Canadian counterpart. And this despite the near monopoly of French-Canadians in the bureaucratic ramparts of the provincial government of Québec. This narrow vision is the result of a Québec-styled intellectual progeny—a mentality echoing Jesuitan *self-righteous* manipulative implementation and pontification of a religious based mission metamorphosed and indoctrinated in a secular fashion after "la grande noirceur". It is reflected further in the self-centered sense of specialness expressed and exhibited by the religious class along with the petty bourgeoisie of a few decades ago, and now mirrored in the parents of the original Parti Québécois' elite and the more committed part of the membership at that time. You can however still find remnants of that retrograde detrimental mentality as Québec's hardcore separatists transmogrify their sermons into a more politically correct dialect, when not diatribes. As if shadows of the xenophobic philosophy and aspirations of "Le Devoir" newspaper in the midst of "la grande noirceur" although presently somewhat less hypocritical in view of a more sophisticated population. And now—like all *self-righteous* groups, the Parti Québécois' fundamentalist crowd tends to ridicule, if not attack outright, anyone challenging their exclusive and proprietary conclusions. Although Québec immigrants scare Québec separatists, most of these come along with a view of living a freer life than the one experienced in their country of origin. In such a context Québec separatists refuse to understand other points of view, although many pretend to be inclusive in order to reach that manipulative '50% + 1' magic formula, because their super ordinate *Immaculate Perception* is that of a people wronged—an untouchable dogma—as if separate and superior to all other concerns. Therefore, by not openly and repeatedly recognizing the reality of ignoring the '50% - 1' excluded from such a social project that disagree with them should they succeed in this manner, they will have shortchanged their own succeeding generations of French-Canadians in Québec, who will thereby be ghettoized from the rest of the North American continent rather than fully participate in it. An unnecessary problem which, say, the compulsory learning of English, although used worldwide in business and by the elite of all nations, as a second language at all school levels for example, would ease the future of Québec's upcoming generations, and bring it on a par with the rest of successful ethnic groups and nations.

Hard Core Québec Separatists.

Hardcore Québec separatists believing themselves victimized:

1. Purposely and dishonestly ignore that English is the language of the planet and that it will remain as such for several generations at least.

2. Refuse to see that their plight in the past was due to the politics of old conflicts, and that their negative attitude blocks their aspirations as free people, whom they already really are.

3. Intentionally forget altogether that England by default allowed them to keep their language and belief system for crass political calculations of course but true, nonetheless.

4. Deliberately disregard that France, their mother country, abandoned them to their plight as collateral damage – unworthy of protection – in the pursuit of national French interests of the day and in exchange of sugar supplied from some small islands.

5. Calculatedly overlook that their local Catholic Church, made up of their own people, separately and for political gains betrayed them several times; not only with the old French regime but also with the English one as well, and continued to do so in a third phase of their betrayal in the 19th and 20th centuries this time with the complicity of their own bourgeoisie—their own doctors, lawyers, priestly class, journalists, and politicians.

6. Knowingly disregard the fact that they geographically live next to the most powerful and still richest nation in the whole

course of human history to this day – a dreamt of for opportunity for any entrepreneur.

7.   Discount the fact that far too many French-Canadian French-speaking people of Québec are still the authors of their shortcomings in many instances—by for far too long snubbing entrepreneurship (a religious leftover social control program of inaction left to a secular Québec); as well as creating sluggish, problematic, and powerful bureaucracies preventing dynamic growth meant to ignore opportunities represented and implied by geographically being smack against the USA as well as being an integral part of the free country of Canada (another religious social control program bequeathed to a secular Québec).

In the meantime, Québec goes on instead creating one of the biggest national debts, while separatist act as phony victims of mostly self-inflicted problems, especially in the last decades, with worse ones to come from those "enfants-roi" they raised.

Raising Its Hideous Head.

The faux intellectual *self-righteous* essays occasionally bordering much too close on anti-Semitism together with a penchant for fascism found in "Le Devoir" newspaper of the 1930s and 1940s in the province of Québec in Canada was a direct reflection of the Québec elite class with the fanatical support of its Roman Catholic clergy. Without a doubt, the yellow journalism spewed out by "Le Devoir" represented the abhorrent attitude of its elite at that time.

Along With ....
Along with an intense religious indoctrination and propagandist preaching when I attended primary school in the Forties that paralleled many of the same ideas I later discovered in "Le Devoir" newspaper.
These notions still reverberate today as subtexts in emotionally charged expressions such as "pure laine" and "vielles souches" found in the glossary of too many Québec's entrenched separatists ... as well as statements worthy of "la grande noirceur" evidenced in 2007 with the ecclesiastical pronouncements expressed not so

subtly by that bitter, pompous, retrograde, self-serving and naturally ultra-conservative cardinal Marc Ouellette of Québec City at "La commission sur les accommodements raisonnables".

The 'Laurentien' Fascism.

Let us recall the utopian and exclusively French-Canadian Roman Catholic Fascist State dreamt of and promoted by that rapacious Jew hater and intense misogynist: chanoine Lionel Groulx. The fascist State he conceived was meant to be at the disposal of the Roman Catholic Church of Québec and also predestined to exclude all those not fitting in – beginning with 'Anglos' and Jews. Not very different indeed than the call to all French-Canadians "de souche" (it's in the subtext again) by cardinal Marc Ouellette of Québec City urging French-Canadians "de souche" to return to the fold of that nasty ecclesiastical elite. No doubt that rabid misogynist imagined and was hoping for the good old days when clerics could run the show once more and lead their "flock" to re-embark as xenophobic fascist-minded followers once more—on their way to that ever fading "Lauretien" utopia he so achingly wished for.

Reflection of Jesuits Fantasies.

As if consisting of a reflection of Jesuits fantasies, the Québec of the last three hundred and fifty years or so was xenophobic, anti-Semitic, anti-entrepreneurship, fearful of business, preferred ignorance, accorded a kind of sainthood to large families, and promoted a saintly poverty. This was the situation of a once highly indoctrinated French-speaking people culturally brainwashed to remain ignorant and abandoned by their mother country in an English-speaking ocean in a dislocated medieval outpost of the Roman Catholic Church right up to the middle of the 20th century. Until then these somnambulistic Quebecers had been troubled by fundamentalist views clothed in religious and ethnocentric visions of the world. That is the reason private Jesuit-run Collège Jean-de-Brébeuf so ardently embraced chauvinistic francophone nationalism from the time of its foundation until recently. It in fact originally contributed along with other similar establishments to the construction and anchoring of an insularity by privileged members constituting its upcoming *Special Group,* and by default falsely propagated a harmful meme, defining French-Canadians from earliest generations as the only people "de souche" which mattered of that province.

Particular Liberalization of Behavior.

In a less politically important area of our planet, the province of Québec in Canada, in the last sixty years, a psychologically ruthless and highly manipulative Roman Catholic Church supported by narrow-minded professionals of the day ruled a most obedient, highly indoctrinated for centuries, and generally uneducated population. But those artificial pillars of fake logic and disingenuous morality supporting this social system disintegrated with the introduction of technology and increasing freedom observed in the rest of North America, especially with the advent of television. This quickly began to weaken the old elite grasp on power at that precise point in time, and the whole Church establishment collapsed on that territory, while a need for another type of *Immaculate Perception* began to develop from the ashes of the old one, wherein a new political clan emerge. A secular one this time and this in just a few decades.

In My Québec Culture ….

In my Québec French-speaking culture of original *'vielles souche'* French-Canadians, a religiously inspired dogma was reflected in the saying heard dozens of times in my youth of: *"Quand tu es né pour un petit pain, tu n'es pas né pour un gros"!* A plain refusal—under the cover of the moral dictum of victims that had given up at that time—to organize their lives of low expectations in the best way possible with the few cards handed them, because their religion would compensate them as a *'Chosen People'* more or less in an extraordinary eternal afterlife in exchange for the surrender of their individualized *self-actualization* in this one.

Moribund Québec Catholicism.

I reasoned lately that there is still hope, after noting the historically recent and unexpectedly sudden failure of the Roman Catholic Church in Québec—an ultra-Catholic territory for three and a half centuries. It was as if the whole place woke up one morning massively rejecting all the nonsense previous generations had been too afraid to throw away like the trash that it was. And all it took to trigger this was in great part television, where we could easily observe our considerable meekness and extensive subservience to our own petty bourgeoisie and our own arrogant clergy, both of which openly and pompously thought themselves better than the rest of the population. A situation illustrated and underscored among other examples to the population at large in this case by the novel and TV sitcom decades ago of *"Un homme et son péché"* by Claude Henri Grignon and in the same vein in another sitcom and novel called "Le Survenant" by Germaine Guèvremont, among others. Maybe there is still hope for other heavily indoctrinated Western nations such as Ireland and Poland for example.

Another Religious Misogynist Again.

Let us recall the crass proclamation and alleged rationalization of that sociopathic and deeply misogynist cardinal Marc Ouellete of Québec City in Canada in 2010, who deeply believed that even a violently raped woman should keep the child from such a disastrous event in view of what this nincompoop considers "respect for life". And for this form of retrograde thinking, he was promoted to a high post at the Vatican—with a good chance at becoming pope for his dogmatic outlook. It's enough to make you puke.

Jean-Charles Harvey.

Let us remember a freethinking individual and an extraordinary Québécois – an example to all professional journalists everywhere! I refer to a man-of-the-world known to us Canadians and particularly those of us from the province of Québec as Jean-

Charles Harvey. A man who insisted on being an ethical human being, at a great cost to himself and those who loved him, amid the then *self-righteous* ultra-xenophobic Québec society with a definite fascist leaning elite, and a medieval like local Roman Catholic Church, prior to the so-called *'révolution tranquille'*. I speak of a man I admire, and who should be emulated. A brave individual whose courage and determination stood front and center against a ruthless domineering Québec elite toward a typically brainwashed and docile population, managed by a self-involved self-serving petty bourgeoisie of Roman Catholic priests, lawyers, doctors, and servile politicians. Yes! Jean-Charles Harvey was a person of ethical convictions, who:

1. Confronted a truly backward subservient education system.

2. Lifted the veil on his ethnic group's unworldly, servile, parochial, and ultra-religious population indoctrinated with medieval standards.

3. Lifted the veil of an ultraconservative reward looking Roman Catholic Church.

4. Showed the machinations of an ultra-nationalist establishment bent on suspecting anything of English consonance.

5. Disclosed Quebec's elite's support of fascists such as Franco of Spain and the Nazi intervention in 1937, as well as Petain of France with his cooperation with Hitler, Benito Mussolini, along with its own home made fascist leader, Adrian Arcand.

6. Brought the light over that vile anti-Semite, chanoine Lionel Groulx, although that unrepentant racist was given a national funeral in 1967, and whose name until a few months ago was proudly petitioned to remain as is in a subway station, college, CEGEP, street, and even a Sportmax.

All of this intellectually encouraged by the Quebec's French-Canadian elite newspaper "Le Devoir". Oh yes! I introduce you to Jean-Charles Harvey, a man fired by the Premier of that province, the xenophobic Maurice Duplessis, for daring to tell the truth, and unethically relegated as a traitor to the cause of French-Canadians by the elite class of the day. And so, I proclaim in my humble way:

"Vive Jean-Charles Harvey! A brave man who expressed that most special courage required in taking the ethical stand he heroically and deliberately took—despite penalties meted against him for this valorous acts of affirmation."

And yet we continue to ignore his memory. Shame on us all dear Quebecers!

Esther Delisle.

Let us keep in mind courageous Esther Delisle, who recently in Québec history, bravely and stubbornly went on debunking the shame of what was considered normal in the 1930s and 1940s in the province of Québec particularly. I speak of a medieval-based, shamefully inspired, religiously managed, and petty-bourgeoisie-concocted political fascist philosophy of the day tied into an anti-Semitic bent, with remnants still alive within a faction of Québec's separatist movements. People whose views are summed up in the notion of *"Le Québec au Québécois"* regardless of political affiliation, and which in my interpretation implies French-speaking Roman Catholic *'pure laine'* Québécois first and above all others as the *'Chosen People'* on that territory of our planet.

Rare nanny state among the few.

In my own province of Québec in Canada the Nanny State has now replaced in all of its excesses the medieval Roman Catholic Church of a few decades ago, which for several centuries acted as dictatorial meta-parents, and now apparently because its population psychologically still requires the illusive protection of a 'super other'. That is why, political correctitude is the unofficial belief system of the present Québec establishment and at the heart of all its political processes. And because of this, massive bureaucratic protocols now exist with the support of a complex managerial methodology pompously and pretentiously identified as "le modèle Québécois" by vielles souches French-speaking Quebecers considering themselves at times superior and much different from Americans and English-speaking Canadians. It also now forms an integral part and function of the special languages of all professionals and bureaucrats in that province. This is routinely characterized with patronizing expressions before answering almost anything, generally framing their opinions and statements, as if these were meant for quasi-illiterate or an already submissive population with such traditional patronizing sayings as: "Il faut d'abords comprendre que ...", and others similar to this. As if the listeners were unable or had serious difficulties to assess a particular point or context, whenever expressed by an expert or professional, while drowning regular folks in torrents of bureaucratic verbiage.

Somehow like the good old days of religious hegemony in that province when opinions or diktats of priests and bishops were accepted as valid no matter their insignificance, paltriness, inconsequentiality, and triviality in the control of a submissive French-Canadian population of the time and place.

A situation now evident in the ever-growing Nanny-State favored by French-speaking Quebecois, reminiscent of the condescending parlance of their previous religious masters, and in fact has now replaced it with a secular version the ecclesiastical modus operandi of their previous masters, which they now so punctiliously mimic in various secular formats.

I am ashamed of....

I am ashamed of the tolerance afforded to arrogant, pompous, and often mediocre bureaucrats in fact running the province of Québec in Canada. A self-serving group now bringing it to the unforgivable chasm of economic and directional mismanagement. An issue worsening and ever more predictable with the contribution of retrograde and greedy labor unions.

Traditional québec elite class

The traditional Québec elite class considers itself worldly, sophisticated, and cosmopolitan despite the fact it is generally and merely bent on short term tactical gains of parochial significance instead of a long term strategic continental mission and supporting objectives.

Newspaper 'le devoir' - 01.

Remember 'chers Québécois' that the well thought out articles and analyses of "Le Devoir" newspaper about the conflict between England and Germany prior to and during the Second World War, proclaimed it *"a mere commercial and economic misunderstanding"*, as I remember reading some time ago. Somehow, it seems, journalists and editors of the day could not see the blindingly obvious conflicts unfolding at that time against freedom and liberty. Or dare I say: *"they did"*. Yea! Read the hypocritical essays constituting the André Laurendeau doctrine, among others.

Newspaper 'le devoir' - 02.

As free human beings let us never forget that 'Le Devoir' newspaper <u>agreed with Nazis</u>, when it noted that the wearing of the infamous "Yellow Star of David" was appropriate. Despondently, I admit being thoroughly ashamed as I realize that the people who believed and uttered these thoughts were also 'pure laine' French-speaking French-Canadians like me. The intense sense of ethical betrayal I feel about this issue, makes me understand most profoundly what many ethical Germans, Italians, Serbs, and others felt at that time. In our local case, only Jean-Charles Harvey had the courage to stand front and center at that time, reprimanding this rag of yellow journalism among other things—and sadly paid dearly for this brave ethical stand.

Bureaucratic mediocrity.

You surely noticed an obvious mediocrity inherent to many bureaucratic occupations, but if you wish to observe a mediocracy ossified in an élan vital of sanctified incompetence and pomposity, despite its membership within the Western tradition but with the camouflage of a socially shallow but sophisticated technology to keep them from participating in the political estate at its disposal, go on and deal with the Québec provincial government bureaucracy in Canada! Or far worse and far more detrimental yet, look into kick-back oriented government bureaucracies and their markedly worse Sub-Saharan African counterparts among others.

The Planetary Decline of 'La Francophonie'

The time has arrived for all Quebecers to adopt efficiency and effectiveness in the world as it really is, while ignoring once and for all their inherited dogmas and ideology.

Like Unwanted Junk

Québec's French-Canadian traditional sense of inferiority is founded on a fallacy and the result in great part of their treatment by their 'mother country' of origin, which is summed up here in seven points:

1. France has never truly helped French-Canadians since abandoning them as French citizens to guarantee their own supply of sugar in 1769.

2. French-Canadians as then French citizens were cast *à la dérive* like unwanted junk by a troubled, ineffective, inefficient, and uncaring France centuries ago.

3. France instead cut them loose centuries ago, only to come back occasionally in the second half of the 20th century to rub it in, treating that province as if a second class colonial subset of *La Francophonie* – a quaint cousin of sort in North America thought and treated as such.

Yet, many attributes can be assigned to Québec:

4. Québec alone, to identify the biggest concentration of French-Canadians in Canada, is:

(a) More than three time the geographical size of France.

(b) Immensely richer in resources.

(c) Better positioned for future development sharing a long frontier with the United States and the rest of Canada and because of that proximity possesses more opportunities to carry on business with them.

5. French-Canadians do not share the same worldview with their European French cousins, because they are by temperament and in fact North Americans in perception and connotation and are not European French-speaking citizens in that respect.

6. French-Canadians are in fact both Canadianized and Americanized more than they care to admit.

7. There is France's habit of occasionally and strategically intervening in the business of its ex-colonies, exemplified in a galling and pompous way once demonstrated by Charles De Gaulle in his *"Vive le Québec libre"* proclamation in Montréal. As if Québec was somehow still a colony of France, or at least a forgotten relative that might be useful someday.

Self-Inflicted Mythology of Victimization

Broad aspects of Québec's shortcomings are based on a true legacy of and yet in the last few decades are founded on a self-inflicted mythology of victimization.

These can be summed up in the following three examples:

1. Various separatist Québec provincial administrations have done summersaults, showing off as it tried to compete with other ex-French colonies for France's condescending attention—a truly embarrassing situation to witness.

2. The weird habit by the Québec government of all too often benchmarking, what is allegedly best in the government practices and policies of France, is an emotional illusion—not a sound approach of doing business.

Indeed, to only copy or giving preference to what Québec politicians and bureaucrats consider the best in France, ignores what is better elsewhere – including the rest of Canada. It is in fact:

1. An illogical approach to business decisions and project management.

2. A most irresponsible financial and overall economic attitude.

3. A mistake the Chinese in their long range and highly disciplined wisdom did not commit in the accelerated growth of their manufacturing and developing economy in all sectors and still does not commit nowadays.

French-Canadians in Québec should above all award all major contracts to advance the construction of its infrastructure and economy based on a planetary bidding format – so that the best in the world with the best overall costs and reputation for on-time delivery and quality of execution can be selected.

In this way Québec would finally stop rewarding incompetents and thieves among its local contractors and engineering firms, for example, who know full well the bias inherently indoctrinated in government bureaucrats to select only locals along with their profoundly inbred fear of entrepreneurship and a culture of systemic kickbacks.

That is why among numerous examples which could be cited, the cost of roads per capita in Québec is much higher, less effective, less efficient, and inferior to its neighbor province, Ontario.

Yet, very few in Québec pay the slightest bit of attention to this most obvious phenomenon.

Until About 1967, When …

Until about 1967, when Montréal reached its apogee, this city was indeed Canada's cultural epicenter along with its mostly separate English-speaking business center. Its effervescence became a trademark and a light of freedom after centuries-long of a *grande noirceur*.

A most welcomed sense of relief by all French-Canadians both in and outside Québec, when they came out of their centuries-long elite-imposed and self-induced isolation.

Montréal was then at last recognized as a world class city often internationally referred to in the news as a most decent place to live.

However, a sluggish process of development has slowed down its evolution since then. The reason for this is four-fold:

Reason 1.

PRAGMATIC SOLUTIONS TO QUÉBEC'S SERIOUS ECONOMIC PROBLEMS

The provincial government failed at the beginning of the *révolution tranquille* to adopt and implement pragmatic solutions to Québec's serious economic problems – preferring to pay for extravagant projects and programs it could not afford – doing so from borrowed money and ever-increasing severe deficits – living so to speak on their credit cards. And this while hiding their dire financial position and sadly with this continuing attitude the worst is yet to come.

Doing so through accounting trickeries worthy of the best prestidigitators along with structured Machiavellian taxation schemes meant to bleed its population dry, while receiving massive unearned *welfare payments* in the billions of dollars from the most productive areas of Canada.

The province of Québec receives such extraordinary benefits for simply being a financially low performing province in a federated Canada, wherein national tax surpluses in a complex federal agreement are shared with no strings attached with the poorer provinces.

Reason 2.

AN UNNECESSARY AND MASSIVE BUREAUCRATIC LABYRINTH

Second, Québec's unnecessary and massive bureaucratic labyrinth created in support of its ideology of instituting a *politically correct* <u>de-Canadianized</u> French-speaking *'société distincte'*, added to overly complex governing silo-intensive administrative structures, both, ensuring a continuing asphyxiation of entrepreneurship.

As well as heavily discouraging businesses from establishing themselves in this beautiful province because of obstructing and complex bureaucratic conditions.

It is as if the Québec political class along with its traditional professional crowd were aiming at complete failure – ignoring the developing economies around the planet, cherry picking only those notions supporting their way of understanding the world – regardless of costs and future financial demands required by such schemes, while passing on this crucial financial cost to future generations to solve if not simply drown in debts.

It is as if driving a car blindfolded at full speed, so to speak, with the certitude that one's ideology is correct and does indeed trump everything ... and will nonetheless guide and protect us in the end.

Reason 3.

A PROVINCIAL CAPITAL WITH NO TRUE BUSINESS REVENUES

Politicians and bureaucrats living in Québec City and surrounding area, have funneled an exaggerated of level of funds in the development of the capital city and concentrated an inappropriate number of government jobs at the expense of the Montréal metropolitan area, the economic engine of the province.

Doing so just because it could and so it could admire an idealized capital for a future republic.

A provincial capital still nevertheless, with next to none in true business revenues, paid in great part by its better off French- and English-speaking segments—citizens and business organizations alike from the greater Montréal— which largely per capita contributes to the provincial tax base.

A shameful money and job grabs blinding the politicians in Québec City to the province's serious systemic economic problems.

Reason 4.

PROJECT AND PROGRAM FAILURES OF
'LA MÉTHODE QUÉBÉCOISE'

The whole governmental behavior toward the planning and execution of its projects and programs has generally been inefficient, ineffective, qualitatively inferior, and often corrupt. This attitude along with its poor performance and comportment have constructed a Nanny-State and a debt-ridden province.

It is therefore high time Québec adopted a pragmatic world view – one that finally understands that all dreams and ambitious undertakings <u>must</u> rest on realistic planning, the real flow of money, and sound resources management among other things.

And that in our specific case, we also cannot pretend that about 600,000 Quebecers in addition to the majority of newcomers from other lands, who in spite of fear-ridden and narrow-minded language laws, nevertheless live in English in that province, and that the whole English-speaking segment of the population earns more per capita and therefore contributes more per capita to the provincial tax burden.

Québec culture: 21st century ce.

In Québec you can easily be impaled on thorns of bureaucracy, as if the State existed as a hybrid combination of a meta-bully and a super-nanny organization legally established to squeeze the most it can out of you as a taxpayer, while continuingly preaching and teaching you what your *politically correct* thinking and behavior ought to be.

In effect minding your business at all times.

This explains, in part, expansive and expensive multi-levelled bureaucratic labor forces draining public funds, thanks to inbred and unaffordable government managed programs, congenital incompetence, and a generalized fundamental lack of business sense and applications—giving preference to ideology and protocols in support of unsustainable programs and therefore at the expense of future Québec generations.

Québec's Original Lack of Entrepreneurship

Many French-Canadians in Québec retained their Gallic habit of sequencing and parsing their collective memory, so that only what meets their highly *politically correct* view of history and a hyper-bureaucratic approach to management policies, execution of projects, programs, and general multitudinous and all too often supercilious administration protocols substitute themselves for a lack of entrepreneurship.

No wonder Quebecers often developed a habit of blaming others for their shortcomings and for an accelerated debt problem that will eventually cripple them financially and in every other way.

No wonder also that the separatist class consists in great part of *The Bombastic, The Cantankerous, The Vain, The-Often-Hysterical* and *The Unwise* – generally those afraid or unable to make it in the world at large, ready to blame someone else for their shortcomings.

What Lurks in the Background

What lurks in the background of Québec's future is its inherited taste for radical solutions set early on, at least since 1608, and its predisposition and predilection for rules based on an ideological blindness that disregard economic consequences.

This has been shown in the course of its history, demonstrated by what could be called a penchant for strong leaders, and robust governing rules applied universally and expectantly without exceptions – as taught by their former and unforgiving Church edicts to which they are still addicted but this time in a secular fashion, context, and model – and this without ever admitting it.

Hence, the highly politicized *politically correct* world of Québec bureaucrats and professionals, and the unwavering ever-growing number of protocols in their robotized administrative mazes and rules along with circular bureaucratic algorithms of controls.

A Losing Strategy of Exclusivity

Daring to question the mythology of Québec's ideology of exclusive separation at the expense and against the will of all others in Québec unwilling to abide by it—especially its nascent entrepreneurial French-Canadian communities and its English-speaking population.

QUÉBEC SEPARATISTS – 01.

In the ideology of their branch of French sovereignty in the entirety of the Québec territory, hardcore Québec separatists are generally impassioned Anglophobes.

Despite their proclaimed and often deeply felt respect for democratic processes, along with an over the top adherence to political correctitude, they in fact despise democracies.

Québec separatists use this approach to hypocritically reduce, if not simply ignore, the *Inalienable Individual Rights* of hundreds of thousands of Québécois functioning in English either at home or at work or with each other or all of these.

Filled, as Québec separatists are, with pathological obfuscation and frustration, their parochial wrath has unhinged their common sense and the reality of global history and planetary economy.

Undeniably, Québec separatists, full of the pomposity borrowed from their French cousins of old, continue nonetheless to speak in the new quasi-religious language of political correctitude in order to rationalize their ideology.

"How very Jesuitical of you guys indeed!" An intellectually liberated Quebecois could then proclaim.

QUÉBEC SEPARATISTS – 02.

Québec's mother country abandoned them centuries ago to the benefit of their English enemy.

France in fact cut them off from their culture, without protection, leaving them at the mercy of their then enemy, England, to fend for themselves, as France did with their brothers and sisters similarly victimized in the Louisiana Purchase and elsewhere in the world before and after that.

And yet incomprehensibly the French-Canadian Québec bourgeoisie with separatist aspirations nevertheless continues to display trails of a misplaced Anglophobia, wherever they go and whenever they speak rather than assess the blow delivered to them by their mother country.

Indeed, the unilingual French-speaking Québec bourgeoisie particularly, which replaced the former French aristocracy after its departure in 1760, transmogrified itself into the traditional professional class of old still arming themselves with a classical education until the end of *la grande noirceur*.

Over time this new bourgeoisie developed to include 21st century ultra-bureaucrats and new professionals – a large segment that sees itself as the future *Special Group;* a sort of *Chosen People* reminiscent of biblical stories, that would govern a separate Québec allegedly without too much challenges from its English-speaking population in Québec as well as in the rest of Canada, and the United States.

A group of mostly French-speaking French-Canadians stakeholders and a few owners, who in fact and at every opportunity prefer to adopt for themselves the well-known although never admitted belly-gazing metaphor:

"To be a big fish in a smaller pond rather than a small fish in a larger pond".

And always it seems this self-promoted class still perambulates with a sort of messianic complex ready to educate us poor ignorant peasants, as they pronounce claims of specialness and make incendiary statements.

Exhibiting a sort of pomposity of the self-promoted self-righteousness of their cause, while completing report after report with the now usual decoration of politically correct terminology tailored to its ideology.

"JE ME SOUVIENS": A FAILED STRATEGY.

For about two centuries a great number of French-Canadians have gone through life as life goes through them, unaware of opportunities passing them by, while bitching rather than taking some initiative to improve their lot.

Indeed, the *"Je me souviens"* social class is bent on remembering their past losses to the English from both England and the US in the early course of their history, while purposely forgetting their abandonment decided and carried out by their mother country. And now separatist-leaning politicians expect in their best wet dreams to rule over a republic constituted of unilingual French-speaking Quebecers first at the expense of those other French-Canadians generally fluent in English along with its large English-speaking minority – with an emphasis on 'Québécois de souche'.

Separatists in addition further expect to rule a republic at their own negative economic costs, since its bourgeoisie prefers classic professions to the detriment of future business development and economic prosperity, based on the globalization of business.

Indeed, while most doctors, lawyers, notaries, priests (although these latter ones are now few nowadays) all continue as in the good old days to spend their life entirely in French, while the rest of the population has to negotiate with reality on the ground with English, and not through the protected financial sanctuary of these traditional professions or that of over-staffed provincial government bureaucrats at the near exclusion of English-speaking Quebecers feeding on revenues from taxes of all sorts.

***

Yet, inexplicably many, within the *"Je me souviens"* social class of French-Canadians, still see themselves as victims, which they in fact are no longer – except when willingly positioning themselves in such a situation on purpose, or when saddling their mind with an ideology that shapes their attitude and structures their comportment as victims.

***

True! French-Canadians were once a conquered people, abandoned by their mother country, and badly treated emotionally and intellectually by their Church, their own petty bourgeoisie, and their conquerors.

In this respect their original subjugated situation was real and most certainly not their fault.

As such it was and remains simply, sadly, and plainly a social form of the *Personal Calamity Syndrome,* although it can no longer remain an excuse for lack of entrepreneurship in this 21st century with all the opportunities literally at our doors.

NO MORE...

The present and future of French-Canadians in the province of Québec are their responsibility – no one else. They have been without a doubt accountable for it, particularly since the paradigm shift that launched the *révolution tranquille.* Look! Although by accident of, both, fortunate circumstances and history, Quebecers found themselves in the 20th and continue now to find themselves in this 21st century in an envious and advantageous business and economic position, which, unless they recognize and capitalize upon this ASAP, they will forever be penalized to their greatest regrets. In fact:

1. They are, like most provinces in Canada, smack against the USA.
2. They live in a free democracy wherein human rights predominate.
3. They have been free to retain and speak their ethnic tongue, while offered the unique opportunity to learn English as a second language through a variety of sources. And this with existing English-Canadians and Americans as neighbors.
4. They possess their own radio and television stations, as well as being free to benchmark regular English classes at all levels in their school systems, similar to Scandinavian countries if they so wished it, particularly since English has become the language of the educated as well as the foundation of business and communication networks along with elite groups across the globe.

But no. The political separatist determination, still heavily influenced and blinded by their ideology, prevented them from living in the real world. Their mythology of sovereign independence still trumped it all.

Yet, every French-Canadian is free to do as she/he pleases and grab opportunities as they present themselves, if not create these for themselves in the first place.

That is why, in spite of Québec's provincial government's historical reluctance to do so, a new and young generation is now moving on the bandwagon of socio-economic success.

Grabbing those opportunities which English is also bringing to them, and de facto moving away from the mythological aspiration of financial success of their parents and grandparents to one that is factual.

So, the *"Je me souviens"* social class should surrender their complacency, depart from their *souveraineté* concept, and join the rest of the human race, because isolation never paid off in the course of history. Québec is no exception to that rule of human existence and the latest generation understands it. Yet, a political truism still remains:

> Now that Québec is a multicultural province, the tribal urge for national independence of French-Canadians, secretly preferred by many of the unilingual 'vielles souches' type on that territory especially outside major urban centers, cannot be founded on the sociopolitical disease of victimization and political ideology of a *'Chosen People'*.

It must be based on the willingness of the vast majority of its citizens from all cultures within it – including both widely spoken languages – whether extreme nationalists recognize it or not.

After all is said and done, reality is reality.

Québec Separatists' Political Mismanagement

*Daring to question
the 'Laurentia' vision mythology.*

THEN, NOW AND BEYOND.

The larger issue that intellectually imprisoned French-Canadians especially in the province of Québec into restrictive cultural folkways and mores, consists of the thinking social machinery that created this unbending inwardness for so long.

An intellectual apparatus constructed and managed through the intellectual brutality of both religion and local politics exercised via the exceptionally and almost impregnable social structures and psychological walls originally created by these.

THE REAL 'GRANDE NOIRCEUR'.

The quasi-medieval French-Canadian environment, which existed in Québec since its beginnings in 1608 until the Sixties, is in fact the <u>real</u> *grande noirceur.*

It created among many other things the ghettos found all over Montréal during that time, which nurtured and fostered people located there into their various subservient positions.

In order to abstract themselves out of this compliant, differential, and obedient rolé, the whole Québec society had to change this attitude, while careful of not falling for another form of dictatorship of the mind as in the good old days of Church hegemony.

STRANGLEHOLD OF RELIGIOUS INFRASTRUCTURE.

While French-Canadians in Québec were marking time with their rather backward economy, overly cautious financial investments by a scarce infrastructure projects, an unchanging and unquestionable medieval-like dogmatic believe system, and their inward looking folkways and mores; English-speaking North-America in the meantime was growing economically and industrially, becoming a world class financial force as well as culturally evolving at an accelerated pace into a new form of society.

Therefore, something decisive had to take place to release the stranglehold keeping French-Canadians unquestionably docile and obedient to authorities generally and the clerical class in particular.

The first and most difficult step – the one that truly enslaves people if it is dogmatic – had to be and was indeed for French-Canadians the shedding of the domination of its own religion.

This oddly enough was unexpectedly accomplished in record time in the province of Québec.

Unfortunately, enough of a skeletal structure of that old control system remained, probably because little time existed to fully develop a secular one at the speed changes were taking place when the *révolution tranquille* was triggered.

The old style elite class in that society was left almost intact in the hands the remaining establishment comprising of lawyers, notaries, medical doctors, university professors, journalists, and politicians, who continued their lessening but nevertheless still commanding influence to their own advantage (admittedly in limited ways) in the management of French-Canadians in Québec, doing so by retaining their authoritarian grip via an allegedly independent new protocol of thinking and behavior with new filters for thoughts and behavior of a nascent political correctness and the stocking of the continuing mythology of victimhood.

And this even though French-Canadians were gradually and quickly breaking all ties with their previous arrogant religious masters and that their future was now fully in their hands with the safety of financial survival in a generous federation of provinces supporting one another.

This time traditional professionals along new ones coming in on account of an accelerating technological world would gradually institute their new and modern hold over the population in an aura of equality, but which would be tightly controlled through brand new secularized, expansive, expensive, complex, and rigid bureaucratic protocols and algorithms.

It seems to have taken place, as if to retain admittedly in different ways, old patterns such as the certainty of another form of *Immaculate Perception* replacing the one overbearing religious Parent-State with a Nanny-State—another meta-parent, nevertheless.

And this while continuing to dictate specific behavior that kept the population at large feel safe and protected and from which the so-called "modèle Québécois" emerged in that province and for which nationalists are so fond to refer to, as the modus operandi of a special people—a *Chosen People* of sort.

And so, three questions remain:

How can Quebecers get out of this quirky way of thinking?

Is it simply by ignoring the 'old school' educated class for a generation or so – letting the unaffected younger generation begin to think anew and on its own?

Is it now taking place with the ultra-connected small entrepreneurial groups found in and around the greater Montréal and Beauce areas at this moment?

RELIGIOUS INFRASTRUCTURE COLLAPSE.

As the once solid local religious structures of control went through their collapse, French-Canadians' attitude toward a new future in Québec regrettably began to cater to another unquestionable belief system—a secular one this time.

A purported reorientation alas intellectually reminiscent in some ways to the medieval reasoning structure to which they had been subjected, and which had already suffocated all of their ambitions and aspirations for centuries.

It was and still is as if enough of the old skeletal template remained, as if it had somehow replicated itself to a larger degree in the construction of their next paradigm shift of beliefs with all the new conventions, procedures, and protocol such a shift demands but in a 20th century context—admittedly in the form of a looser but nevertheless progressively, unquestionable, and dogmatic belief system – although in a secular form this time.

Despite all the efforts spent by French-Canadians so far in extirpating themselves out of the psychological cul-de-sac, in which they had been lodged into for so long, it must be said that once more that:

> *Unless a significant segment of that society, insists on getting out of that new secular conundrum, a quasi-dogmatic one in some ways in its structure, still blocking serious forms of independent thought and behavior, it is doomed to a most hazardous future.*

REVOLUTIONARY PROCESS.

Thankfully, the first step in any societal evolution requires the elimination of all dogmas and unquestionable beliefs—ancient and new ones alike. This revolutionary process took place in the course of only a few decades in Québec– although this liberating movement has been slower outside its urban centers.

Nonetheless once and where it was accomplished, a world of incredible opportunities begged them to do something to improve their situation and a whole generation did just that. Indeed, once Quebecers were finally out of the darkness of medieval thinking and in the sunshine of a North-American world that had gone ahead of them in just about every way, it became advantageous to act freely with no more religious based social barriers in the way.

As French-Canadians divested themselves of the yolk of religion and readied themselves to institute a paradigm shift and rebuild their culture on another more rational basis, a more pragmatic belief system emerged, and the only roadblock left was emotional.

Not an easy task indeed.

French-speaking French-Canadians in Québec now had as a society to overcome five things:

1. Their ingrained habit for ready-made solutions thought out by the authority in place has remained, with a tendency still to look for prêt-a-porter products, solutions, or results. And so, they have a tendency to look for a strong leader and or government, a meta parent of sort, to handle all social issues and problems that previously were the purview of the religious class.

2. Their national phobia of English, the language of their conquerors, which has ironically and coincidentally now become the communication language of international business, diplomacy, information technology, science, and that of the world's elite by default nearly everywhere. A fact that developed quite independently from the Québec situation and which a significant segment of unilingual French-speaking French-Canadians in Québec have not yet been able or unwilling to discern.

3. Their inferiority complex constructed co-dependently with their being dumped by their mother country in exchanged for a few small Pacific islands, while being forgotten from then

on, as if an illegitimate child in a pitiless Roman Catholic environment.

4. An ingrained habit of ignoring finances, economics, the management of money generally, and the fear of entrepreneurship in nearly all of its forms literally taught to them by their own Roman Catholic Church, which not only controlled their school system but their private lives as well.

QUÉBEC SEPARATISTS' MYTHOLOGY – 01.

The problem so far illustrated by the mythology expounded by the Parti Québécois – those who envisaged Québec as a separate nation regardless of costs, and ideally a self-sufficient republic, where only French would be spoken, is that they irrationally believe:

1. That the ideology promoted openly by their writers, journalists, artists, radio personalities and local one-dimension entertainment stars was one of a romanticized French-Canadian utopia on Earth, where the labor unions would set the tone and adequate revenues would also flow in support of a new so-called "modèle Québécois" in labor relations and an unparallel 'rapport de force' for all workers.

An ideology promoted by the sort of people that hardly ever entered in contact with, both, the business and the English-speaking world in their very own towns, province, country, and continent.

A people often dreaming of and suggesting that a sort of *"de-Canadianization"* of Québec could magically take place, and that Canada and the USA would just stand aside. An illusion allegedly in support of the greater interest of and benefits of vieilles souche Quebecers.

2. That reaching such a vision could almost immediately and miraculously solve all political difficulties, present severe financial problems, and correct real and mythological inequities. An idea surreptitiously promoted as well by their old-fashioned bourgeoisie during the Thirties, Forties and Fifties, and now repeated ad nauseam since then by the new reinvented but nevertheless traditional medical, legal, journalistic, and several other professorial classes.

3. That they could survive as a small and totally independent French-speaking country and this as an economically minor player on the entire English-speaking continent of North America with the most powerful nation on earth smack against its frontiers.

4. That assumed its younger savvier French-Canadian population would vote *en masse* for this ghettoized political proposal.

5. That they could pretend that its English-speaking population would eventually side with them once their organization could win a '50% + 1' referendum – including its wide-awake migrant population, which generally favors English at least for external communications simply as a survival tactic for the job market among other factors.

6. That they could make up the financial difference once Québec no longer could get equalization payments from more prosperous provinces.

7. That they could ignore the English-speaking reality in all domains on the entire North American continent including its significant English-speaking Québec population

8. That they would retain their entire present territory as is, and that Canada would agree to be geographically split into two portions <u>without a corridor</u>, especially since the majority of its Anglophones citizens are already located within such a corridor.

9. That they assume France would cooperate with them on the international scene and come to their rescue if lodged into a jam of some sort—forgetting that France had the tendency in the course of its history of abandoning its own citizens in time of crisis or defeat, including French-Canadians and Acadians.

Planning to do so as if to 'prove' like a petulant teenager to an uncaring 'parent', France in this case, among other reasons, the superiority of those that France unceremoniously dumped in the 1759-1760 period. As if to proclaim in a sort of rebellious adolescent manner: *"See! We didn't need you ... Don't need you still ... And can <u>now</u> deal with you 'equal to equal'!"*

QUÉBEC SEPARATISTS' MYTHOLOGY – 02.

What has been purposely ignored by Québec separatists in their discourse over the last decades following *la révolution tranquille* was that English had by then gained planetary acceptance by the educated, business, and scientific classes in all significant nations of our planet – independent of what had happened to French-Canadians.

Québec separatists, whether they recognize and accept that reality or not, have no other pragmatic choice but accept it – and yet they won't or at least have great difficulties accepting its possibility.

If they do not, they will burden the whole national group they purportedly claim to represent, making them pay an additional and unnecessary high price for ignoring the world as it really is in this regard.

Indeed, in the course of the *grande noirceur* as history unfolded independently, quietly, and ironically, English became the lingua franca of the planet – pardon the pun here.

A language now used by international commerce and business among many other global activities – with the power center of the

English-speaking community shifting from the UK to the USA in the course of the 20th century.

And that to refuse to use English as a secondary language – especially for Quebecers – becomes an act of sheer insanity in the midst of an accelerated global economy and planetary communication network based in great part on English and certainly not on a significant planetary decreasing utilization of French since the Treaty of Versailles in 1919 and more so since World War Two.

This is something Québec separatists get indigestions when thinking about it – and because of their unbending ideology most cannot emotionally admit to it, and go to great length and pains to avoid it in political discourses .

And yet, because Québec shares a long geographical frontier with the USA, it cannot avoid both contacts with it, and the extraordinary opportunities this represents – including those economic and business prospects held at bay for so long and which are still there for the picking.

This also includes Ontario, the largest, richest, and most populated province in Canada, a next door neighbor as well, in which more than close to a million other French-Canadians also reside, bilingual French-Canadians that is, in addition to the rest of a growing and vibrant economy in the rest of English-speaking Canada, which also includes tens of thousands of other fully bilingual, when not simply now unilingual English-speaking French-Canadians.

Opportunities a great number of countries and ethnic groups around the world would most certainly capitalize upon, should they be so lucky as to possess the same prospects.

RESISTED ALL FORMS OF ENTREPRENEURSHIP.

Until the Sixties French-Canadians generally were led by an ultra-fundamentalist Roman Catholic Church with the support in

Québec of a well-paid class formed of the medical, legal, educational, journalistic, professorial, and political establishments.

A group that stupidly resisted all forms of entrepreneurship for fear of losing their hierarchical rank and the control this provided them over their national community.

That is likely why:

> *The French-speaking Québec population nowadays still tends by <u>sheer prior indoctrination</u> – passed onto them often by the parents – to give more credence to, and easily submits itself still at the hands of, officialdom, professionals, petty bureaucrats, and above all to complex protocols of 'Political Correctitude'.*

And another reason why as well:

> *The Québec chapter of the French-Canadian community generally prefers a map of procedures and borrowed cash rather than deal with the actual execution of real projects in real time with real earned money of their own. In effect a classic response to and expectations of self-appointed victims.*

Although a slowly growing exception within that group began with those who attended English-speaking Canadian or American universities or undertook serious business administration degrees in the very few emerging French-speaking centers of learning now providing these or simply attended English-speaking universities to facilitate their education in this respect. A group that has now been followed lately by a more global thinking generation.

WHEREIN NO ONE IS ACCOUNTABLE.

In order to feel that they were now in charge of their destiny, while literally dumping their unflinching and unforgiving religious masters, French-speaking Quebecois *'de souches'* sadly attached themselves to the 'procedural manual' of *'Political Correctitude',* way before it had been given a name in the USA and the rest of the world.

Doing so on rules and regulations, which in effect replaced old religious ones on a template somewhat resembling them but in a secular context instead.

So, in Québec nowadays the new creed that replaced the authoritarian Roman Catholic Church has become the belief system of *'Political Correctitude'.* A quasi-religious addictive process and methodology especially visible in the complex structure of its institutions and the labyrinthine protocols of its bureaucratic organizations. And this with a set of meanings, values and standards demanding the absolute applications of predetermined thinking and behavior, rather than creative ones.

A process that demands an ideological application of principles regardless of what the present demands or future economic brutalities will cause, for example.

And this just so a given *politically correct* principle or other can be maintained <u>in a pre-scripted protocol</u> **<u>wherein no one is accountable</u>**.

Therefore, in 21st century Québec, for example, while its government regulates and finances daycare centers at a great loss, it provides no true fundamental means to attract and retain sound business investments or research and development.

On the contrary it chases these away with the inevitable disastrous results this inevitably brings to future generations.

This now 21st century French-Canadian government still blinded to the realities and benefits of entrepreneurship—by centuries of punishing isolation, combined with a previously crippling and profoundly damaging religious brainwashing—rather than change the situation now that it can to its interests and benefits in this land of peace and opportunity, worsens it instead by:

1. Still blindly and aggressively creating Machiavellian taxations schemes of every kind in the hope of creating an ideal society without critical business participation and a sound revenue base.

2. Still behaves, like a gigantic corporate welfare bum, by legally getting money **it never earned** from the more financially successful provinces generation after generation – acting in parasitical ways throughout its history from the efforts, efficiencies, and effectiveness of better off provinces through the federal government agreements: that of 'Péréquation' as it is called in Québec.

3. Still downgrades concepts of business and entrepreneurship in favor of government subsidies.

A LAUDABLE SOCIAL OBJECTIVE.

While the overall Québec social objective is laudable, the means to get there are self-destructive since it ignores the principle of pragmatic long-term development that may inevitably lead to the obliteration of such a society. In the end their visionless approach to problem-solving, if it remains unchanged, will most likely bankrupt this particular national community. As its various governmental administrations keep on dumping future financial disasters on the next generations, simply because the tax base cannot support such goals; or by strangling commercial ventures in the face of unnecessary robotized bureaucratic rules along with smothering taxation; or by a population at large generally still shy if not simply afraid of venturing in entrepreneurial enterprises.

RATHER THAN ACT ON THESE IN REAL TIME.

By its ideological attempts to produce permanent change and despite its progress, Québec has demonstrated for decades since the *révolution tranquille,* its tendency to mismanage most of its projects and programs in real time and within its financial means.

That is why, since the Sixties Québec authorities as a whole along with their support class of professionals and technocrats, tended to endorse pretentious ideological and mythological goals without assessing the nature and structure of its enormous management problems.

Doing so for immediate political rewards especially among those dreaming of an independent French-speaking North American nation.

Doing so as well against long term strategic planning, while neglecting revenue creation – choosing Machiavellian tax schemes against its very own people and free handouts from the rest of Canada.

Copying in many respects the Church's management style that French-Canadian Quebecers had found so despicable just a few decades before.

Partial Context and Background

Ad hoc references, quotations, comments, and notes are reproduced here in no particular order or degree of importance about French-Canadians generally and Québec particularly.

These were abstracted from previous works by this author, so as to provide further context and background for the non-initiated to the politically incorrect discussions and opinions contained in this specific essay.

A NEWSPAPER CALLED 'LE DEVOIR' – 02.

As free human beings let us never forget that 'Le Devoir' newspaper agreed with Nazis, when it noted that the wearing of the infamous 'Yellow Star of David' was appropriate.

Despondently, I admit being thoroughly ashamed as I realize that the people who believed and uttered these thoughts were also 'pure laine' French-Canadians like me.

The intense sense of ethical betrayal I feel about this issue, makes me understand most profoundly what many ethical Germans, Italians, Serbs, and others felt not so many years ago.

Only Jean-Charles Harvey had the courage to stand center stage it seems at that time, reprimanding this sad episode of yellow journalism among other things he highlighted.

VICTIMHOOD: QUÉBEC STYLE.

While I readily admit that Quebecers were treated as inferior beings by the English conquerors in cahoots with their very own French-Canadian Roman Catholic clergy, it worsened even more after the creation of Canada, when this same clergy cooperated together with its own bourgeoisie, continuing their intense control of a rather docile religiously brainwashed population to their interests and benefits.

What astounds me today however is that Québec's separatists still behave as if still victims at the beginning of this 21st century—faced as they are with an incredible array of opportunities most can only dream about elsewhere in the world—such as the biggest set of potential customers for any business smack against their political border still refusing as a decreasing minority of about 2% to fluently speak the language of a continent where 98 % speak English.

So, instead of capitalizing on their incredible freedom of thought and behavior along with astonishing economics and business opportunities offered them by living smack against the most powerful country in the world at present, with all the advantages this provides any good entrepreneur, aside from being an integral part of a steadily growing highly democratic Canada, too many French-speaking Quebecers do nothing but complain about the good old days when they were truly victimized.

Yet, effective religious and other social controls ceased several decades ago, but many independence-minded Quebecers won't admit it, or worse yet cannot see it, and do nothing to get out of their psychological cul-de-sac. Doing so, while pretending that their own elite would be kinder to them and would also spend their regular and new revenues if any to the greater advantage of the population they allegedly serve—forgetting innumerable historical lessons, so blinded are they with their ideology.

SEEDS OF QUÉBEC FASCISM.

Not so many years ago in the province of Québec, Canada, in my lifetime:

1. Divorce was nearly impossible.

2. Pétain was considered brave.

3. Chanoine Lionel Groulx's xenophobic ideologue logic and profound anti-Semitism seemed correct and enough to dedicate his name to a metro station, streets, schools, etc.

4. In my primary school classes, we accused Jews of the vile crime of crucifying our godly figure himself a Jew, and anti-Semitism was quietly de rigueur.

5. The world was divided into Catholics *(i.e., the Chosen People)* led by god's chosen elite (i.e., the Roman Catholic Church as *The Most Special Group*), and all those who were not part of this group 'but really wanted to be' of course, according to those indoctrinating children through Catholic catechism and stories based on holy scriptures.

6. Many Québécois liked and considered fascism a worthwhile alternative, having been in a form of intellectual medieval totalitarianism themselves from 1608 to the 1960's.

7. Le Devoir newspaper, the one favored by the Québec elite, supported, and encouraged rationalized xenophobic outlooks, and seriously flirted with, if not adopted outright, a penchant for fascism, through pompous supposedly scholarly exercises or blunt articles written at times under pseudonyms—always with a penchant for authoritative solutions under the cover of a type of elitist intellectualism combined with a despicable attitude over democratic British style institutions.

8. "Les enfants de Duplessis" happened because it was considered reasonable and a normal procedure by the Québec elite and its Québec style Roman Catholic Church of the time.

No better than the beginnings of Nazi Germany in its first years, I sometime conclude. So, from time to time, I ask myself this scary question:

When will those seeds of hate, and others not mentioned, germinate further in my land of birth?

I admit to shaking in my boots at that very question.

That is why: courageous Esther Delisle is reviled by diehard Québec separatists; treated as a traitor by the "pure laine" Québec elite; and ignored or ridiculed by its inbred academic community, since she dared to openly bring into the light of day the unmentionable and shameful Québec history of the 1930's and 1940's particularly.

She forced us to clearly see our cowardice in the face of an undeniable Holocaust in Europe and our unadmitted quiet glee in some respects over its execution by many of us at that time among other things.

> **Although …**
> It must be admitted however that Esther Delisle's presentation was rather clunky, but she was nevertheless accurate.

Yea! I know there existed a strong anti-Semitic current throughout Canada in those days as well, but it certainly did not become the mythological affirmation it did in Roman Catholic French-Canadian circles in the province of Québec at that time. Oh yea! I know. I was there. I witnessed it. I lived through a portion of it.

QUÉBEC AS A RECENT SEMI-FASCIST STATE.

Recently in their history Québécois rejected en masse their isolation from the rest of the world and distanced themselves from the domineering Roman Catholic Church, that had shackled them spiritually, ethically, politically and every other way for so long in a quasi-medieval mode of life.

Oh yes! Not so very long ago in my younger life and much before that, the province of Québec in Canada functioned more or less under a sort of Canon law at home, school and church—having done so first since the foundation of New France in 1608 , then again after its defeat at the hands of England in 1759, while during, in between, and after these two events operating as a more or less a semi-fascist religious State until the so-called "révolution tranquille".

If in doubt think of the following easy considerations among many others:

1. The British and the Québec Roman Catholic Church reached an agreement to control the French-Canadian population of the day that would benefit both these stakeholders and protect their interests.

2. Both State and Church combined forces again to suppress the freedom of French-Canadians (i.e., especially in Québec) with the pernicious involvement of their petty bourgeoisie: attaining a high point during 'la grande noirceur', just before its collapse after the death of Maurice Duplessis and his era.

3. An invasive program of violent interference was created throughout that time to protect the interests of the Roman Catholic Church and special laws were created to that effect.

4. Communism—the Church's sworn archenemy at the time; the new Jews so to speak—was hailed enemy number one with the so-called "Padlock Law", which was used liberally against them and any other group or person the Québec government or the Roman Catholic Church proclaimed as "heretics" of one kind or another.

5. In many quarters including my neighborhood as a child before and during the Second World War, Pétain was considered a 'reasonable man' and Mussolini a 'strong leader'.

6. The *curés* in nearly all villages, towns, and cities as well as newspapers generally, surreptitiously, if not openly, supported and promoted fascist ideas.

Shush! We, French-Canadians tagged as so-called "vielles souches", are not supposed to recall these things, lest we be considered traitors to 'the cause'.

THE PARTI QUEBECOIS IS TRIBAL AND RACIST.

The Parti Québécois is racist. The reason is evidenced in its exclusivist undercurrents known and felt by its Roman Catholic 'vieilles souches' and 'pure laine' notions, which imagine Québec's future decided strictly by those specifically identified as such, while ignoring the will and aspirations of all other Québec citizens in principle and in fact – except lately out of desperation.

Indeed, with it more than a million non-French-Canadians located in the province of Québec, separatist-minded Quebecers until most recently behaved as if these people did not exist, or as if most did not significantly contributed to their tax base. Although ironically tax contributions from non-French-Canadian Québécois 'pure laine' exceeded at least for the last two centuries a per capita income superior to that of their French-Canadian counterpart – and this despite the near monopoly of French-Canadians in the bureaucratic ramparts of the provincial government of Québec.

This narrow vision is the result of a Québec-styled intellectual progeny—a mentality echoing Jesuitan self-righteous pontification and manipulative implementation of a religious based mission metamorphosed and indoctrinated in a secular fashion after 'la grande noirceur'.

It is further reflected in the self-centered sense of 'specialness' exhibited by the religious class along with the petty bourgeoisie of a few decades ago, and now mirrored in the parents of the original Parti Québécois elite and the more committed part of the membership at that time.

You can however still find remnants of that retrograde detrimental mentality as Québec's hardcore separatists transmogrify their sermons into a more *politically correct* dialect, when not diatribes.

As if shadows of the philosophy and aspirations of 'Le Devoir' newspaper in the midst of 'la grande noirceur' – but now somewhat less hypocritical in view of a more sophisticated population.

And now—like all xenophobic self-righteous groups—the Parti Québécois' fundamentalist crowd tends to ridicule, if not attack outright, anyone who challenges their exclusive separatist and proprietary conclusions. That is why:

> *Québec immigrants scare them so much since many of these come in with various and often vastly different worldviews and attitudes.*

In such a context:

> *Québec separatists refuse to understand other points of view, although many pretend to be inclusive in order to reach that manipulative '50% + 1' magic formula, because their super ordinate 'Immaculate Perception' is that of a people wronged—an untouchable dogma—as if separate and superior to all other concerns.*

Therefore, by not openly and repeatedly recognizing the reality of ignoring the 49.9 % excluded from such a social project that disagreed with them should they succeed in this manner, they will have shortchanged their own offspring and succeeding generations of French-Canadians in Québec, who will thereby be ghettoized from the rest of the North American continent rather than fully participate in it.

An unnecessary problem which, say, the compulsory learning of English, also used worldwide in business and by the elite of all nations, as a second language at all school levels for example would ease the future of Québec's upcoming generations, and bring it on a par with the rest of successful ethnic groups and nations around the world.

HARD CORE QUÉBEC SEPARATISTS.

Hard core Québec separatists believe themselves victimized while:

1. Purposely and dishonestly ignoring that English is the language of the planet and that it will remain as such for several generations.

2. Refusing to see that their plight in the past was due to the politics of old conflicts, and that this attitude blocks off their aspirations as free people, whom they really are.

3. Intentionally 'forgetting' altogether that England by default allowed them to keep their language and belief system.

4. Deliberately disregarding that France, their mother country, abandoned them to their plight as collateral damage – unworthy of protection – in the pursuit of national French interests of the day—a supply of sugar from some small islands. Surrendering the whole of Canada. A truly stupid political decision.

5. Calculatedly overlooking that their local Catholic Church made up of their own people separately and for political gains betrayed them several times; not only in cahoots with the old French regime but also with the English one as well, and continued to do so in a third phase of their betrayal in the 19th and 20th centuries this time with complicity of their own petty bourgeoisie.

6. Knowingly disregarding the fact that they geographically live next to the most powerful and still richest nation in the whole course of human history to this day – a dreamt for opportunity for any entrepreneur.

7. Designedly discounting that the French-speaking people of Québec are now the authors of their shortcomings in most in-

stances—by snubbing entrepreneurship, ignoring opportunities represented and implied by being smack against the USA as well as being an integral part of the free country of Canada.

Oh no! They go on creating one of the biggest national debts instead, while acting as phony victims. Now grown up 'enfants-roi' with mostly self-inflicted problems, especially in the last decades.

AS I GO ON WITH MY SELF-ASSIGNED TASK.

While a child I was intellectually in the throes of the tenacious grips—with the rest of French-Canadians in Canada—of the medieval minded Québec's priests-ridden society of the Thirties, Forties, and Fifties.

In this respect I obviously have a serious grudge against religions generally and have openly questioned their raison d'être since age eleven.

Having said this, what I have already proposed and continue to advocate is the removal of those people whose mission and objectives is to physically or psychologically bully others to think and behave like them, if not as exactly instructed by them, through the self-assertion of our own personalized and ethics-based meanings, values, and standards in the exercise of all our *Inalienable Individual Rights*.

Beyond my initial grudge you will continue to find an attempt at understanding where we as a species are headed for, on account of this and other philosophies of domination there to predatorily rule us all.

Here then are many other pieces of that gigantic puzzle used to create one overall image as well as various sub-images forming our reality.

'LAURENTIEN' FASCISM.

Let us recall the utopian and exclusively French-Canadian Catholic Fascist State dreamt of and promoted by that rapacious Jew hater and intense misogynist: chanoine Lionel Groulx.

The fascist State he conceived was meant to be at the disposal of the Roman Catholic Church of Québec and also predestined to exclude all those not fitting in – beginning with 'Anglos' and Jews.

Not very different indeed than the recent call to all French-Canadians *'de souche'* (it's in the subtext again) by cardinal Marc Ouellette of Québec City urging French-Canadians *'de souche'* to return to the fold of that nasty ecclesiastical elite.

No doubt that rabid misogynist imagined and was hoping for the good old days were clerics could run the show once more and lead their flock to re-embark as xenophobic fascist-minded followers once more—on their way to that ever fading 'Lauretien' utopia.

IN MY OWN POLITICAL UNIVERSE...

In my own political universe, separatist-leaning members of my society in the province of Québec, Canada, tell me, <u>not</u> to consider myself as a French-Canadian but only as a Québécois – although largely benefiting from the privileges, interests, and benefits of belonging to the Canadian federation compared to the rest of Canadians.

THE SEMITIC LAND QUAGMIRE – 06.

Undeniably, the concept of special rights for one group (*The Chosen People*) over others ultimately implies that; the battle cry of *Barbarism* of "The end justifies the means" is ethically correct as far as Israel, Aboriginals, and other groups are concerned.

Special rights by French-Canadians from Québec in Canada are in fact founded of a similar philosophy of victimhood on a scale of victimization, where seniority and or a *'Chosen People'* concept reign supreme.

VULGARIC-SPEAKING PEOPLE OF THE US & CANADA.

This group now beginning to grow exponentially exposes their intense despair and utter frustration – it had no other choice – in the form of foul language meant to assault the professed values of the established order first as re-enforcer of their own values and meanings among themselves generally, and also addressed to those outside their group particularly.

I choose to call it *"Vulgaric"*, just to give it a name.

The most obvious group of 'Vulgaric-speaking people now coalescing together in North America and Europe consist of *Street People* abandoned by their societies as human trash as well as the *'Working Poor'* usually paid minimum wage in the official economy and less so in the underground one—and aware of their precarious position near the abyss of becoming *Street People*.

Indeed, note *The Poor, The Disenfranchised, The Socially Defrocked, The Despised,* and *The Ostracized,* now speaking the language of despair and helplessness.

Pay attention!

These are people now also beginning to wear the Western-styled uniform of tattoos and piercings representing their situation—readying themselves either for their last and ultimate battle for survival as human beings, or simply dressing up for their inevitable early slide into oblivion much before their time.

We also find Vulgaric-speaking people among the once sexually repressed English-speaking world in which sexual pleasures were considered and coercively controlled as 'unnatural' and violently managed by the Church establishment, and wherein, for example, the word 'fuck' and anything dealing with sexual activities became taboo and took on a negative importance, itself invested with a blasphemous value vastly disproportionate to its basic nature—although social controls in our days are slowly and gradually devolving in this area into a more or less vestigial legacy.

A similar situation also occurred with French-speaking Quebecers, where Roman Catholic religious paraphernalia attached as they were to their local, moral and fanatical religious dictators for about four centuries, became another source of negative importance and utter blasphemy, and wherein words such as 'ciboire' and 'tabarnak' (i.e., tabernacle) considered as holy objects of celebration by the Roman Catholic Church, became most offensive to the religious establishment.

Social controls nowadays, however, have thankfully almost totally devolved in this area, and the use of such words to spice up a conversation is clearly sliding into a vestigial legacy as well.

THE JOUAL-SPEAKING PEOPLE OF CANADA.

Note the *"Joual"* spoken by many French-speaking Canadians from my districts of origin of St. Henri, and other ghettos such as Hocholaga in Montréal by people continuously betrayed by the Roman Catholic Church of their locality as well as their own petty bourgeoisie.

A people now hell-bent in indebting themselves without regard to the future regrettably indoctrinated into them by their nasty and highly domineering medieval-like local Roman Catholics Church establishment until the 1960's with the promise of an eternal life, now metamorphosed into, and operational in, the secular arena in a highly bureaucratic *Political Correctness*.

A lose-lose proposition presently found in the hyperbolic economic illusions of many *"vielles souches"* French-speaking Quebecers that will go on until bankruptcy kills their irrational aspirations or the population faces the realities of our present unfolding world economy.

Hopefully my will soon wake up and capitalize on the outstanding opportunities offered them on this North American continent.

I speak of a group of people who—until they decided otherwise—had been mentally isolated from the rest of the world for over four hundred years or so, giving enough time to their local governing elites and government to sponsor xenophobic attitudes, create crushing bureaucracies, invent Machiavellian and devastating taxation, and construct a racist attitude toward anything English, despite the overwhelming status of that tongue as the language of the planet and that of the most powerful nation on Earth at the moment right next door to them. A situation geographically located on the Québec-US doorstep wherever they turn—a fact noted by everybody else in the world.

I refer to a people often bent on a cult of victimization, while sadly living beyond their means in one of the best countries of the world, located next to the most powerful and most advanced country in the history of the world so far.

Pay also attention to the sort of *"Joual à l'Acadienne"*, as I call it.

I do not here refer to the "pure Acadian" with so many beautiful ancient words used by the few, spoken by their sisters and brothers in New Brunswick, Nova Scotia and elsewhere in the Canadian maritime region.

No! I speak of the badly Anglicized French spoken by a segment of Acadians in the Maritimes. Yes! In these examples, we are in the presence of another historically recent minority, which by its own accord and which under its own terms speaks another version of the language of the weak – a sort of bastardized Anglo-French found in many localities—exhibiting their self-deprecating appreciation of their lower social position for generations by now vis-à-vis their traditional English counterpart.

These few obviously selected examples and others represent those numerous cracks or initial fissures in the edifice of our Western tradition.

But if you think this is bad, it is nevertheless immensely dwarfed by the horror, morbidity, and terror, found elsewhere outside advanced civilizations.

QUEBEC'S "VIELLES SOUCHES" TYPE BOURGEOISIE.

Those 'vielles souches' notions of the Québec bourgeoisie about proper French grammar and its alleged correct pronunciation are among other things motivated by inbred snobbery and perceived class difference, since this specific class of bourgeois have elected themselves, and insists on being identified with their 'exclusive' European ancestry. In this self-assigned context, it then considers itself as the educated segment of the chapter of *The Special Group* that ought to rule that particular section of Earthly landmass called Québec.

BETRAYAL OF QUÉBÉCOIS - 01.

Many people of French extraction in Québec rightly proclaim their political independence as all ethnic groups and sub-groups throughout the planet do at a certain stage of their development.

Sadly, many of them also irrationally believe that such a successful undertaking would free them from their alleged oppressors, forgetting all those lessons recorded throughout the annals of history.

Yes! Many politically committed Quebecers still assume that their own petty bourgeoisie would be kinder to them, overlooking of course that the bourgeoisie everywhere on Earth forms the most importantly integrated group in the planetary-wide daily application and management of social and political controls everywhere and throughout history.

I speak of course of the special role played by the *barbaric* segment of *The Planetary Managerial-Professional Class*—whatever the specialty—in their active involvement toward the implementation and maintenance of the status quo on behalf of society's owners and stakeholders.

BETRAYAL OF QUÉBÉCOIS - 02.

In early Québec history the slow development of Quebecers of French extraction began with the premeditated betrayal by their clergy along with their political masters in France; then the same clergy again associated itself with similar allies from England; and after that for the third time, the Catholic clergy of Québec did it again with the continued coercive implementation of the Catholic doctrine with those who could profit the most within their very own culture, such as lawyers, doctors, and politicians. So, I say, let us not fail here in Québec and elsewhere for that matter, now that we've finally begun to overcome that gang of scoundrels; that older subset of dogmatic belief system administrators for society's owners and stakeholders. I refer of course to the local chapter, or if you prefer the Québec franchise, of *The Planetary Managerial-Professional Class*.

REFLECTION OF JESUITS FANTASIES.

As if consisting of a reflection of Jesuits fantasies, the Québec of the last four hundred years or so was xenophobic, anti-Semitic, anti-entrepreneurship, fearful of business, preferred ignorance, and accorded a kind of sainthood to large families and poverty.

A situation of a once highly indoctrinated people abandoned in an English-speaking ocean as a dislocated medieval outpost of the Roman Catholic Church right up to the middle of the 20th century. Until then these somnambulistic Quebecers were haunted by fundamentalist views clothed in religious and ethnocentric visions of the world.

That is why:

The private Jesuit-run Collège Jean-de-Brébeuf so ardently embraced chauvinistic francophone nationalism from the time of its foundation until recently. It originally contributed along with other similar establishments to the construction and anchoring of an insularity by as privileged members constituting its upcoming Special Group, and by default falsely propagated this harmful meme, as if it was only the people "de souche" of course that mattered in that province.

ESTHER DELISLE.

Let us keep in mind courageous Esther Delisle, who recently in Québec history, bravely and stubbornly went on debunking the unmentionable shame of what was considered normal in the 1930s and 1940s in the province of Québec. I speak of a medieval-based, shamefully inspired, religiously managed and petty-bourgeoisie-concocted political fascist philosophy of the day tied into an anti-Semitic bent—with remnants still alive within a faction of Québec's separatist movements. People whose views are summed up in the notion of *"Le Québec au Québécois"* regardless of political affiliation, and which in my interpretation implies French-speaking Roman Catholic *'pure laine'* Québécois first and above all others as the only *Chosen People* on that territory of our planet.

LANGUAGES AND MANITOBA.

In Manitoba, Ukrainian is a widespread second language. German is also one of the popular second languages spoken, and there is even a radio station in southern Manitoba, which broadcasts in German every day. And just like their country cousins in those days particularly, Ukrainians, Germans, Russians and others, French-Canadians were also predisposed to speak their mother tongue on the farm or in the privacy of their homes.

Nevertheless, like them they also tended to automatically switch to English the instant they step off the farm or village or their city dwelling.

It is not because they were ashamed of their mother tongue, but simply that it was easier to get along with their neighbors. Indeed, a characteristic of Manitobans is their genuine sense of cooperation and friendliness.

MANITOBA'S FRENCH-CANADIANS.

Manitoba's French-Canadians are particularly ticklish, if not simply ill-at ease about their place in that province; first in view of those chronic emotional reactions, which surfaced from time to time since the creation of that province, and the fact that *"the French"*, as they were called, were never accepted as equal partners with the Anglos for a long time, as the saying goes, since they too from the very beginning were also intent on establishing that territory as a cultural and political entity of their own.

That is; the English-speaking segment of this area of Canada with the political support of the John A. MacDonald administration, was intensely against a French-speaking province based on a template provided by the Metis leader, Louis Riel.

In the course of this political struggle French-speaking people were outplayed by the English-speaking segment of that province in their attempt at a takeover and governance.

It failed for a variety of reasons.

The principal one being the underhanded and miscalculated takeover by the French-speaking Catholic Church in the management of the so-called French-speaking political cause on behalf of the French-speaking population—including the rather coarse and ungainly tactic adopted by that Church in giving French sounding names to all aboriginals they could either directly or surreptitiously baptize – and recording these as an additional and official part of the local French-speaking Roman Catholic nation.

But in spite of the realpolitik practiced by the Roman Catholic Church in these parts, local average French-Canadians didn't really participate much in that process; except for the few, whose future would particularly benefit from that venture and therefore become a privileged class should they have succeeded—especially the clerical class with the support of lawyers, doctors and a few successful merchants.

Nonetheless, French-Canadians ended up shabbily treated by the ever greater number of English settlers, and then, eventually ignored, if not simply regarded as a quaint oddity by other Manitobans until late in the 20th century.

But surprisingly and ultimately to those observing a steady maturing of a whole provincial civilization; a more sophisticated, developed and remarkably friendly English-speaking Manitoban culture did what few societies do at any time.

They admitted their past behavior, accepted their errors and recognized Louis Riel as the founder of Manitoba.

A mature political admission indeed.

They even erected a monument to him right next to the Legislative Building in Winnipeg and instituted a statutory holiday called the Louis Riel Day.

So, gone gradually were old prejudices about local French-Canadians.

But while quietly working their way into the English-speaking Manitoban society and despite this exemplary acceptance and recognition, French-Canadians of Manitoba again felt ill-at-ease with the political trouble from their cousins in the province of Québec throughout the last half of the 20th century. Indeed, it stirred a lot of discussions and even brought back some of the old hatred from those, who could not bring themselves to treat everyone equally in the first place on both sides of the fence.

On the whole nowadays despite events taking place in Quebec, peace has settled back again and Manitoba remains a superb example of cooperation and acceptance.

WHERE THE "ASSINIBOINE" AND THE "RED" MEET.

In the geographic center of North America about half way between the island of Vancouver in the west and Newfoundland in the east in Canada, where the Assiniboine and the Red rivers meet – exists a place, just across from downtown Winnipeg, called St. Boniface.

There the body of Louis Riel, the Metis leader of the Western Canada Rebellion, lies in the St. Boniface cemetery next to the St. Boniface cathedral.

A body stolen out of reverence and brought from Regina, Saskatchewan to St. Boniface, Manitoba to provide Riel a decent burial in the eyes of Roman Catholic French-Canadian patriots and Metis people. And through this process symbolically return to him his human dignity.

There, a simple and yet provocative reminder of a bitter defeat is boldly written on his headstone, "RIEL, 16 NOVEMBRE". The date he was hanged.

And a piece of the rope, which was allegedly used to hang him, also lies in a small museum a block away or so, as another bitter reminder of what could have been.

Aside from this rather important incident, however, nothing rebellious has ever happened in this quiet, subdued, self-effacing and yet proud previous suburb of Winnipeg.

Yet there is little doubt that St. Boniface has been tested; has been intellectually attacked; and has been unfairly treated for a long time by the English-speaking population of Winnipeg.

Indeed, its French culture was mortally wounded years ago. What remains is merely the morbid rattling of an accelerating cultural disappearance in the form of a soft ethnocide, quietly inflicted from within as well as from outside of this chapter of the French-Canadian population.

The sad events, which have led to this, cannot be blamed on such things as the cultural worth of English and French. That would be unfair, intellectually dishonest and far too simplistic a conclusion.

Nor can it be blamed on just intolerance of the English-speaking segment of that regional population toward its French-speaking population.

MANITOBA.

Let us not risk the creation of a misunderstanding here. Manitobans are good people. They live in a beautiful province. Although they don't put up with bullshit—such as when Torontonians boringly complain about severe cold spells. Manitobans are otherwise polite, friendly, helpful and cooperative.

Manitoba is also a region of Canada that the whole country—indeed the whole world—can be proud of.

The death of the French culture in Manitoba happened simply because people with intolerant attitudes on both sides permitted it to happen. And because people, who since the conquest of Western Canada from its North American Aborigines, have wanted to establish their particular belief system at the expense of all others.

First, the French took over, then the English.

And later on, as everywhere else in North America, a whole spectrum of ethnic groups choosing English as their language of communication, continued in the gradual takeover of the province from the Aboriginal people – as was being done on the rest of the continent.

The English-speaking tide was simply too strong, too overwhelming, too attractive, too easy to adapt to and adopt, too pervasive everywhere and too massively imbued with growth and momentum, for the all too focused inward looking French-speaking Manitoba culture to survive as the language of the ways and means of functioning in that beautiful part of Canadian land.

A process helped in great part by France, and more particularly its governing elite, in the course of its history, which never made the right decisions in the establishment of its culture since 1608 – either abandoning its established colony in what is now Brazil, or losing one third of what is presently the continental territory of the United States, or walking away from the immense Canadian territory for lack of long range planning and general interest.

In addition, the inflexible local Roman Catholic Church-based controls, exercised over French-Canadians in every aspects of their private and public life, was too suffocating to give ordinary citizens a chance at overcoming the English tide of progress and liberalism.

And let's face it.

Any other language and culture caught up in a similar situation at that time would have under similar objectives and situation suffered the same fate despite the introduction of a far too late constitutional right.

It is sad, but this is a historical reality, and one must accept reality as is, if one wishes to remain sane.

In addition, aside from fringe groups on both sides, which insist on making self-serving noises from time to time, nothing bad or negative has ever happened out west to trigger world attention.

And it is this fact, which focuses our attention on a land where world calamities have not taken root, where the smell of the wheat permeates the country side and where friendliness is an active reality—not just PR bullshit.

Look! Manitoba is a land of immeasurable possibilities; enormous natural wealth; and beautiful countryside. And as in many other places in Canada, it is also filled with an innate, incredible and seemingly ever lasting peace.

As if the violence of Iran, Columbia, Mexico, South Africa, Iraq, and Afghanistan and so on, did not exist; and as if the muggings of New York City, the serial murders of California and Florida, and all those faraway places were not occurring.

JEWS AND FRENCH-CANADIANS.

Jews were believed in small communities of the day to abuse the weakened political position of French-Canadians generally everywhere in Canada, and particularly weakening the wobbly place of French outside the province of Québec in order to strengthen their position in the Anglo communities.

No proof ever existed for that, but many nonetheless thought so.

And this was taught and reinforced in nearly all of the French-Canadian speaking Roman Catholic schools from the heart of Montréal and Québec City to the most remote settlements, where French-Canadians lived across Canada, as well as in the US where again many would seek work—particularly in the New England states.

This teaching was often subtle, especially with the Jesuits, who have since their inception been masters of propaganda and indoctrination.

But on occasion it would also rise to pure and openly crude prejudices and racism—especially with local clerics, who tended to be less sophisticated and not as highly educated as the Jesuits.

This fire of hatred of Jews all too often became the staple in the sub-texts of newspapers of the Québec bourgeoisie and part of running narratives interwoven in the frustration of the wretched from the ghettos.

Montréal's Le Devoir newspaper in the Thirties and Forties particularly, would peculiarly stoke that fire by augmenting the fear its readers had about the future, and the supposed collusion these alleged traitors would embarked upon against the cause of Roman Catholicism and the overall community of French-Canadians.

So that self-righteous and self-doubting French-Canadians alike would, after due indoctrination, see enemies everywhere, in a world wherein the self-doubting ought to follow the advice and counsel of the self-righteous, who would lead them onto *the right path* by fancying leaders that were *vieilles souches* and Roman Catholic in a style reminiscent of that Jew hater, the cleric Lionel Groulx.

But the truth was that the above average education and business acumen of the Jews scared them to a degree that only a pathology of inferiority could explain.

To that end one could read diatribes camouflaged as literary essays against Jews (although not specifically identifying them), and for a strong French-Canadian Roman Catholic leader to take charge through not so subtle and suggestive notions.

In other words, advocating a home style dictatorship – through the sophistry of a good, sophisticated Jesuit education.

A notion openly supported by elite writers in the French-Canadian community of the province Québec—including that nasty xenophobic Jew hating and anti-English cleric, Lionel Groulx, on the religious and less sophisticated side; and André Laurendeau and others on the secular and far more articulate side, who under the cover of alleged neutral but pseudo-intellectual essays would disguise racial harangues along with other prejudices through pseudo-intellectual discourses, so these could be more acceptable to the Québec bourgeoisie.

ST. LÉON'S COMMUNICATION NETWORK – 01.

As an isolated small community, communications in St. Léon were nevertheless good although limited in great part to its French-speaking channels.

This included the Montréal newspaper *La Presse,* delivered days after its initial publication, which brought the news of the world, as perceived and interpreted of course with the heavy influence of the Roman Catholic Church, which ran just about everything in the province of Québec in those days, either directly or indirectly, legally or morally.

ST. LÉON'S COMMUNICATION NETWORK – 02.

It also involved the Roman Catholic controlled St. Boniface paper, "La Liberté", in fact created in 1913 par Mgr Langevin, bishop of Saint-Boniface, which conveyed local news and other activities along with the religious fulminations that always accompany theologically controlled *information.*

FRENCH-CANADIAN'S COMMUNICATION WEB.

Oddly enough for us living in the 21st century, there existed an effective fifteen-minute Monday to Friday radio program titled *"Un homme et son péché"* broadcast at 7 pm from Montréal.

This radio program, based on a novel by Claude-Henri Grignon, became a template of accepted social attitude and suggested behavior—promoting submission to Church authority, a lower expectation about one's future, an unreasonable dislike for entrepreneurship, and anything financial.

A program regarded by Church authorities at the time as a modern and most efficient way of retaining their control of the entire French-speaking Roman Catholic population across Canada—as well as provide them with a simple minded model of submissive behavior.

This radio program was therefore developed and engineered to continue the indoctrination of French-Canadians in Québec and throughout Canada, so they would continue to obey without questions diktats of their Church, accept without complaints *their place* in the hierarchy of their local societies, and be moralized about the evils of money—although the Church still kept collecting the meager earnings of its "flock" – even though it must be admitted; no one described it that way then. And so powerfully seared into the minds of these people was this radio program that, it still constitutes a function of a major Québec attitude nowadays toward entrepreneurship for profit, which is why, among other factors, this province in so caught up in enormous debts along with a generalized failure to implement long-term sound economic and financial planning.

As if French-Canadians still, if only by proxy from an old religious-oriented brainwashing program, could insanely and irresponsibly continue to borrow money, pushing their accumulating debts to the next generations, whenever it suited them, in order to escape their troubles or lack of entrepreneurship based on the nemesis of that program—Séraphin Poudrier, rather than act as business entrepreneurs.

That is why among other factors of course; so many people from the Québec bourgeoisie prefer the safety of the local traditional professions and tend to avoid the challenging world of business and other global venues for advancing their societies.

ST. LÉON'S COMMUNICATION NETWORK – 04.

And lastly, like in all communities everywhere, communications took place by word of mouth whenever someone came back from the big city with the latest trends—generally Winnipeg or Montréal for the more adventurous.

This and the other means of communications mentioned formed the source of information and knowledge that well-connected French-Canadians in St. Léon, Somerset, Notre Dame-de-Lourdes and other French-speaking communities in the rest of Manitoba disposed of at that time.

GABRIELLE ROY TURNS ON THE LIGHT.

When reading *"The Tin Flute"* first in English and later on *"Bonheur d'occasion"* in French, I could clearly see what Gabrielle Roy was describing in that work.

I had been out that ghetto for three decades by then, but the memories came back loud and unblemished.

First the scenes lived and observed, followed by the smells, and sounds, returned as if no time had elapsed.

Then, those sensations of despair felt so long ago, which permeated the whole place at that time, reemerged – along with the dread of a desperate future felt by each resident within that ghetto.

Indeed, it all came back like a nightmare long buried.

Although just eight years old at that time, I still recall the mean-spirited comments and plain offensive observations made by Saint-Henri residents about Gabrielle Roy shortly after its publication – although, it must be said, the vast majority had not read her book.

Nonetheless many from that ghetto, especially the many an-alphabets in the parishes within the larger Saint-Henri (within which my world of Sainte-Cunégonde and Sainte-Irénée were located), were very offended.

Their hurt came out as questions such as:

"What does she know about us?"

"Why does she bring us down for?"

"She's not from here, she's a bloody Manitoban, what can **'she'** *pretend to know anything about us?"*

"She must have been hired and paid by 'les Anglais' to laugh at us?"

Indeed, many among us (including myself at that time) thought of her as a traitor to the cause of the broader community of French-Canadians across Canada – and on and on it went for several weeks.

No doubt the little bit of pride left among these residents had been crushed by an outsider.

But what was worse, and no one dare speak of at that time was that; Gabrielle Roy had lifted the veil of their poverty, hardships and general unfairness against them on account of the existing social system in place.

Although Gabrielle Roy had done so through a fictitious story, her narrative was sadly recognized by most, and which, in one form or another, had already taken place in real life for them, or was actually occurring in their own family, or that of a next-door neighbor.

In other words, that the world described by Gabrielle Roy was accurate.

This was what hurt them the most – the parting of the curtain, showing for all to see their dreadful and wretched lives, along with the despair that came with it.

She was right, and deep down everybody there knew it, although no one dared admit it.

MICHEL TREMBLAY TURNS ON ANOTHER LIGHT.

When I saw *"Les Belles-Soeurs"* I could also picture my *aunts* Berthe (married to my *uncle* Lucien Bourdeau) and Germaine (married to my *uncle* Donat Bourdeau) and all the other aunts in my family as well as many neighbors in and around Workman Street, where I lived in my early life.

Although I am five years or so older than Michel Tremblay, *"Les Belles-Sœurs"* for example, nonetheless brought me back in many respects to that French-Canadian narrative I had so intimately and so attentively known and listened to.

Indeed, he too emerged from a neighborhood with a struggling working-class atmosphere and Joual as dialect – granted without the smoke belching factories and the constant and intense rail transportation from the large Turcot railway yards (the largest in Canada at that time), and continuous ship circulation on the Lachine Canal that I experienced.

Gentrification
Both neighborhoods ironically have for the last couple decades been in a process of gentrification with Plateau Mont Royal ahead of the game so far.

THE PROVINCE OF QUÉBEC - 02.

French-Canadian Quebecers are a resilient people, which in spite of improbable odds have culturally and linguistically survived, in great part due to a strategic decision of their new English masters after the conquests of 1759 and 1760 (Officially recorded in Montréal in 'The Articles of Capitulation of Montreal') – added to their inherent Gallic stubbornness to be who they were.

Nonetheless, French-Canadian Quebecers particularly retained enough of a sense of who they are as a people to possess a sort of unexpurgated culture of their own in spite of their complete isolation from their mother country until recently in history.

Until a few decades ago, French-Canadians' isolation over the centuries in addition to their general lack of intercourse with most with their English-speaking comrades on the North American continent (including those living in the same urban centers as them if not on the next street such as in Montréal) contributed a sort of self-imposed Apartheid.

However, in a quickly evolving world of communications along with global business and manufacturing opportunities acting as catalysts, more and more French-Canadians slowly and gradually became conscious of their predicament and began to join the group of winners.

Although their sense of cultural belonging had remained and their language had survived, they had been, since the incredibly stupid surrender by their Mother Country, nonetheless (to use a metaphor), found themselves *à la dérive,* so to speak, on a large French-speaking island in a vast sea of English-speaking people.

Only to realize recently for many, that most in North America, like them, were also; regularly caught up with the same daily job of surviving one more day; like them they also dreamt of economic independence and freedom to be who they really were; as well as building a future for their children. All universal objectives found nearly everywhere for that matter – regardless of origin and language.

Other French-Canadians
Smaller French-Canadian settlements outside the province Québec quickly adapted to and adopted the Canadian English-speaking way of life in order to survive – although an ever smaller sub-segment continues to varying degrees to privately function in French at home in a few scattered areas across Canada.

But in the case of the English-speaking communities, greater successes were to be witnessed – especially in the US – than in the French-Canadian community, where it was common practice to attribute economic superiority to greed and usury, rather than perseverance in the implementation of an idea, a project, a proposal, a program, a notion, and so on, often way out of the ordinary – beyond the acceptance of the status quo.

Sadly, for French-Canadians everywhere the status quo set by their Church centuries ago was supreme, and a fear of change based on this notion settled in for a long time, with severe ramifications still for many today – including a tendency to look down on financially successful people.

Admittedly this anomalous Church-influenced characteristic has significantly diminished in the last five decades, but much remains still for reversing this attitude entirely.

Indeed, a general conversion about and a true overall adaptation to entrepreneurship has yet to take flight.

THE PROVINCE OF QUÉBEC - 03.

To understand the context of French-Canadian life in Québec, we begin by looking at a form of thinking set in concrete long ago, along with rigid social controls that kept a whole group of human beings in check for centuries. A process that purposely separated French-Canadians in many respects from the rest of the North American population and from the rest of the world for that matter.

THE PROVINCE OF QUÉBEC - 04.

The province of Québec is nonetheless a peaceful territory, wherein sadly a deep sense of insecurity has existed for centuries in a once profoundly indoctrinated population.

A situation which at last – once Québec woke up from its long slumber – circa 1960 when it came face-to-face with its profound economic deficiencies and restrictive societal shortcomings.

A time wherein the conclusion of a very dark period for French-Canadians was ending and a brand new one filled with opportunities was emerging.

A period brought to everyone's attention under the label of *révolution tranquille*.

***

We pay particular attention to three decades in the first half of the 20th century CE, in which the story about to begin took place.

A period marking the paroxysm of the power of the Church and its codependent partners, and the end of that cooperative 'monopoly.'

This is the context wherein five segments of the Québec establishment routinely participated.

Indeed, what caused the self-inflicted province-wide situation in Québec before the *révolution tranquille* was the result of coordinated activities by five groups of codependent partners, deliberately acting as one *cooperative community of social controllers*.

They were the Roman Catholic Church, politicians, the early professions, the police, and a complex of victimization within the general population.

FRENCH-CANADIAN CATHOLIC CHURCH - 01.

To say that the French-speaking Roman Catholic Church was an arrogant and pompous organization in Québec, particularly in the first half of the 20th century, for example, is an understatement.

Indeed, the incoherent beliefs and medieval superstitions rammed into the thinking of its *flock* for four hundred years by the Roman Catholic Church throughout Québec were mind-numbing and took its toll.

The rigorous political interference and sheer manipulation of the French-Canadian population by the Roman Catholic Church was indeed vast and psychologically crushing.

The myth promoting a terrorizing fear of eternal suffering after death if disobedient to Church edicts, along with the dread of losing one's language and personal freedom in this life, both, were relentlessly being fed by the organizationally mature and powerful institution which the Roman Catholic Church represented and constituted.

FRENCH-CANADIAN CATHOLIC CHURCH - 02.

At the very beginnings of the colony of Nouvelle-France, the mother country had made sure that only very devout (highly indoctrinated) Roman Catholics would be sent there. Hence, strategically ensuring that only the most obedient applicants would become part of their venture in Québec, for easier supervision and control by the '*petite aristocracie*' sent to that colony as well.

> **An 'Aristocracie' That Once …**
> An 'aristocracie' that once included Gouverneur Frontenac, whose teenage wife was a favorite of the King of France, for example, which is why the latter sent Frontenac as far as he could – and that truly was far in those days.

It took centuries and an accumulation of ridiculous enunciations, stupid fairy tales, over-the-top brainwashing of children, and manipulative social controls, in order to trigger an eventual quiet intellectual rebellion that took at least a half a dozen decades to bear fruit after it began to simmer– ending with the *révolution tranquille* of the sixties.

Indeed, during the preceding centuries the clergy exercised a most powerful censorship and a total control over the life of residents of this colony – particularly the economically poor – the majority.

FRENCH-CANADIAN CATHOLIC CHURCH - 03.

In practice the Québec establishment (at first made up of the original *petite aristocracie,* and then consisting of its leftover remaining support staff when the British governance took over) always supported Church's requests for children's indoctrination and tax free existence as an organization, since the ecclesiastical class acted on their behalf in the behavioral control of the residents, preventing any form of rebellion that might take place, by first controlling each parish through Sunday sermons and compulsory mass attendance. Secondly most importantly, no better place existed for a micro-management of behavior than the Roman Catholic confessional.

GROWING DISRESPECT TOWARD THE CHURCH – 01.

Nevertheless, and despite all social controls, revolutionary intellectual memes no doubt took roots as in all cases where a repressed population is targeted.

As everywhere else it likely began in the normal conversation of people at get-togethers, taking place mostly within family compacts, mainly by French-Canadian mothers in this case for the last few decades of the 19th century and the first six decades of the 20th – by women who were thrice subjugated by the Church and State institutions – if we are to give credence to our great-grandmothers, grandmothers and mothers.

First, generations of French-Canadian mothers were clearly assigned a permanent and openly known subservient role at best by religion. A role further reinforced by the State in reaffirming the religious position of men as head of their family. A role reconfirmed each year when the Church suggested and supported a ritual benediction by the father (as head of the family) of his family, during which mother and children had to get on their knees so they could understand their place in this hierarchy.

Secondly, French-Canadian mothers were pressured by institutionalized social and psychological mores to bear as many children as possible in a desperate effort to multiplying themselves in order to overcome their *enemy* – the English communities in whatever locality they found themselves, whether in a small village such as, say, Saint-Léon in Manitoba or Hawkesbury in Ontario or Montréal, Canada's metropolis at that time.

As if these women consisted of biological production machines and conscripted warriors of a kind, once brainwashed or unwilling and coerced to get pregnant by social convention and shaming.

No wonder so many women were pregnant between the ages of fourteen and mid-forties; unmarried women were harassed and dealt with as unworthy or possessed of loose morals; and the laws in Québec considered women as chattel longer than anywhere else in Canada.

Sadly, like soldiers, but in this case, in a weird field of battle, many died in childbirths, because of that policy.

Thirdly, the largest burden of all in the massive physical work of bringing up large families was born by women, which led most of them to age prematurely, weathered and withered by heavy work, and others ills that led them to die much before their time or otherwise live a miserable old age – like their Irish Roman Catholic cousins for that matter in similar circumstances.

GROWING DISRESPECT TOWARD THE CHURCH – 02.

As in all other nations, whenever frustration comes to the forefront, blasphemy in the form of an open show of disrespect toward those running a society comes out in swearing as a relief valve of sort as well as a harbinger of things to come.

***

In the case of English-speaking peoples around the world their frustrations came against the heavy censorship over practices and expression in all things to do with sex – a process still ongoing in this 21st century. So, swearing in that cultural world deals mainly with sexual references (e.g., *"Fuck you!", "Fuck face!", "You're a cunt!" "You're a prick!"* Etcetera.)

As for French-Canadians their extreme frustrations emerged from an anti-religious stand.

So, demoting and belittling anything considered blasphemous by the Church establishment became the norm the more their own mothers questioned the Church, and the more French-Canadians felt subjugated by that Church and the State by ricochet.

And this in spite of the ecclesiastical class's aberrant and consuming focus of the minutia of normal sexual activities of others over the centuries, while the Vatican ignored the abhorrent pedophilic activities – among other callous sexual misdeeds – of its officers and priests and religious brotherhoods over the centuries to this day.

Nonetheless, French-Canadians in the area of sex were, despite various sustained interdictions and edicts, able to enjoy themselves in this domain more that the average it seems – and no one was more liberated in this area than mothers as time evolved, which is why; sex never became a blasphemous issue.

So, long ago – as if a forerunner of a liberation to come – French-Canadians began to use religious terms and items to insult or downgrade the religious institution through sayings (in Joual) such as *"Mon tabarnak"* or *"Mon hostie"* or *"Mon sacrement"* in order to refer to, say, someone who had betrayed you, or had committed some despicable act against you, etc. It meant you were no better than the rotten Church institution – represented by its obvious sacred items of worship in this case – the tools of the trade in the rituals, which in the end were used by those restraining your freedom through brainwashing, the confessional, the mass, vespers, and other means of influence and control.

A form of swearing, which has been radically reduced since the *révolution tranquille* – given that the power of the Church has now been demoted to near insignificance. This disrespect and irreverence toward the Church establishment matured far more rapidly in urban centers – particularly in Montréal, which is where the greatest evolution of individual independence of thought grew and remains to this day – while in the more remote regions the divestment of Church controls took longer and is still ongoing in some isolated parts. As another proof of this devolving phenomenon more and more churches have been closing since the Sixties. Many have been demolished. Others used as cultural centers. Others yet utilized for a variety of reasons such gyms, art studios, condos, etc.

GROWING DISRESPECT TOWARD THE CHURCH – 03.

This gain could not have happened however without the gradual lack of respect for the Church as an institution by many of the women from the working class – especially in neighborhoods such as Sainte-Cunégonde and Sainte-Irénée.

Conversations between women were particularly cutting and highly disrespectful of the Church establishment and its officers throughout the Thirties and Forties, and seemed to boil over in the Fifties.

No doubt these mothers, directly or indirectly, knowingly or unknowingly, influenced their children over the generations – especially in the last few decades before the *révolution tranquille.*

Indeed, that powerful urge to be free at last; and to think and behave as one pleases without the sanctimonious approval of the Church, took on proportions that had never been observed before.

And like a flammable gas, this longing contained the potential explosion of the very social fabric in place – that collective intellectual membrane that had imprisoned them since their arrival on the North American continent.

All that was needed was someone to strike a match. That metaphorical match was lit on the death of Maurice Duplessis, then Premier of the province of Québec and at that time the near absolute ruler of that province, with the openly expressed, unabashed and special cooperation of the Church establishment.

MAURICE DUPLESSIS.

Maurice Duplessis was a man, who got what he wanted or otherwise ensured that those who did not cooperate with him were demoted, disbanded, resigned, or otherwise fired or removed from exercising influence.

His death nonetheless signaled the official end of *la grande noirceur,* and the opportunity at last to walk into the bright light of the world as it really was.

Québec had at last decided to free itself from the shackles of religion.

The psychological wall that held it back from thinking and acting independently for centuries collapsed within one generation.

All folkways and mores, which had blocked what otherwise would have been its normal development, began to break down, although you could not tell so at first – with a nervous emphasis in showy theatrical rituals by the Church.

GROWING DISRESPECT TOWARD THE CHURCH – 04.

All along, however, what assaulted young Ti-Jean's common sense at all times was that these fundamentalist ultra-Roman Catholics – like most Christians with a similar degree of blind commitment – knew everything about guilt and self-sacrifice and absolutely nothing about human compassion and self-fulfillment.

The Church generally and falsely marketed itself as an empathetic and sympathetic caring organization. But what disturbed young Ti-Jean as well was that Church officials and administrators committed premeditated fraud on the minds and lives of innocent people with cockamamie notions and contempt for the *flock*.

GROWING DISRESPECT TOWARD THE CHURCH – 05.

Another issue, which very early on infuriated Ti-Jean, was the way priests talked about the stupidity of their parishioners without the slightest concern for altar boys surrounding them in the preparation room of the presbytery, as they readied themselves for a religious service.

The same attitude was also prevalent in the presbytery office – except that it became more evident.

For example, when dealing with a man, the priest on duty would be polite and most officious – ensuring he protected the paying of fees for whatever service was contracted with or due the Church.

Soon after that man's departure depreciatory comments dealing with the low education and dullness of the parishioners were often uttered.

It was worse for women of course, who were generally treated as children, or as if possessed of a lower intelligence.

Women were sadly indoctrinated and coerced to consider themselves as a mere adjunct of their husband.

In both situations, priests acted, as if those altar boys surrounding them (whether one or two at the time) were deft, or insignificant, or worse yet, as if they did not exist.

These lessons about religious hypocrisy remained seared in most of the in the south-west area of Montreal.

GROWING DISRESPECT TOWARD THE CHURCH – 06.

Nonetheless, despite a generally growing disrespect of clerical arrogance and disapproval of the clerical methodology, which became clearer the more one paid attention to their behavior. Indeed, people in the south-west area of Montreal were astonished at the grandeur of the embroidered and greater-than-life religious rituals that would take place on Sundays and particularly on special religious holidays such as Christmas and Easter.

The first two such extraordinary spectacles of which he was aware, because he, by default, participated in them, was his Confirmation and First Communion.

Both were splendid ceremonies carried out in grandiose majesty by the local bishop in the magnificent église Sainte-Cunégonde on Saint-Jacques Street on the corner of Vinet Street– a ritual he still clearly remembers to this day.

Ceremonies, nonetheless, which oddly enough, began Ti-Jean's attachment to rituals, in spite of his total detachment and repulsion toward addictive fake beliefs system such as religion.

RELIGIOUS REALPOLITIK – 01.

Québec's Roman Catholic Church's arrogance went so far as to insist on whom to vote for, what to eat on Fridays, how much of the meager earnings of the working class should go to the Church establishment, how to think and behave, and to blindly consider ecclesiastical authorities as superior over all others – including scientific facts.

The message conveyed directly or indirectly in all texts, subtexts and utterances was the same: The 'word of god' was superior to everything in all matters.

Hence *Absolute Obedience* to Church authorities was categorical – and that in a perfect Roman Catholic world Canon law should reign supreme.

A secondary tactical message – with the support of their acolytes; medical doctors, notaries, lawyers, and journalists particularly – was the alleged duty for each family to produce as many children as possible in order to *preserve* their nation (i.e., French-speaking Roman Catholics specifically).

Thus, supposedly ensuring among other things the continued flow of revenues of the Church by ricochet and a predictably obedient population.

RELIGIOUS REALPOLITIK – 02.

A similar strategy of political interference was also carried across Canada in all regions, where French-Canadians settlements existed.

Outstanding among these was Saint-Boniface in Manitoba, which as a regional headquarters of the French-Canadian Catholic Church reporting to Montréal, managed all French-Canadian activities in western Canada in this respect. This included the Metis communities over the same territories, who were openly or surreptitiously baptized as soon as possible. As if members of, and de facto furtively adding these Metis to, the so-called French-Canadian Roman Catholic community at large. Although Metis people were rarely treated as equal but nonetheless given French names as often as possible in official papers such as birth certificates in order to up the count.

So, it is no surprise that the local application of the overwhelming religious management in people's affairs on Workman Street was just another urban sub-program of that overall massive religious control.

RELIGIOUS REALPOLITIK – 03.

There was a fear in Québec among many of the men folks that their position as 'head of the family' (regardless how humble their situation in their community), would be abolished, should the legal situation of women change from being mere chattel to a position equal to them in law.

Indeed, the thought which was prevalently held by men; those insecure working class men in Sainte-Cunégonde and the environs of southwest Montréal among others was that: 'if voting rights were given to women, these would likely undermine men's rightful place as the 'head of a household' – a strongly held religious edict at that time hammered into their conscious and subconscious for centuries.

Consensus logic in taverns as well as in presbyteries of the era was that a woman's proper place was in the home, tending to her husband's *needs* and the bringing up of *his* children.

The more macho among the men further proclaimed that 'women did not possess the mental equipment to understand politics and other manly realities of life'.

The more allegedly pragmatic among the masculine gender would paternalistically suggest that women would unnecessarily be exposed to strong emotions, be shoved around by bullies during electoral periods, likely exposed to violence on voting days, or simply be easily influenced in the course of a political campaign like children, when compared to men.

RELIGIOUS REALPOLITIK – 05.

How could a people, generation after generation, although descendants of already brainwashed ultra-Roman Catholics sent to New France on account of their blind unquestionable belief and *Absolute Obedience,* nonetheless continue to accept extreme ethical distortions, such as the treatment of women as inferior to men throughout the almost four centuries spent in North America?

How could they do this as a normal routine in a clearly quickly changing 20th century context of discoveries and advancements of all kinds?

RELIGIOUS REALPOLITIK – 06.

It was advantageous for the social elite and supporting establishment of the day in order to keep the Québec French-speaking population highly obedient to its pronouncements and commands, and that this characteristic continued to retain its potency.

And in order to ensure this population stays within the confines of their authority and power, the Québec elite and supporting establishment, which consisted of a bourgeoisie made up mostly of professionals (i.e., lawyers, notaries, politicians, university professors, journalists and medical doctors) convinced a great part of the population in cahoots with the proposals sponsored by the clerical class, to despise the *"evil"* of business; along with a disregard for money-making that eased an acceptance of their poverty; and a generalized disrespect for entrepreneurship, so that most tended to remain within their preassigned subservient roles.

An aberration still causing the Québec province serious financial difficulties, due to the unavoidable penalties such backward attitude costs future generations.

And unless Québec's latest generation reverses once and for all this perverse disregard for well-grounded economics and financial administration in its general population, it will most likely hit rock bottom before it smartens up.

RELIGIOUS REALPOLITIK – 07.

It was also common practice among the teaching religious orders to beat boys and girls into submission, although boys ended up getting the 'strap' more often than girls, while the latter where humiliated, admonished and brow beaten more regularly.

And throughout one's existence it was also common practice by clerics of all denominations to scold their *brebis* (as if an unthinking bunch of sheep) of all ages.

A practice that seemed most normal in the eyes of these religious officials, since many among them had a strong penchant to abuse children sexually – a practice that was not only tolerated but encouraged each time a pedophile was outed, by either ignoring accusations or simply moving the worst perpetrators elsewhere in areas where knew them. Indeed, the guilty party, a criminal without a doubt ethically speaking, were never brought before criminal courts, able again to carry out his despicable and reprehensible maltreatment and sexual exploitation.

A practice which now in our more open communication systems appears to have been universal within the whole Roman Catholic Church.

RELIGIOUS REALPOLITIK -08.

Quebec's French-Canadians had been for centuries indoctrinated and guided by hatred of non-Roman Catholics generally and Jews particularly – until the death of Maurice Duplessis, then Québec Premier, which signaled the beginning of the end as well as the emergence – until then not accepted – of a new way of looking and appreciating other people outside the periphery of their own closed-in claustrophobic world.

This death acted as the trigger for the beginning of a new Québec expressed in the *révolution tranquille* that followed.

POLITICAL RACKETS – 01.

As in all highly hierarchical, controlled and obedient societies, authority rather than pragmatism took precedence in French-speaking Québec since its very beginnings.

Having transferred mostly ultra-Roman Catholics to its new colony of New France, all of the authoritarian habits of both the imperial establishments of State and Church found in France at that time entered North America untouched.

It remained that way with French-Canadians qualified as *de souche* until a first wave of awakening began to emerge at some time at the start of the 20th century.

A social reality that had also remained mostly unchanged due to their lengthy and wide-ranging isolation.

Consequently, the mediaeval habit of blind obedience to those in charge remained almost untouched until then – leaving the responsibility of their values, meanings and standards to those in authority rather than create one's own.

So complete was French-Canadians' isolation that, not even the French Revolution had an effect upon their everyday life; nor did the American Revolution aside from a military intervention in Canada at that time, and in which they sided with their English masters for fear of losing their language; nor did the Industrial Revolution that took place most spectacularly in England; nor the burgeoning economic growth that was taking place in the USA – especially after World War I – although in this latter case many French-Canadians in Québec followed jobs in New England, wherein most eventually became Americans.

Generally, and throughout French-Canadians remained in their cocoon not only in Québec but throughout the dispersed Francophone community across Canada, as did in this respect their confreres, who had immigrated to the US – although the process of full integration took root much faster and far more thoroughly in the USA.

Nonetheless, at that time still Québec's French-Canadians particularly continued to live as if on another planet, preferring to be treated as children by those in charge, leaving all key decisions to someone else – someone appointed by the society in place at that time, if not a god, whose wishes and orders were *interpreted* by a clerical class – like Delphic pronouncements in some ways.

POLITICAL RACKETS – 02.

But once ever evolving technologies began to be introduced in Québec, beginning with radio, it gave voice to the notices, cautions and caveats from French-Canadian mothers to their children particularly in the first decades of the 20th century.

But what really launched the *révolution tranquille* in the eyes of everyone, unaware of the growing influence of mothers here, was a combination of factors taking place concurrently.

While the publicly noticed spark for the *révolution tranquille* was the death of Maurice Duplessis in 1959 and was seen as if taking place all at once – it in fact resulted from the combined confluence and influence of radio, telephones and television. As if someone had turned several lights all of a sudden upon the dire situation French-Canadiens found themselves in at that time.

POLITICAL RACKETS – 03.

In the minds of the majority, Maurice Duplessis was the epitome of a benevolent dictator anticipated by French-speaking Quebecers – a man who took charge and was bent on *defending* them against all enemies of their tribe – those outside the Roman Catholic Church and especially the 'English' (i.e., English-speaking Canadians were usually all lumped into this group regardless of origin).

Throughout their history, the Québec style French-Canadian notion of a strong leader with a benevolent attitude had been inculcated in them either directly or in subtexts found in sermons and *histoires saintes* along with a variety of other religious forums.

The supreme clerical model of course was Jesus Christ – whether it was openly mentioned or not, along with a plethora of saints and other heroes or personages acting in similar ways – both religious and also secular as they approached the end of *la grande noirceur*.

In daily life this notion was personified by and rested with the Church establishment, and the narrow-minded political establishment that supported it.

It found its apotheosis in Maurice Duplessis.

All nevertheless promoted an *Absolute Obedience* to religious values and the secular ones based on these, which is why Duplessis could rule this province with impunity.

POLITICAL RACKETS – 04.

As all-powerful leaders without opposition Maurice Duplessis committed stupid political blunders.

An example of this was the Québec dream of including the whole Labrador Territory as an integral part of the province of Québec on account of its location on the same geographic landmass. Rather than intelligently and civilly negotiate the amalgamation, and if possible, the transfer of that territory with the full cooperative help of Ottawa and London, prior to the inclusion of Newfoundland as the tenth province of Canada, Maurice Duplessis bombastically assumed and presumed that its location irretrievably meant that it was already part of Québec and would in due course be officially and irretrievably become part of Québec.

On the subject about making Labrador officially an integral part of Québec, Maurice Duplessis was heard to boastfully say that:

"I will do no such things with a territory that already 'belongs' to us".

Or something to that effect.

This again underlines this Gallic lack of long-term planning in a context outside normal practices of plain business negotiations, Ti-Jean had noted from his earliest years, with Québec's French-Canadian way of doing things at that time.

This manner of dealing with others that has so often crippled Québec in the course of its transactions with others, has been exemplified on numerous occasions and on an almost continuing basis through Québec's maladroit, if not ham-fisted dealings, with Ottawa and the confederation of which it is an important part.

POLITICAL RACKETS – 05.

Maurice Duplessis was the first elected Québec leader, who, although cognizant of the necessity of Church support to win elections, nonetheless gradually began to govern more independently.

While Duplessis still supported many Church objectives and paid obvious respect in public to its *moral authority,* his support became conditional for the first time in Québec history.

Maurice Duplessis held the public purse and ensured those who got governmental funds contributed directly to his secular objectives – an obvious change from catering to religious goals and strategies of all previous administrations.

The new condition over the twenty years or so he was in power was that the Church had to play ball with his political objectives and not the other way around. And this rule became increasingly a part of his playbook as time went on.

Many in the clerical class objected, but only a few did so publicly and this to their detriment.

Among these, the then most senior executive of the Roman Catholic Church in Québec, Archbishop Joseph Charbonneau, publicly protested, directly challenging the authoritarian strong-arm tactics used by Duplessis.

POLITICAL RACKETS – 06.

Duplessis' Padlock Law combined a blatant and co-dependent State/Church censorship.

Yet, he was barely eleven when made aware of it.

A law, promoted by both Maurice Duplessis and the Catholic Church, he discovered through his *father*, Ovide, because of both the Church's and Duplessis' fear of communism, combined with their awareness of the poverty and misery encountered by a restless general population, and the temptation such a radical solution might present.

A proposal eagerly accepted and transmogrified by Duplessis as a government sponsored legislation to *protect* French-Canadians against all left-leaning political notions and affiliations as early as 1937.

This broadly applied and ill-defined law denied the presumption of innocence, and clearly deprived citizens of the right to freedom of speech.

While this law was frequently applied against various radical leftist groups, the Duplessis regime also used it to openly and surreptitiously neutralize political opponents.

Indeed, locations, where left-leaning activities took place or was suspected to take place, could literally be padlocked at will, and anyone found *guilty* of involvement in prohibited activities for example could be incarcerated from three to thirteen months for each offence.

POLITICAL RACKETS – 07.

And further that freedom of thought and behavior was a principle in Québec at that time, which came in only after the *law of god* as far as the Church establishment was concerned – the Roman Catholic proprietary god in this case.

In effect that the *law of god* trumped all.

Hence, that the concept of *Inalienable Individual Rights* was considered superfluous if not simply dangerous.

THE REAL GRANDE NOIRCEUR – 01.

The period, traditionally identified by Canadian historians as *la grande noirceur,* included mainly the two-decade long Duplessis regime.

In fact, contrary to the pre-Duplessis era, that later part of *la grande noirceur* consisted of extraordinary efforts by the Union Nationale to catch up with a much-neglected infrastructure.

A time in which Maurice Duplessis, knowing the obvious backwardness of Québec, wanted to promote his province at least to a level equal to Ontario – as the rest of the world was jumping ahead technologically, demonstrated in the accelerating manufacturing sector during and after World War I and World War II.

It implied the accentuating of controls on a population that had by now become more restless, while still being in command of the government for the ultra-conservative goals of the regime in place.

And yet all the while trying to jump ahead economically by improving existing infrastructures and building brand new ones – a basic condition for further development.

THE REAL GRANDE NOIRCEUR – 02.

Predictably, during this process, Duplessis and the regime of politicians and professionals, which supported him, favoured rural areas over city development – introducing a variety of agricultural funding.

The Duplessis government was characterized by patronage and corruption, and its methods in the field also ensured that all was done to keep the opposition party as weak as possible.

So, while progress could be noted such as paved roads or new schools where the locals had voted for Union Nationale, those who had not, remained with their dirt roads and shacks for schools, which made it difficult for them to invite commerce, improve education and provide adequate transportation needs.

And this attitude and way of doing things were replicated in all domains.

THE REAL GRANDE NOIRCEUR – 03.

The traditional method in Québec – as it was nearly everywhere else in allegedly democratic circles – was by vastly over-representing the emptying and far less populated rural counties, wherein a heavy religious and political conservatism was predominant – doing so at the expense of the more populated and more liberalized citizens in urban centres.

This ensured, both, that religious values and their related and expected thinking, behavior, folkways and mores, which maintained the population in check, would be retained through government laws in support of the Church as guardians of the minutia of family life. And that disturbing secular ideas and notions such as strong labor unions and change of style of governance would be quelled before they gained momentum. Indeed, the Duplessis regime was opposed to new ideas and challenges, continuously trying and often succeeding in eliminating philosophies opposed to it. So, a period of stagnation or retardation remained as Québec was working hard at getting out of its catastrophic hole of ignorance and lack of creative endeavors, it had hidden itself into for centuries by now.

THE REAL GRANDE NOIRCEUR – 04.

While hidden in this capsule of ignorance Québec continued its religiously induced negation of business activities as if mere acts of usury and exploitation of the helpless.

And so nearly all of Québec pretended in those days that, it was not necessary to upgrade your station in life through business ventures, capital investments and out-of-the-box projects – admittedly a particularly more difficult message to convey in the last few decades after the Second World War.

THE REAL GRANDE NOIRCEUR – 05.

The transition from *la grande noirceur* to the *révolution tranquille* took place between the Second World War and the death of Maurice Duplessis – an interim period of progress albeit filled with conditional, dislocated, disordered and haphazard projects in the direction of progress.

A period that showed the desperate efforts, made by the Duplessis regime to catch up with the rest of North America.

A period that became an uncoordinated and rushed fifteen years or so of catch-up in infrastructure development particularly after such a long period of isolation and decline.

A period in which many understood at last, the missed opportunities at industrialization and other fields of squandered economic breaks Québec was guilty of.

A period, which also indicated the futility of a classical education that catered to its elite – made up mostly of its old style traditional professions – when business development required and demanded MBAs or some other equivalent economic and financial qualifications and solid engineering and scientific education, if you wanted to get out of the economic hellhole Québec was in.

Hence, a period during which more and more people understood that a major change of education of Québec residents was also greatly overdue, if Québec was not only to catch up with the rest of Canada, the US and the Western World generally, but participate in global development as well.

A period wherein the urge to catch up in every domain – especially for consumer items with the rest of Canada, the US and the rest of the Western world, became an irresistible incentive.

A period of transition from the stagnation that had been the norm for centuries before that, and into the world as it really was – and not that mediaeval world of make-believe values and fake otherworldly *certainties* offered by the Church.

A period of intense modernization and upgrading, which by default brought down the institutions and the control programs that had kept French-Canadians enslaved psychologically and intellectually.

THE REAL GRANDE NOIRCEUR – 06.

The many centuries of stagnation that characterized French-Canadians between 1608 and a decade and a half or so before the Sixties was truly the one that should have been labelled *la grande noirceur*. Hence not just the last twenty years or so before the *révolution tranquille* traditionally assigned by historians.

The period conventionally labelled as such by them is a misnomer, simply because the self-imposed backwardness of French-Canadians dates back centuries.

This French-Canadians' acceptance and habit of taking a backseat to progress to the benefit of the medieval goals of the Roman Catholic Church and its affiliated supporters was a colossal and most stupid centuries-long blunder.

Indeed, their allegiance to the ideology of that Church rather than the realities of the world at large became over the centuries

– and particularly since the end of the 19th to almost the first half of the 20th century – became a prefabricated excuse for not accomplishing very much, while remaining within the parameters of control assigned to them.

Therefore, the dominant lack of enterprise, which characterized much of Québec's French-Canadians for so long, also became a factor in Québec's development after the *révolution tranquille,* since bad habits do not all of sudden disappear, just because one or a whole national group has had an epiphany about its situation and condition.

And despite Québec's desperate efforts to ignore its lackluster past, its inherent lack of 'can do' entrepreneurship was also – although to a lesser extent – a significant factor with the first and second generation coming out of *la grande noirceur.*

The men and women, who were now at the forefront of the *révolution tranquille* in the Sixties, and who also promoted themselves as <u>the</u> agents of change, nevertheless continued to ignore the lessons their mothers had taught them, stubbornly replacing Roman Catholicism by the religious-like ideology of the newly emerging secular bureaucratic belief system of *Political Correctitude.*

Hence, as planners and executors of their ideology, Québec politicians continued to plan with the notion that methodology in support of ideology supersedes future economic ramifications – even if future generations will inevitably be paying the price and eventually brace themselves for bankruptcy if not corrected on time.

So, the questions that kept recurring with Ti-Jean was:

Why do we obey ideological notions and applications of unquestionable dogmatic principles, while ignoring the pragmatism of economic, financial, scientific, and technological realities in the world at large?

Why institute wonderful social programs without the necessary planning for their future financial survival?

Why continue in a secular format the old religious parlance of *'god would provide'* although never admitting to it by blindly instituting programs we clearly cannot afford?

And yet the various separatist administrations when in power have continued to act in the same mode of thinking taught for centuries by their own Roman Catholic Church – as if French-Canadians *vielles souches* were a *Chosen People*, who could and would supersede all without regard to future ramifications of present day decisions.

This notion gained much more significance with the schooled generations that followed the sixties, although it has remained to a large degree in government affairs and bureaucratic administration – where true long-term strategic planning has been largely ignored to this day, although it has often been feigned.

THE REAL GRANDE NOIRCEUR – 07.

The elements, characterizing *la grande noirceur* over the centuries in Québec, epitomized by the paroxysm of over-the-top and sumptuous religious ceremonies in the postwar period between 1945 and 1960, presented a powerful Church at its zenith on a particular territory.

It theatrically camouflaged the grumbling of the population at large, along with a noticeably rapid dissipating respect for an *Absolute Obedience* to Church and associated authority and edicts, as well as a palpable sense of an unstoppable longing to defeat a system that had held French-Canadians down individually and as a society for so long. As if, many wanted and needed that long sought after craving to meet personal objectives, at least for their children, if not for themselves.

Such aspirations emerged in great part from both, the period after the First World War to begin with, and then the Second World War in particular.

During that time French-Canadians in Québec came face-to-face with their dire and unvarnished situation – and they did not like what they saw.

They by then highly resented the limits imposed upon them by their own elite, and finally insisted for the first time since their coming on the North American continent to change this humiliating position.

A position generated by these two major trigger causes, which urged them along with other factors of course to forge their own future.

Indeed, both World Wars had shaken French-speaking Quebecers awake, introducing by default many of the memes for change into that segment of the French-Canadian consciousness, in addition to the cumulative lessons taught by their mothers over the years – a process that would clearly show up in their future.

A process that first visibly expanded with radio broadcasting and was accentuated by the coming of television. And so the roughly four century-long stranglehold of the Roman Catholic Church over the French-Canadian mind began to dissolve with the advent of more advanced communications.

Once Québec's decline at all social and economic levels before the Second World War became common knowledge, it inaugurated a new beginning in segments of that population along with a dream to improve its dire economic and social situation. Indeed, once recognized, it snowballed until it transformed itself into the *révolution tranquille*.

The growing realization, that the whole French-Canadian nation had been imprisoned into a dogmatic belief system and social straitjacket, was usually highlighted by mothers everywhere in Québec – a situation that became particularly significant in triggering the *révolution tranquille.*

Indeed, French-Canadian mothers kept telling their children that, the world belonged to those possessing an education and that the odds resided with those who spoke English – the language of those running the show.

Emphasizing that the accidental fact that France had surrendered Québec to England as a settlement of the Thirty-Year War was just that – a settlement.

And the fact that English was now the predominant language of communication of our planet among the elites, the educated and business had nothing to do with past national conflicts and did not change the reality they had to deal with it in their daily lives.

Two hard pills to swallow indeed among those ideologically disinclined to accept these, but then reality is a difficult thing to acknowledge by many, and French-Canadians were no exception to this.

Although mothers told their children over and over again that, while they should be proud of, and retain, their mother tongue as their primary language, these children were also instructed that they should nonetheless be familiar with, and speak, English, in order to get on the bandwagon of business and employment in this primary English-speaking continent.

And this whether or not French-speaking Canadians from Québec were totally sovereign or not.

Reality is reality and no one can walk away from it without hurting oneself, these children were often told.

A reality that is there and everywhere whether one likes it or not, since English is now recognized as essential for advancement and success in the business world – especially when all your neighbors are English-speaking on the entire North American continent with a significant number in Québec itself.

A view, which in the end proved to be right, and all the more applicable and required as English became the planetary language.

A fact that confirmed what these mothers had been voicing all along, especially when eventually discovering that, the two most significant and best known leaders of the separatist party, le Parti Québécois, their founder René Lévesque as well as Jacques Parizeau, their one time economic tsar, both completed their education by attending English-speaking universities – Lévesque in the US and Parizeau in the UK.

THE REAL GRANDE NOIRCEUR – 09.

It was in this context that Ti-Jean while considering the future life which poverty and ignorance had legated to him – and transmitted from one generation to the next as if a family heirloom – realized he could no longer live in Sainte-Cunégonde without suffocating emotionally and intellectually, and that a decision process in this regard had already begun in his young mind.

A by then already uncomfortable notion particularly troubling for the status quo within working class neighbourhoods of Montréal, then the largest urban centre in Canada – including that parish where much of our story takes place.

A NASCENT NANNY STATE IS BORN – 01.

The vacuum, created by the departing omnipresent influence of the Church in controlling the behavior and thinking of French-Canadians, was filled first by the old traditional professions composed of medical doctors, notaries, lawyers, politicians, university educators, journalists, and accountants, who had supported the Church establishment during its reign.

As the decades unfolded after *la grande noirceur*, provincial government bureaucrats along with new burgeoning professions such as psychologists, psychiatrists, sociologists, and engineers took over the role – leaving old guard medical and legal professions thinking 'they were still in charge'. Indeed, as religious faith became more of a parody, despite its outward spectacle of religiosity, blind secular beliefs oddly enough carried the day nonetheless in Québec, as this province slowly began to transmogrify itself from a Church controlled population to a complex ultra-bureaucratic one.

In addition to the old guard medical and legal professions, each new profession in turn was put on a pedestal, as if – like the priests who preceded them – members of each could deliver the generally uneducated or unsophisticated populace, the certitude the Church had previously pretended to provide them with.

Except that, this was now apportioned in different fields of specialization, rather than in the golden old days, wherein one monolith *Immaculate Perception* centered on a single proprietary belief system that had previously remained on the shoulders of one type of priesthood only.

The result was that the religious habit of indoctrination metamorphosed itself by a reconstituted blind obedience to the ideology of specialized training tied into an over the top respect for the alleged specialness of these professions – traditional and new ones alike.

A Promoted Self-Adulation...
The most original and most prominent beneficiaries of this promoted adulation were members of the medical establishment, at the top of which reigned medical doctors.
For decades this profession – like their colleagues in the clerical class – benefited from an unearned and clearly exaggerated respect it did not deserve, which led to far too much condescendence on

their part – with reverberations still felt nowadays in the mannerism of many a young medical doctor.
A profession originally occupied by men, who like priests saw themselves as all knowing – as if they too had been favored by the gods. An idiosyncrasy being reduced at last with the inflow of females into that profession, but still visible each time I meet my young GP.

A NASCENT NANNY STATE IS BORN – 02.

Nevertheless, for too many decades the older professions favored; the patriarchal concepts of large family, obedience to the Church in place, along with a conservative view of life, which left women in a servile role especially within working class French-Canadian families – with no prospect whatsoever for them for fulfillment. Hence, that everyone had to know their place – especially women. A reality significantly lessened at last by the influx of a large proportion of women into all professions and the work force generally, and now made even more visible by a superior and still increasing university attendance by women.

A NASCENT NANNY STATE IS BORN – 03.

And yet, even nowadays one can still easily witness self-righteous paternalistic conversations and comments from well-meaning, intelligent and dedicated female general practitioners, who still carried with them, part of that indoctrination passed on to them from past generations of misogynistic male confrèrerie, even in the truly advanced medical school of the université de Montréal.

Rather than ...
It was more important for Ti-Jean's wife's GP for example – a good and decent person – to reduce the amount of morphine that would have otherwise lessened to a minimum the pains suffered by his wife, Helen, rather than relieve all of her pains.
And this for the ideological notion of not allegedly turning this seventy-something woman into a drug addict (her comment) – about a woman who did not even smoke a joint in her entire life.
It was reminiscent of those doctors and nuns during *la grande noirceur*, who insisted patients *"offer their pains to god"* in order to *reduce* their time in purgatory.

In such cases the logic was (again excluding sound independent human judgment as in the religious days) to abide by principles of *Political Correctitude* influenced by our contemporary 'zero tolerance' concepts in effect in the world at large – and not from pragmatic ethical grounding about the reduction of pain prior to an impending death – about which we are all bound to sooner or later.

A NASCENT NANNY STATE IS BORN – 04.

There were few doctors, lawyers, professors, notaries and so on in the good old days of *la grande noirceur*, when the vast majority of the French-Canadian population was both poor and uneducated – therefore set up to be in awe and at the mercy of anyone, who allegedly or in fact knew far more than them.

The normal and all too often impertinent if not simply disrespectful professional attitude of members of the old professions toward Quebec's poor, like their previous master from France and those of the religious class, showed even in their public mannerism, as they generally perambulated and acted as if chosen by their predecessors, as most special and superior to the rest of the population. A process that accentuated the normalcy of obedience to authority regardless of the content and purpose – religious or secular.

This professional attitude of olden days privileged a stance of authority, copied in several ways from the original aristocracy that governed them and the Church's posture of *knowing it all*, then gradually replaced by a rational form of knowledge instead of old megalomaniac royal demands and religious cockamamie gobbledygook. But the gob smacked effect remained the same however, since simply the object of adoration and the fragmentation of their unquestionable new knowledge had changed from the perspective of the population caught in its poverty and utter ignorance.

A NASCENT NANNY STATE IS BORN – 05.

Each specialty by its nature, definition and in fact covers a very narrow spectrum of knowledge – usually ignoring the numerous and broader fields of knowledge and judgment often required in the wise survival strategy of everyday life.

This silo type knowledge sadly became the accepted stance by nearly all professions in Québec until recently.

Over the decades this stance carried with it a disrespect of the population at large.

A form of disrespect which assumed in its discourses that, professionals had to teach and mold a docile and slow thinking populace.

Just like you would a child (or their *flock* as their religious predecessors habitually considered their parishioners).

A NASCENT NANNY STATE IS BORN – 06.

Particularly in the Thirties, Forties and Fifties all you had to do to understand Quebec's professional stance toward its population was simply to pay attention.

Whenever involved in a one-on-one encounter with one of them, or simply listen to the pomposity of their comments on the radio or television or read newspapers and magazine articles or professional journals of that era, their attitude came out clearly.

Indeed, the implementation of a sort of professional *Political Correctness* emerged, as each group in turn adopted over the decades an attitude and a bureaucratic stance in very many ways reminiscent of the religious approach to things.

The world, from that platform it seemed (their new 'bible' in some way), could only be explained through the lens of each of the narrow narratives abstracted from their sphere of knowledge.

Even children of the Forties and Fifties loathed the pompous sense of social superiority, and on occasion the intellectualism of those insisting they be addressed with a formal title of authority – whether valid or not as a real segment of knowledge.

People wearing their State assigned designations, as if a toga worn by Roman senators of old, or the ostentatious clothes displayed by a Louis XIV's court or a priest at mass, irritated him.

A resentment emerging out of that arrogance that existed and had presumably been more deeply inculcated in all early professions everywhere in Québec.

An attitude that spread to nearly all other professions afterward but without the preceding obvious honorific titles for the newer ones.

An attitude, which still today contributes through cultural memes, … later on, … assumed to take it upon themselves to comment on events or situations clearly out of their control and their purview – in some ways similar to deluding Hollywood stars in the US.

As if their knowledge in the narrow specialty of each of their professions, also miraculously provided them with a special outlook on the rest of data, information and knowledge at large.

Therefore, and throughout, the questions it suggested being:

Is this a remnant of the massive indoctrination and know-it-all philosophy inculcated in so many generations, still showing its ugly head into new forms of contempt in Québec for those with less opportunities or with less technical data and information in a particular area of knowledge?

Is this indeed also an unfortunate vestigial attitude legated by the Church through the teaching institutions of Québec –

transferring a sort of no responsibility and no accountability memes through the new religion of *Political Correctitude*?

FAKED SPECIALNESS OF A PETTY BOURGEOISIE.

From its beginnings the Québec bourgeoisie supported the ruling English establishment running the Québec territory from the time of its conquest of 1759-1760 to the days of the *révolution tranquille*.

In this process the Québec bourgeoisie coincidently kept adopting the pompous airs of their original French aristocratic masters that had preceded them, carrying this attitude through an assumed and evolving bureaucratic language approaching in an altered form, the religious lingua in some ways of its previous religious dictators. A characteristic, which can still be observed, when dealing with professionals of all stripes but particularly obvious in the traditional ones such as lawyers, notaries, medical doctors, and the few remaining priests.

A trait observed as well with provincial bureaucrats and other government officials and politicians generally, and which sadly in this case appears to be spreading still.

> **As If Precursors of ...**
> A peculiarity guessed at when a radio station dear to this class of more or less privileged individuals and want-to-be leaders of a proposed Québec republic, brings them into a virtual aristocratic make-believe world in a daily musical program for the last several years titled *"Pour les soupers du roi"*.
> As if a precursor of things to come, if not an imaginary monarchy of sort like the good old days, or at least a republic, where the Québec bourgeoisie (especially its older professional class) seeing itself as an aristocracy of sort.
> As if they could and would eventually be an integral part of *The Most Special Group* running the show in an alleged North American French-speaking independent country.

It is exhibited in a manner meant to suggest a marked superiority over consulting clients, if not simply imply their own self-assigned superiority as a *Special Group*, often accompanied with excessively officious tones couched in patronizing and paternalistic conversations. An arrogance that routinely seeps through their discourses, as if their academic indoctrination – like remnants or a specter of the religious brainwashing of the parents and grandparents before them, once combined – could not be hidden in spite of efforts by many to camouflage their self-righteousness and other strong prejudices through fine manners, and a language designed to avoid responsibilities and accountabilities.

BRUTAL POLICE UNIT AT ALL LEVELS IN ALL AREAS.

The concept of human rights was not part of regular consideration in the first part of the 20th century in south-west Montréal or anywhere else in Québec for that matter.

What counted, for the constabulary throughout the province was fear of authority erroneously tagged by them as respect.

A reality found especially in regions wherein poverty was concentrated in ghettos such as in Sainte-Cunégonde.

IF THE PLAINTIFF …

If the plaintiff about a criminal act, for example (in south-west Montréal), was a local, he had to remain humble in making his case, otherwise he would literally be dragged into to the police station for a beating, allegedly for lack of proper respect for the badge, and put in a cell for a few hours or for the night to 'teach that fellow a lesson'.

If considered belligerent, some charge or other would be laid against him – one of which generally included resisting arrest.

But if it was a professional such as a medical doctor, lawyer, or one of the local politicians that complained about someone from the working-class ghettos, then all hell broke loose, and nothing was spared to arrest and beat into submission, whoever had been identified as an alleged offender.

A SUBMISSIVE QUÉBEC CULTURE – 01.

Sadly, a significant segment of French-Canadians from a *vielle souche* origin are still indoctrinated to muddle through aimlessly and without insight.

They generally blamed others for their own lack of enterprise, while continually ignoring that it was their Mother Country, which had exchanged them for a few backward natives and tiny islands. And also, as if the religious brainwashing imposed on all previous generations contributed to their blindness about the Church's cooperation with their masters – French or English.

A SUBMISSIVE QUÉBEC CULTURE – 03.

The vast majority of French-Canadians pursued an existence of low expectancy from life's rewards in view of their near complete obedience to a form of morality set by the Church – an *Absolute Obedience* to a set of clearly medieval notions and principles.

The carrot used generally was that in following Church edicts, they would avoid suffering eternal torture for serious disobedience to Church dictates.

If that did not work, then the Church marketed the idea that with its help and support, French-Canadians would not have to struggle so much in the use their mother tongue, and that it would eventually facilitate their use of French across Canada – often citing Saint-Boniface in Manitoba as an example, if not a *proof*, of that progress.

It was all a lie of course, and the Church knew it, but hope is eternal, and an unsophisticated population believed it.

BETRAYING THEIR OWN COMMUNITY – 01.

Once the Fleurs-de-lys was substituted for the Union Jack as the provincial flag and the term Québécois was substituted for French-Canadians in Québec, a split in the French-Canadian community across Canada took place. Two decisions that cut off French-Canadians in Québec from the rest of that community in the rest of Canada.

This in turn set these isolated smaller communities *à la dérive*, just as France, their Mother Country, had done with their whole community in 1760.

BETRAYING THEIR OWN COMMUNITY – 02.

At that point, the intellectual disease of victimization lying latent since 1760, took deep roots in Québec – and the real Québec urge to separate truly began.

As if separation from the rest – the vast majority –on a brand-new territory could and would miraculously resolve all their shortcomings.

As if their very own elite would be kinder and more understanding – ignoring of course the lessons taught by history everywhere in this respect.

Conveniently forgetting as well that their Church worked in cahoots with the English authorities in the old days, so they could continue their imperial control over the thoughts and forms of behavior over all French-Canadians everywhere in Québec. And hoping they could continue their isolation, undisturbed in a world that kept on changing – out of fear of a world outside their perimeters that kept on advancing in just about every way.

POINTE ST-CHARLES AND GRIFFINTOWN.

Pointe St. Charles – like Griffintown – was considered a mostly 'English' territory by uneducated residents from Sainte-Cunégonde and Sainte-Irénée.

Those so-called "English', as they referred to them, those alleged outsiders, consisted in the vast majority of poor Irish immigrants. These people of Irish descent were also uneducated just like them, although this did not somehow enter their perception bias. A thought that never came to the mind of most French-Canadians in that area—perceiving anyone speaking English at that time and place as English. And this no matter how badly English was spoken by some – by most newly arrived immigrants choosing English as their new means of communications.

THE REALITY WAS …

The reality was that both groups were poor and struggled – although the Irish often ended up as first line supervisors (usually first level foremen on a shop floor or on a loading dock) to the detriment of most French-Canadians, which is probably why a sort of resentment existed in the first place. Otherwise, the majority of French-Canadians rarely communicated or dealt with the Irish side – as was the case in a different way with the Black railway workers from the Passengers department of both Canadian Pacific and Canadian National.

There, however, never existed an overall conspiracy to promote Irish only at this first level of supervision on the part of business owners and managers.

It was simply the way of least resistance.

An approach similar in the US for several decades with Hispanics but in a reversed fashion, wherein bilingual Spanish-speaking people usually end up with first level foremen jobs over those who do not possess such a skill.

Indeed, because owners and bosses were Anglophones, they expected their first line supervisors to easily understand them, since factory owners and the management staff had no inclination nor a need or an obligation to speak French – and had figured out that the Irish, whom, many of them looked down upon, would nevertheless find a way to make their wishes and orders understood by the "frogs" – as French-Canadians were often prejudicially referred to at that time.

Although that term changed in the Fifties to "Pepsies" in view of the inclination by the "French" to drink that soda pop rather than Coca Cola.

MARCH OF 'THE CONDEMNED'.

The indoctrinated local residents of Sainte-Cunégonde and Sainte-Irénée – and let's face it, nearly all had been thoroughly brainwashed – regularly went to mass like robotized puppets, occasionally by themselves but generally as a family or in larger monolithic groups, if they belonged to a religious order.

In the Thirties, Forties and Fifties, in all parishes found in *La Petite Bourgogne,* mass was scheduled daily, to meet various agendas, generally beginning at six o'clock in the morning and every half-hour after that until the last one at nine o'clock during the week.

After this, nine, ten and occasionally eleven o 'clock, were reserved for funerals from Monday to Saturday, while on Sunday a more elaborate mass was scheduled every hour from six in the morning until eleven.

No mass was ever celebrated from noon on at that time, because local priests never missed their Sunday feast prepared since early morning each Sunday, wherein the best of wines was chilled and added to an extraordinary inventory of victuals worthy of a well-assigned gastronomic table.

THE BLACK ENGLISH-SPEAKING PRESENCE – 01.

Black residents in Sainte-Cunégonde and Sainte-Irénée were located mainly on streets near their workstations, because of the short a walking distance to the two national railways that employed them.

These people held jobs, which were better remunerated than the ones French-Canadians generally occupied, first because Blacks spoke English, but also because they were not afraid to leave home for a couple of days or more on trains that traveled all over Canada and parts of the US.

French-Canadians at that time rarely considered such jobs even when they could speak English.

The proof is that most applied for laborer jobs instead since most in these two parishes had not finished their primary school and many among them were almost analphabets.

WORKMAN STREET - 03.

Workman Street was considered by its resident to be the center of their lives, wherein the surrounding streets were at times or when necessary, part of the geography they also considered a familiar terrain – although less comfortable there than being on their own street.

Nevertheless, the general parameter of this area wherein the Workman Street people felt at home – their world so to speak – consisted of the Lachine Canal, Rose-de-Lima Street, Saint-Antoine Street and Dominion Street and occasionally a bit beyond that.

WORKMAN STREET - 04.

Life on Workman Street was harsh for nearly all, wherein a couple of beers and a pack of cigarettes crowned a workweek for men folks at a tavern located at the corner of Notre-Dame and Charlevoix or on Notre-Dame near Atwater or at the corner of Atwater Avenue and Notre Dame – especially after a week of arduous labor.

A tavern was where working-class men stuck in low paying labor intensive jobs gathered with other men of their kind.

Knowing that, they too held similar arduous jobs like you, meant you were somewhat successful.

You had a job.

You were surviving.

You were considered a 'good provider' in this world of low expectations.

You were part of the average.

You did not stand out.

And you most certainly did not go out of your neighborhood for fear of witnessing a better way of life – although never admitting to it.

No! That would be too much. Much too hurtful. So, you generally lived and died in the neighborhood you were born into.

WORKMAN STREET - 05.

What drove the wretched people on Workman Street and the environs was dread and fear.

Fear of not having enough food or money to pay for rent or wood or coal for heating or electricity.

Added to the dread of going straight to a hell of eternal torture for disobeying "god's laws", inculcated into these people for hundreds of years by then.

These were people torn away and disconnected from their natural culture, immersed in an English-speaking environment, scared out of their wits about the future, and centered only on itself as a shaky means of communal survival.

NOTRE-DAME STREET – 01.

French-Canadians men from working class neighborhoods were often humiliated at work, while women found their embarrassment in stores such as Eaton's on Sainte-Catherine Street in Montréal and many other stores where clerks generally did not or would not speak French to unilingual French-Canadian clients and generally look down at them, in spite of the fact that millions of them lived and had been there for centuries.

In the first case, first line supervisors – nearly always unilingual English-speaking foremen and occasionally bilingual ones – would convey to the workers what had to be done.

This was generally carried out with a tone indicating their contempt of French-Canadians, usually by people of Irish origin roughly of the same low level of education but with a slightly better economic background.

When done in English only, those orders were translated by one of the workers as best he could and conveyed it to the rest.

Indeed, French-Canadians from the big city lucky enough to find employment in one of the factories in *La Petite Bourgogne* were considered a sort lower class of citizens – uneducated and unable to speak the language of business and that of the majority on the North American continent, as if a group of odd balls, abandoned by their mother country, and still ignoring the language of the majority on that continent.

In the second case, working class women struggled as best they could with the little money and little English they knew, or simply gestured to identify items chosen, when that was possible, if they could not express themselves in English – otherwise store clerks would ignore them.

The Eaton's department store on Sainte-Catherine has remained the worst example in this regard in French-Canadian memory and narrative – although this behavior was common practice throughout both central and western parts of Montréal particularly.

HIGH LEVEL OF FRUSTRATION.

Both situations created a high level of frustration, which was alleviated by smaller stores lining up Notre-Dame Street, where

French would be used, as was generally the case east of Saint-Lawrence Street in Montréal.

These were owned in great part by Jewish-Canadians and a few French-Canadians.

As evidence, there and throughout Montréal, those of Jewish origin obviously had a better sense of the retail business at hand, accommodating themselves to the needs of the population they catered to – and speaking the language of their customers once in *la petite Bourgogne.*

NOTRE-DAME STREET – 03.

Within a short stretch on Notre-Dame Street you could also find three cinemas, the Lido and Corona in Sainte-Cunégonde and the Cartier a bit further.

These entertained a densely populated area, when only radio existed as another form of mass entertainment.

Two of these provided two feature films twice a day seven days a week.

The third, the Lido, the oldest and grubbiest, showed three features in order to attract customers, intent on getting more for their money.

The craziest thing however was that all films were in English including news and cartoons.

So, the population did its best to understand movie plots along with news of the week, cartoons, and upcoming features, shown on the screen by visual clues rather than speech. While the price paid was right, the language was not, but they in practice had no other choice.

They put up with it, because there was nothing else of real value for them or in accord with their expectations of movies in French, except a few cinemas situated outside their comfort zone.

These few cinemas showed French films from Europe, which were also out of sync even that far back with the North-American mentality of the French-speaking population of Québec, which without realizing it at that time, was more North American than European.

Indeed, French-Canadians had become, without noticing it at the time, French-speaking North Americans in mind and spirit, which is the reason they disliked most of those films, preferring Hollywood productions by far.

Unlike their English Canadian compatriots but similar to Americans, French-Canadians, at least from the province of Québec, generally felt no attachment to Europe or their mother country.

The exception to this consisted of those belonging to the small bourgeoisie of the day, which even then saw itself in some dreamt of future, as the ruling class of a French-speaking country called something like *'la république de Québec'*, if not the dream of *Laurentia* advocated by that rabid Anglophobe and Jew hater, the Roman Catholic cleric, chanoine Lionel Groulx.

This small bourgeoisie came mostly from the ranks of those who had attended *université Laval* and *université de Montréal* – a particularly ardent group of this political ideology.

A group who favored strong leaders – especially with themselves at the helm as *The Chosen Ones*.

Typically exhibited at the *université de Montréal,* among numerous examples, by that pompous Jean-Louis Roux.

A French-Canadian actor with an adopted faked cultured Parisian accent that nobody in Québec then and now dares mention.

An ostentatious self-centered individual for a short while promoted as Lieutenant Governor of the province of Québec (because he favored and obtained those substantial federal grants over the years), and who chose at least once to wear a swastika on his lab coat in protest against conscription, when it was already obvious Jews were suffering ignoble humiliation that inevitably lead to a genocidal apocalypse. An event among others, probably due to the newspaper Le Devoir, the favorite of the intelligentsia in Québec, which was already molding the minds of Québec's intellectuals and pseudo-intellectuals.

THOUGHTS FROM AN OLD MAN.

While most easily admit that an overtly religious presence has been shed off by the vast majority of French-Canadians in Québec from the Sixties on, one thing remained certain:

The original religious blueprints – particularly the Jesuitan schematic way of analyzing, synthesizing, and controlling a population and a prevalent belief system by whatever means available – have remained firmly transferred and implanted to this day at the secular level in the mind of a majority of professionals, bureaucrats, and politicians.

All you have to do in order to observe this phenomenon is talk to them and they soon reveal their ideological thinking – masqueraded as democratic protocols and hyperbolic financial scenarios out of context with today's global economy – just so this group can retain control over the population.

So, the question remains:

Will Québec get out of the Jesuitan structured thinking – now secularized – in which it is imprisoned?

The potential answer could be:

Because a system of reason imbued with such ideological inward self-rigorousness purposely allows us to ignore, among other things, the future negative economic impli-

cations of its decisions – as if a new god would still magically 'provide for us' despite our self-imposed blindness to reality as it really is.

THEN, NOW AND BEYOND.

The accepted societal belief system and its codependent political machinery, which together neutralized so completely all French-Canadians for centuries, having finally collapsed in the Sixties, must not be replaced with another although different stultifying one.

That is why; the Jesuitan logic still residing in our new religion of *Political Correctness* now unnecessarily complicates our existence in Québec today.

That is why also; our one-sided favoring of, if not near-addictive intra-cultural search for, allegedly effective and efficient benchmarking principally from members of the *Francophonie* must immediately be extended to the absolute best in the rest of the world.

Otherwise, both of these ideological strategies, if they remain unchanged, will threaten our future, because they heavily diminish our full participation with everyone, and reduce our ability to grow more fully in all other aspects and respects with the best in the rest of the world.

In the vivid example of China, our approach must consist of the best there exist on our planet – nothing less. To do less is to shortchange ourselves.

Otherwise, we will have purposely compromised our entire future to the benefit of a narrow-minded cultural myopia.

IDEOLOGY, RECOGNIZED OR NOT, DESTROYS ALL.

Let us be clear here.

It is always an enforced ideology that creates poverty and brutality, whether in the *bidon villes* of Brazil, Zimbabwe, India, Pakistan, the Gaza Strip, and Bangladesh for example.

It is also ideology, which creates ghettos in lands of plenty, such as those found in the more democratic nations, including those with enormous resources at their beck and call.

Sainte-Cunégonde and Sainte-Irénée of the Thirties, Forties and Fifties are examples of that, as is Hocholaga still nowadays.

Although Québec has accomplished the nearly impossible by shedding its addiction to *Absolute Obedience* to a religious belief, it must not replace this ideology with another – even if secular – since both types are enslaving systems of control.

QUÉBEC'S AND CANADA'S FUTURE.

A reasonably level-headed person continuously integrates those lessons, life inevitably teaches us all in the course of our existence. But what frightens Quebecois the most about our future is that the average among them in fact accepts the unfounded pronouncements and unsubstantiated allegations of mad men and psychopathic leaders – religious and secular alike.

And that we, therefore, deliberately, and insanely choose to live according to the level of madness these insist we live with.

History everywhere is witness to this lunacy.

Indeed, the mad utterances of a J. Edgar Hoover; or a fundamentalist born-again Christian such as G.W. Bush; or Tea Party members; or Mormons; or Roman Catholic officials in the USA; or the fumed ravings of a Hezbollah imam; or a Taliban extremist; or an ISIS barbarous genocide, or the calculated takeover of a Machiavellian planner and supreme leader in Iran, or a desperately acting Prime Minister of Israel, and so on – all predict, through their behavior and attitude, a post-apocalyptic future for us all.

Where it will end no one really knows.

That is why; economic issues and the anti-business attitude in Québec seem small in comparison.

And yet these are directly connected to the rest of the world and must be resolved in accord with the reality of the North American world particularly and at large generally, since they together affect whatever is to take place in Québec.

That is also why: we in Québec must open up our mind and see the world as it is – at least on our North American continent where we are located.

On that enormous land mass markets are open, freedom flourishes and the language in communication, business and research is English.

Not to capitalize on this is an act of insanity.

Above all we must never substitute one unquestionable ideology for another.

Political Correctness and the complex ultra-bureaucratic establishments promoted, must never take over.

Yet that is precisely what we're doing right now in the province of Québec … and that scare me.

IMPORTANT POINTS.

First, if we are to advance with a bright future ahead of us as a species with a total respect of all of our *Inalienable Individual Rights* fully protected, we must become sane and kind as societies.

Second, the first order of business must then consist of dislodging the curse of all forms of an alleged and unquestionable *Immaculate Perception* that has enslaved humanity to this day – such as religion as well as any other forms of dictatorial control of mind and body.

Thirdly, if fascism could take root in a highly civilized country such as Germany in the 20th century CE; and if I sensed and witnessed the first burgeoning heartbeats of fascism in my very own community of French-Canadians of the Thirties, Forties and Fifties; I must then presume that fascism can take root whenever and wherever dogmatic attitudes exist.

All this implies by definition that such potential malevolent force exists nearly everywhere at this very instant.

That is what scares me the most at the moment.

HISTORY KEEPS ON TEACHING US.

History keeps on teaching us that those in charge as well as those in support of the status quo of a society, which they together rule and manage; generally understood little or refused to accept or vastly underrated momentous social changes to come – even when these were about to take place – and that such societies paid dearly for both the ignorance and arrogance of their elite.

That is why; history has continuously taught us that an ideologically governing a subjected population through manipulation and /or coercion always paid a highly punitive price.

Therefore, unless Québec changes its strategy for survival, it will be no exception to this lesson of history. Although I admit that from time to time a flicker of hope surfaces, when I consider the extraordinary potential inherent in all of us in Québec, and especially with the 'can do' attitude of a segment of our latest generation.

A RAY OF HOPE.

In the end, all honest narratives bring out a ray of hope by suggesting that, similar to the first group of entrepreneurs of the Beauce region – those original and inspiring 'can do' people of Québec – a generalized underground movement has at last begun an original creativity and economic development, bypassing the previous limits of language, stifling religion, and <u>the ideological self-imposed traditional barriers to entrepreneurship and business</u> legated to us French-Canadians through our submission to our own chapter of Roman Catholicism.

A paradigm shift demonstrated particularly with a second expanding and groundbreaking generation during the Nineties and the present millennium age group – all of a sudden beginning to take their rightful place.

But my nagging questions nevertheless remain:

Will it take flight?

Knowing our peculiar French-Canadian historical pattern of putting down independent thinkers – even decades after the *révolution tranquille*, will our new attitude toward free thought swerve us away from our newly found religion of *'Political Correctitude'*?

Will this newfound ideological monopoly continue to gain momentum and slow us down one more time?

Will the ingrained traditional self-destructive attitude of French-Canadians in Québec change for a more positive and a lesser *Politically Correct* one to our benefit and open-ended future?

My tentative answer to these questions is simply this:

> *The harbinger signaling my community's intent to make a paradigm shift away from the prescriptions triggered by the ideology of their newly found religion of robotized bureaucratic 'Political Correctitude' that replaced among a significant number among us the diktats of the Roman Catholic Church, which had so completely ruled us for centuries, will show up among other things, when – a significant reduction at least, if not its unnecessarily complex bureaucratic processes are totally*

eliminated, while business is truly encouraged, while financial solvency, science and technology take precedence.

Epilogue

Evaluating
A Society's Ethics

If you want to evaluate a society's ethics, examine the way it treats its most vulnerable people – its children and old folks. To resolve this societal problem, we can at least consider five issues.

Issue 1.
Pretend to Prepare Our Children

In Québec, we pretend to prepare our children to manage their adult life effectively better. Yet, we do this through an out-of-touch educational system, despite a forever changing world and repeated reforms that never got rid of the roadblocks preventing it from truly upgrading itself, along with a massive bureaucracy that cannot be dislodged, and the sacred cow that pedagogy trumps everything.

As we deny our students the spirit of curiosity and adventure, the thrill of discovery, and the skills required along with the means to get there at all levels but especially early in their formative years, we program them for failure.

Issue 2.
Paying Lip Service to A Sound Knowledge of...

We pay lip service to a sound knowledge of money, financial transactions, markets, economy, and entrepreneurship. Those very subjects so crucial to reach those objectives beyond the limits set by the traditional Québec community. All of which is owed to all students, and which ought to be thoroughly integrated into a comprehensive educational curriculum.

Issue 3.

Planetary Communications Presently Means English

In the case of all territories, where the local language is not English, children should learn it early on, as shown in the more socially and/or business savvy and advanced nations – simply because the language of planetary communications presently is English for all intent and purposes at the moment and for the foreseeable future.

Quebecers **ought not** for short-sighted ideological views on this issue prevent their children from learning it early and from using it at work in their adult life for the same myopic insular logic.

Issue 4.

We Must Not Labor Unions Ruin Our Economy

Labor unions should be prevented by law from ruining the Québec economy and obligated to readjust their salaries and benefits with an overall mission and objectives in line with the Québec, Canadian and world economies.

Issue 5.

Pretend to Care for The Vulnerable

Within a nursing home (i.e., whether government-run or private) for those whose life is ending, routine bureaucratic work protocols ought not contain directives instructing workers to be insensitive to *The Vulnerable* of our society and rob them of their human dignity—especially in a society such as Québec conceitedly, insincerely and deceitfully marketing and selling to one and all the notion that it truly cares for its most vulnerable citizens.

Ad hoc Addendums

Addendum 1.

Note: **Consider This Illustration …**

To get an appreciation of this murky issue let us consider this illustration. In my own French-speaking Canadian tradition, a young teenager and a few of his buddies went out on a drunk, and then foolishly or imprudently or accidentally fought Mohawk warriors about a couple hundred years ago and were all killed in that encounter.

You guessed right!

My culture, which intensely feared Mohawks at that time as well as needing home grown heroes, elevated these belligerent and/or foolish teenagers as patriots of the first order, who had allegedly selflessly sacrificed themselves in the surrendering of their lives supposedly for the good of the community of the time.

What a crock of shit that was, and yet, for a few of my tender years, I believed it.

Realizing this was a sham that could no longer be believed as time went on especially in urban areas, a new general "patriotic" holiday was instituted to replace this myth cautiously and gradually and it has generally succeeded.

Anyway, my point here is that: Each time I departed from my original coerced acculturation (i.e., tribal brainwashing) from this belief, other beliefs like this one, or others much more serious than this one – because they no longer made sense to me – I nevertheless felt a sense of treason toward French-Canadians generally and Quebecers in particular.

Such is the power of myths my friends.

Note: **In Québec, Canada - 1**

In Québec, Canada—in addition to the natural on-going Anglicization of French in Europe—you are also caught up with "Joual" … where you can easily be understood in Montréal, if you would say, using overly easy street examples, *"J'ai **fucké** mon **tire** quand j'ai eu un **flat**"*, … or *"J'adore les **hamburgers**, les **hot-dogs** et les **scores** de **hockey**"*, … or *"As-tu **watché** la **game** hier soir?"* … and still claim to speak French as well.

While many well-schooled French-Canadians will shudder at these sayings, this remains true, nonetheless

Note: **In Québec, Canada - 2**

Contrary to France, French-speaking Canadians are drowning in a sea of English, so to speak.

The pressure is immense.

This explains in part why a significant number of French-speaking Canadians entered into some form of schizophrenic episode, demonstrated by separatist Québec government administration creating a nationalist law for visual signs to mask that fact in spite of that reality.

But regardless of that law, we all know we are constantly and irretrievably very influenced by English, because we find ourselves culturally on a sort of a mostly "French-speaking island" in an immense English-speaking ocean—with English Canada surrounding us from without and from within along with English American smack against us and all over us in every way.

Like a mouse sleeping and living next to an elephant away from its long-lost parents, who with premeditation and callousness abandoned them on the other side of the world, we are further continuously bombarded by the ever present and ever immediate American cultural influence more than anywhere else on Earth, through regular and satellite TV, radio, magazines, movies, sporting events, internet, etc., on our door step, over our roofs and within our homes literally.

And many among us routinely make the USA a home of choice such as those "snowbirds" in Florida and California.

It's a no-brainer, and we all know it, except for the usual fanatics in such cases along with the mostly unilingual classic professionals within the Québec elite, which would benefit the most from a political separation from Canada, but not for long I suppose, since even their children would have to speak decent English to make it in this globalizing world—particularly here in North-America.

Note: **The 'Joual' of Québec**

The 'Joual' of the province of Québec, like the Veneziano of Italy, the Cockney of East London, the Häme or the Savo of Finland, the Kandri of Northern India, and all other varieties of sublanguages and dialects, are coherent narratives nonetheless – like the rings seen on a cut up tree.

Such means of expression de facto reflect more or less what happened to the people speaking such a marked variation of a given language.

In each case a local narrative shaping the presentation of a local culture and language associated with it has thrived over the generations when such a group developed a forward-looking attitude, rendering their present social reality, political situation, and vibrant culture, exceptionally their own.

Québec has been no exception to this universal reality and has benefited from this peculiarity in shaping its society as a cohesive group.

Note: **In My Québec Culture …**

In my Québec French-speaking culture of original *'vielles souche'* French-Canadians, it is reflected in the saying heard dozens of times in my youth of: *"Quand tu es né pour un petit pain, tu n'es pas né pour un gros"!*

In fact, a plain refusal—under the cover of the moral dictum of victims that had given up at that time—to organize their lives in the best way possible with the cards handed them.

Addendum 2.

· The largely baseless political protests from Quebec's French-speaking, spoiled, demanding, ill-mannered, and insolents 'enfants-roi' now in college causing mayhem.

· Doing all this either just for entertainment at the expense of their fragile provincial economy, or simply to annoy the population at large and hard-working stiffs in particular – for dubious, out of context, and manipulated democratic principles … and the sport of abusing practices taught to them for so long by successful labor unions.

Addendum 3.

Note: **Speaking of a Nanny State …**

In Québec the Nanny State has now replaced in all of its excesses the medieval Roman Catholic Church of a few decades ago, which for several centuries acted as dictatorial meta-parents – apparently because its population psychologically still required the illusive protection of a 'super other". That is why the new religion of *'Political Correctitude'* is the unofficial belief system of the present Quebec establishment and at the heart of its political processes. And because of this, massive bureaucratic protocols now exist with the support of a complex managerial methodology pompously identified as *"le modèle Québécois"* by French-speaking Quebecers considering themselves different from Americans and English-speaking Canadians. It also now forms an integral part and function of the special languages of all professionals and bureaucrats in that province.

This is routinely characterized with patronizing expressions before answering almost anything – generally framing their opinions and statements, as if these were meant for quasi-illiterate or an already submissive population with such traditional patronizing saying as: *Il faut comprendre d'abords que …,* and so on, as if the listeners were unable or had serious difficulties to assess a particular point or context, whenever expressed by an 'expert' or professional.

A situation reminiscent of the condescending parlance of their previous religious masters, which they in fact replaced with a secular version and now mimic.

Addendum 4.

Note: **Consider This Illustration …**

To get an appreciation of this murky issue let us consider this illustration. In my own French-speaking Canadian tradition, a young teenager and a few of his buddies went out on a drunk, and then foolishly or imprudently or accidentally fought Mohawk warriors about a couple hundred years ago and were all killed in that encounter. You guessed right! My culture, which intensely feared Mohawks at that time as well as needing home grown heroes, elevated these belligerent and/or foolish teenagers as patriots of the first order, who had allegedly selflessly sacrificed themselves in the surrendering of their lives supposedly for the good of the community of the time. What a crock of shit that was, and yet, for a few of my tender years, I believed it. Realizing this was a sham that could no longer be believed as time went on especially in urban areas, a new general "patriotic" holiday was instituted to cautiously and gradually replace this myth … and it has generally succeeded. Anyway, my point here is that: Each time I departed from my original coerced acculturation (i.e., tribal brainwashing) from this belief, other beliefs like this one, or others much more serious than this one – because they no longer made sense to me – I nevertheless felt a sense of treason toward French-Canadians generally and Quebecers in particular. Such is the power of myths my friends.

Note: **A Personal Irritant, Nothing More…**

Now here is a term (the word "gay") which as a French-speaking person I admit resenting. This misuse of a fine word from my native tongue was clearly unnecessary, but there it is nevertheless forever part of our terminology whether I like it or not. Thus, this question:

Does this imply that all non-heterosexual individuals—the vast majority of human beings—are not or less joyful, merry, cheerful, and bright?

How condescending indeed to have, not only adopted such a word, but to disfigure its meanings, rather than create or adopt one reflecting the natural reality of what non-heterosexuality implies at this time of our history, and to represent an ever-advancing sophistication of many societies along with the valid shift demanded of our intellectual and moral values?

Addendum 5.

Note: **Hard Core Québec Separatists.**

Hard core Québec separatists—to believe themselves victimized:

1. Purposely and dishonestly ignoring that English is the language of the planet and that it will remain as such for several generations.

2. Refusing to see that their plight in the past was due to the politics of old conflicts, and that this attitude blocks off their aspirations as free people, whom they really are.

3. Intentionally 'forgetting' altogether that England by default allowed them to keep their language and belief system.

4. Deliberately disregarding that France, their mother country, abandoned them to their plight as collateral damage – unworthy of protection – in the pursuit of national French interests of the day and for a supply of sugar for some islands.

5. Calculatedly overlooking that their local Catholic Church made up of their own people separately and for political gains betrayed them several times; not only with the old French regime but also with the English one as well, and continued to do so in a third phase of their betrayal in the 19th and 20th centuries this time with complicity of their own bourgeoisie.

> o Knowingly disregarding the fact that they geographically live next

to the most powerful and still richest nation in the whole course of human history to this day – a dreamt for opportunity for any entrepreneur.

6. Designedly discounting that the French-speaking people of Québec are now the authors of their shortcomings in most instances—by snubbing entrepreneurship, ignoring opportunities represented and implied by being smack against the USA as well as being an integral part of the free country of Canada.

Oh no! They go on creating one of the biggest national debts instead, while acting as phony victims. Like an 'enfants-roi' about mostly self-inflicted problems, especially in the last decades.

Addendum 6.

Note: **In My Québec Culture …**

In my Québec French-speaking culture of original *'vielles souche'* French-Canadians, it is reflected in the saying heard dozens of times in my youth of: *"Quand tu es né pour un petit pain, tu n'es pas né pour un gros"!* In fact, a plain refusal—under the cover of the moral dictum of victims that had given up at that time—to organize their lives in the best way possible with the cards handed them.

Note: **Speaking of a Nanny State …**

In Québec the Nanny State has now replaced in all of its excesses the medieval Roman Catholic Church of a few decades ago, which for several centuries acted as dictatorial meta-parents – apparently because its population psychologically still required the illusive protection of a 'super other". That is why the new religion of *'Political Correctitude'* is the unofficial belief system of the present Quebec establishment and at the heart of its political processes. And because of this, massive bureaucratic protocols now exist with the support of a complex managerial methodology pompously identified as *"le modèle Québécois"* by French-speaking Quebecers considering themselves different from Americans and English-speaking Canadians. It also now forms an integral part and function of the special languages of all professionals and bureaucrats in that province.

This is routinely characterized with patronizing expressions before answering almost anything – generally framing their opinions and statements, as if these were meant for quasi-illiterate or an already submissive population with such traditional patronizing saying as: *Il faut comprendre d'abords que ...,* and so on, as if the listeners were unable or had serious difficulties to assess a particular point or context, whenever expressed by an 'expert' or professional.

A situation reminiscent of the condescending parlance of their previous religious masters, which they in fact replaced with a secular version and now mimic.

Addendum 7.

It was indeed in the paroxysm of grand and sumptuous religious ceremonies, the political stranglehold of the Duplessis regime, and the hopelessness these two forces created, that Ti-Jean decided, the time had come to leave not only his neighbourhood but his province. In his naïve and evolving young mind it was more than high time to escape, if he wanted a normal life and far better chances in life. The grass indeed seemed greener on the other side at that time.

Addendum 8.

By the time Ti-Jean left Sainte-Cunégonde, he'd already been working full time at near starvation wages and supporting himself financially since age fourteen.

Under those circumstances he felt he had no other choice but to break away from drowning in the gasping throes, which *la grande noirceur* reserved for him and those in similar situations.

He was in no position to know about the upcoming *révolution tranquille,* or if such event would take place within his own lifespan, because it seemed at that time that *la grande noirceur* would continue on and on – well beyond his own generation.

Ti-Jean was seventeen years old when he left his ghetto – never to return except for a couple visits.

Addendum 9.

Indeed, there existed a quiet antagonism against everything and anything with an English connotation or association bordering one could say a sort of quiet jealousy, occasionally expressed but never violently in regular life – except in bars and taverns from time to time after imbibing too much alcohol. Although the Irish exhibited a bit more entrepreneurship than their French-Canadian neighbors at that time, it was obvious to all that they too had lousy lodgings and were also submitted to a harsh life and an oppressing Roman Catholic influence – otherwise the Irish would have moved out of there much sooner than they did decades later.

So, this area never became a sort of Belfast, because the antagonism felt by French-Canadians was more of an irritant about their own condition, which in their programmed ignorance and without knowledge of English, rarely considered their Irish neighbors as poor 'Anglos', unwittingly nearly always misidentified as part of the governing English class – at a lower level mind you but part of that group nonetheless.

Hence in some odd ways acting as if the Irish were de facto automatically somewhat superior to them, or at least as speaking the language of those running the show. Although a small sense of superiority, exhibited from time to time by many of the poor Canadians of Irish descent in *'The Pointe'* (as it has always been called by the locals) and Griffintown toward their French-Canadian fellow citizens, did not help this vision and at times worsened it.

Addendum 10.

The State, among other things, had traditionally transferred several of its bureaucratic controls to the Church – saving itself a lot of administrative time, staff, and money in the process – in the recording of births, marriages, and deaths.

This gave the Church an assumed authority by churchgoers in the choosing of names, the setting of moral standards and so on.

That is why; most French-Canadians ended up with "Joseph" as a first name if they were males and "Marie" if they were females – a way for the Church to tag (like an intellectual skin tattoo) its members in official documents, and to tell these same members of the allegiance they owed to their Church and which they should unquestionably obey.

Addendum 11.

This and other tactics to retain membership also provided the Church with a constant source of revenues for services rendered in baptismal, wedding, funeral costs and other money collecting arrangements. Whatever, once part of that membership, social rules, laws (including Canon Law), mores and folklore, made it socially difficult to leave it.

Addendum 12.

All of this created a slowly evolving but nonetheless rebellious nature in French-Canadian women much before it became stylish with their men, who generally had remained compliant, and who unfairly took much of the credit for the *révolution tranquille*.

Indeed, while French-Canadian men dreamt of a strong and decisive victory over their English-speaking masters through violent revolution such as the failed 1837 Rebellion and their last stand in Saint-Eustache, women did not have the leisure or vision of such pyrrhic triumphs.

Later on, the more educated men would write intellectual essays for newspapers or local magazines in the Thirties and Forties particularly (the 'blogs' of those decades) especially in Le Devoir newspaper.

These were often veiled diatribes against those perceived as enemies of French-Canadians – often camouflaged as intellectual essays and articles.

These often enough included attacks on Jews and *Les Anglais* by a bunch of narrow-minded pseudo intellectuals too timid to be entrepreneurs, several hiding under pseudonyms, while rejoicing in the assurance that their classic education exceptionally provided them with – unbeknownst to them perhaps but nonetheless at the expense of Québec's future—it was a favored societal position and role within a stagnant and servile culture of little importance and unenviable future.

Addendum 13.

Unlike the timidity of most men and the hypocrisy and pompous sense of superiority of classically educated ones, Québec mothers' quiet insurgency was to successfully weaken the very foundations supporting the institutions controlling them.

Doing so at that tender age when children are most susceptible and extremely dependent on their mother – before the compulsory religious indoctrination took place.

A period during which mothers urged them to change things, once they grew up, and to stop obeying stupid notions and orders.

A process that took place in those early years when mother and child possess a most special relationship – the only period of time they could significantly influence their children.

Indeed, it was because their contribution took place in the formative years of their children, generation after generation, that it became all the more effective, efficient and above all cumulative.

It became more intense during the last few decades before the *révolution tranquille,* wherein children became far more aware of their mother's extreme frustrations and strong recommendations; the clear unfairness at the way they were being treated as chattel; the burden of the work prejudicially assigned to them; and the servile vocation generally expected of them.

French-Canadian children – especially in Québec – were continually influenced by their mother's constant refrain to get an education of sort in order to get a better job. But blasphemy of all blasphemies felt among the stolid and solid Québec establishment was the notion inculcated by mothers in many struggling families, to learn English in order to build a much improved future in a world of business and manufacturing that was then clearly dominated by English-speaking entrepreneurs and clients – much before English became the planetary language of business and communications among the earth's elite and the educated – gaining momentum after the Second World War. And although it took a few generations to mobilize the young, it did not fall on deaf ears.

Addendum 14.

That is why among other things on radio and TV, and in news programs of the Fifties and early Sixties, English-Canadian broadcasters presented Québécois as a quaint group with a submissive preponderance for large families and an over-the-top reliance on their clerics – remnants of which still, decades later, well after the collapse of the Roman Catholic Church in Québec, occasionally show up.

Such as when Cardinal Ouellette, the leader of the Québec clergy a few years ago offered medieval-minded comments, admonitions and remarks along with patronizing religious family values. As if hoping one day to return to their golden years of total control over the mind and behavior of that whole national group, and again refocus their energies on the flow of money and other resources into Church coffers.

Addendum 15.

And all of this took place along with the will of its near-dictator, Maurice Duplessis, who, acting according to his national secular objectives, finally began the construction of an infrastructure Québec had never had in all of its existence until then. Although in great part all of this was the result of those strong foundational bedrock questions, cautions and hopes French-Canadian mothers communicated to their children over the last few generations – particularly in the early decades of the 20th century CE. In other words, average French-Canadian fathers, while officially promoted by both Church and State as head of the family, were in fact generally weak, timid and lazy – leaving everything other than their narrowly assigned workload to women.

Addendum 16

As a countermove and in flamboyant example of his authority and power, Maurice Duplessis demanded and obtained from the Holy See in Rome, the removal of that most senior ecclesiastical authority in the province, for getting openly involved in the Asbestos Strike particularly (and other political issues), which reflected badly on Duplessis' handling in cahoots with its owners, of that important labor problem.

Duplessis also did this, because he had had enough of archbishop Charbonneau's steadily mounting interference and general opposition to the reactionary policies of his regime.

In fact, shortly after Maurice Duplessis visited the most senior ecclesiastical authorities in Rome, Archbishop Joseph Charbonneau *resigned.*

The date was February 9, 1950.

He was then made titular Archbishop of Bosphorus.

And had therefore *accepted* a pyrrhic transfer and a drastic demotion, *agreeing* to work in Victoria, British Columbia – about 5000 kilometers away – as a hospital chaplain.

The furthest he could be sent in Canada from his lavish residence in Montréal and lodged into a humble abode – from a portfolio with enormous authority and palatial splendor to one without any of either.

No one heard about Archbishop Joseph Charbonneau after that, until advised of his death on November 19, 1959.

Addendum 17.

The Duplessis regime also excelled in vote-fixing. So, bags of groceries and bottles of alcohol in poor rural districts particularly were not uncommon for buying votes.

In more affluent areas, where the votes of certain people were strategically important, kitchen appliances were provided in exchange for their votes.

Index